MIND FACTORY

edited by
LOUIS ARMAND

þ
Litteraria Pragensia
Prague 2005

Published 2005 by Litteraria Pragensia
Faculty of Philosophy, Charles University
Náměstí Jana Palacha 2, 116 38 Prague 1
Czech Republic

The publication of this book has been supported by research grant MSM0021620824 "Foundations of the Modern World as Reflected in Literature and Philosophy" awarded to the Faculty of Philosophy, Charles University, Prague, by the Czech Ministry of Education.

Cataloguing in Publication Data

Mind Factory, edited by Louis Armand.—1st ed.
        p.   cm.
    ISBN 80-7308-104-0 (pb)
    1. Theory.   2. Psychology.   3. Philosophy.   4. Cognitive Science.
    I. Armand, Louis. II. Title

Printed in the Czech Republic by PB Tisk
Design by lazarus
Cover image: Synapse 1

ANTITHESIS OF AMBI-
DUAL ANTICIPATION
THE MIND FACTORY,
ITS GIVE AND TAKE.

—James Joyce, *Finnegans Wake*

Contents

Introduction

Our high-end technologies leave us on the cusp of a best- and worst-case scenario as previously imagined in doomsday films and futurist fiction. How can we contend with the hand of artifice that is the postmillennial condition?
—Max Henry, *Portraits of Robots*

In testimony recorded in the 24 February 1974 edition of the US *Congressional Record* (no. 26, vol. 118, p. 4475), José Delgado— former director of neuropsychiatry at Yale University Medical School—said the following:

We need a programme of psychosurgery for political control of our society. The purpose is physical control of the mind. Everyone who deviates from the given norm can be surgically mutilated.

The individual may think that the most important reality is his own existence, but this is only his personal point of view. This lacks historical perspective.

Man does not have the right to develop his own mind. This kind of liberal orientation has great appeal. We must electrically control the brain. Someday, armies and generals will be controlled by electric stimulation of the brain.

Author of *Physical Control of the Mind: Toward a Psychocivilised Society* (1971) and over 200 scientific papers, Delgado's major methodological innovations included the permanent implantation of electrodes in the brain; intracerebral chemitrodes and dialytrodes; cardiac pacemaker implantation; brain pacemakers; brain radio stimulators; two-way radio

1

communication brain-to-computer; time-lapse recording of social behaviour in monkey colonies; and the design and application of non-invasive electromagnetic devices for the investigation of biological effects and therapeutic application. Delgado is also widely believed to have co-operated with US government agencies with the objective of developing means of direct electro-technical control of mental activity and hence of individual and social behaviour. Yet the remarks attributed to Delgado, and the nature and orientation of his accredited research, no longer appear as problematic or ambiguous today as perhaps they ought to, considering the ever increasing prevalence of bio-technologies such as genetic modification, RNAi, cloning, robotics, bionics, global telecommunications and surveillance, and the whole multiplicity of micro-, macro- and nano-technologies. The ideal of technological "accountability"—or of a technological "public domain"—has long vanished behind a smoke screen of international patents and a renewed military-industrial progressivist rhetoric, despite a resurgence in US public moralism with regard to such things as stem-cell research, abortion and the medical use of human embryos, and despite a broad non-US scepticism with regard to the motives of corporations engaged in vivisection, bio-genetics and research into animal or artificial intelligence.

Whether utopia or doomsday scenario, the globalised, post-Cold War state of technological innovation has effectively reconstituted the very idea of mind, and of "mind control," in ways that even half a century ago would have appeared science fiction, just as it has transformed the critical and ethical paradigms for determining the limits and nature of the so-called "mind problem." The advent of computing science, cybernetics, systems and information theory in the ten years following WWII, gave rise to the notion that characteristics of mind, and above all "intelligence," could be affected by technical means, thereby initiating the most radical phase of industrialisation yet: the industrialisation of "consciousness" and the transition from machine age to information age (—and

2

Chimpanzees Paddy (left) and Carlos at Yale University Medical School, each with two intracerebral electrodes and boxes for instrumentation. From José Delgado, *Physical Control of the Mind: Toward a Psychocivilised Society*, ed. Ruth N. Anshen (Irvington: 1971).

with it, the renewed contest for global informatic, economic and political hegemony). While commentators like Marshall McLuhan sought to locate antecedents for this transition in the earlier technologisation of literacy, by way of the mechanised printing press (the "Gutenberg effect"), and the advent by way of television and telemedia of a post-"typographic man," others like Claude Shannon identified within the idea of language itself the technological basis for the changes at hand.

In 1948 Shannon published his landmark "A Mathematical Theory of Communication," which established the industry standard of information theory, and in 1949 he published a paper entitled "Communication Theory of Secrecy Systems," in which language is defined as being represented by a "stochastic process which produces a discrete sequence of symbols in accordance with some system of probability." Along with Alan Turing's pioneer work on cryptanalysis, computing and artificial intelligence, Shannon's theoretical papers have provided the basis for rethinking "cognition" in terms of programmatics and recursive codes, and of identifying "information" with effects of disturbance intrinsic to any language system or system of sign operations. The implication here being that programmes or computing codes, like language, are not simply "error prone," but rather error-determined, with the consequence—as we may better appreciate today—that despite the most rigorous forms of dataveillance every system is inherently susceptible to "viral" interference. Moreover, Shannon's work on communication and unpredictability proved to be one of the major forerunners of more recent "chaos" theories which, along with quantum mechanics, have offered some of the more persuasive accounts of neural structures and the constitution of intelligence or "mind." In light of such developments, cognitive linguists, like George Lakoff and Gilles Fauconnier, have similarly proposed that language and human thought processes are both "non-logical" and "non-generative," instead being defined by endless idiosyncrasies of patterning and distribution—or what we might call, following Ted Nelson, *hypertextuality*.

Shannon's other major publication, *A Symbolic Analysis of Relay and Switching Circuits*, extended the notion of recursive language systems and cryptanalysis to problems dealing with computing and programmatics, by applying Boolean algebra to establish the theoretical underpinnings of digital circuits. This work has had broad significance due to the fact that digital circuits are fundamental to the operation of modern computers and telecommunications systems. As information technologies have becoming increasingly networked in complex ways, and "intelligent" systems increasingly come to mimic neural structures of parallel processing, the circuit has come to be a paradigm case not only for understanding cognitive structures, but for mapping contemporary social organisation—from the power grids and computerised transit systems that allow our cities to function, to the advent of "global" information systems like GPS and the World Wide Web.

First proposed by Tim Berners-Lee at the Centre Européenne pour la Recherche Nucléaire in Switzerland in March 1989, and based upon a distributed hypertext system, the World Wide Web has often been regarded as something analogous to a *global mind*, organised across an almost countless array of computing nodes. This idea was foreshadowed in a proposal by US science administrator Vannevar Bush, entitled "As We May Think" (1945), which called for new, non-linear technical means of managing the industrial output of information—an output dramatically accelerated by the recent war. The development of the Web at CERN was initially prompted by similar concerns of information management and the need to discover means of linking remotely distributed information together across heterogeneous systems in an unconstrained way.

As a multi-user system with a radically decentred structure, the Web can more easily be considered analogous to certain non-human "neural structures"—such as those of various types of insects—rather than to the singular brain-centredness of humans. Biomimetics has explored structures similar to those of the Web in invertebrates and insects like the cricket, whose localised, networked "intelligence" is comprised of multiple ganglia located across the cricket's body, capable of the rapid assimilation and processing of information before it is able to reach the central "brain." In practical terms, this provides the organism with a vastly enhanced reaction time (or what Berners-Lee termed "automatic analysis"), just as the organisation of microprocessors is designed to speed up the circulation of "information" in computing circuits. Similar phenomena have been noted in the perceptory systems of locusts and bees, whose multiple lens structures give their optical centres the capacity to isolate photo-effects of a frequency of 50,000 times per second. In similar ways, biomimetics—which seeks to develop imitative technologies for use by humans (such as the adaptation of ultrasonic devices,

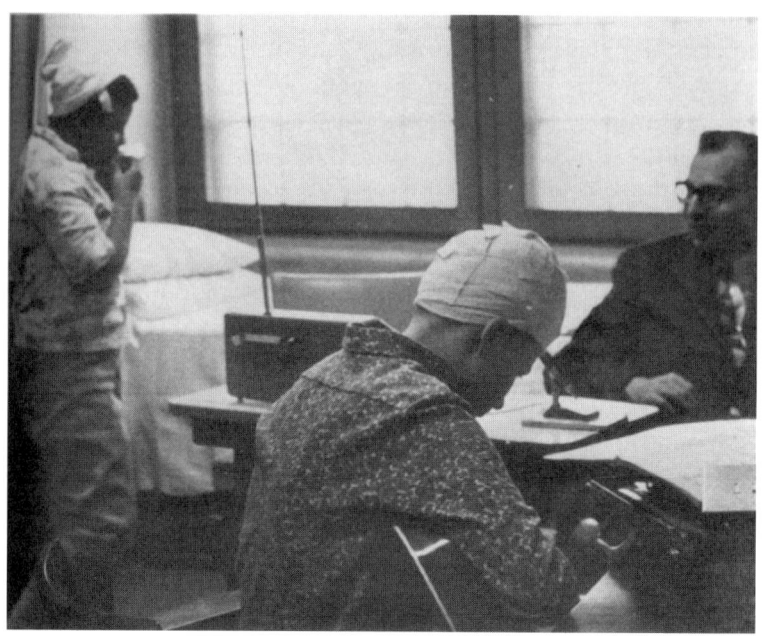

Two girls who were suffering from epileptic seizures and behavioural disturbances requiring implantation of electrodes in the brain for diagnostic and therapeutic purposes. Under the cap, each patient wears a "stimoceiver," used to stimulate the brain by radio and to send electrical signals of brain activity by telemetry while the patients are completely free within the hospital ward. From José Delgado, *Physical Control of the Mind.*

like those employed by bats in order to "see" in the dark, as prostheses for blind people)—points to a broad understanding of cognition on the basis of enhanced, networked, pan-sensory (synaesthetic) experience, "re-coded" in human terms as a type of *virtual reality* grounded in actual, quantitative, material phenomena.

The manufacture of "mind" has long represented the apotheosis of human technical ambition, whether by way of literacy, philosophy, education or indoctrination, or by various instruments of belief, physical or psychic control and coercion, or by way of technology itself. In the 1930s, procedures had already been devised, for example, to implant very fine wires within the brains of anesthetised cats (W.R. Hess)—a direct antecedent to the later neurophysiological work of José Delgado. By the 1950s, the reduced size of electrodes and the invention of micromanipulators made it possible to establish direct communication between brain and computer, circumventing normal sensory organs. In this way, "automatic learning" was discovered to be possible by feeding signals directly into specific neuronal structures without the conscious participation of the test subject.

Already in 1971 Delgado was able to write: "The technology for nonsensory communication between brains and computers through the intact skin is already at our fingertips, and its consequences are difficult to predict. In the past the progress of civilisation has tremendously magnified the power of our senses, muscles, and skills. Now we are adding a new dimension: the direct interface between brains and machines."

One of the legacies of Delgado's project is that, while no consensus as to what objectively constitutes "mind" yet exists, we are nevertheless confronted at every juncture with its technological *invention*. That is to say, as technē or artifice. This has led to the idea that what we call mind is nothing other than an effect of techno-symbiosis, mediated by particular neural networks or "structural properties." Consequently mind—as an object of enquiry—has assumed an *analogical* character, based upon our capacity to *represent* our experiential relation to our environment, or to theorise about other forms of experience beyond the limits of the human sensorium. Or, indeed, to determine the practical and ethical limits of what it is that *mind* represents for us: be it in terms of free will, consciousness, or civil liberty, even as these terms are complicated by any materialist definition of conscious, or admission—vis-à-vis Freud—of a determining, *unconscious* agency at work in the life-world of man.

And while the philosophy of mind may have evolved on the basis of a false premise—the desire to explain the seemingly mysterious qualities of experience and intellection—it may be that there is nothing *other* than this "false premise," that *mind* is

7

constituted solely in the separation or interface of the representable and the unrepresentable, on the cusp of verifiability, analogy, metaphor or mimesis, or as the division between that which thinks and that which makes thinking possible.

Louis Armand
New York, October, 2005

Slavoj Žižek

The De-Sublimated Object of Post-Ideology

The latest ethical "crisis" apropos biogenetics created the need
for what one is fully justified in calling a "state philosophy": a
philosophy that would, on the one hand, condone scientific
research and technical process, and, on the other hand, contain
its full socio-symbolic impact, i.e., prevent it from posing a
threat to the existing theologico-ethical constellation. No
wonder those who come closest to meeting these demands are
neo-Kantians: Kant himself was focused on the problem of how,
while fully taking into account the Newtonian science,
guaranteeing that there is a space of ethical responsibility
exempted from the reach of science, i.e., as Kant himself put it,
he limited the scope of knowledge to create the space for faith
and morality. And are today's state philosophers not facing the
same task? Is their effort not focused on how, through different
versions of transcendental reflection, to restrict science to its
preordained horizon of meaning and thus to denounce as
"illegitimate" its consequences for the ethico-religious sphere?
It is interesting to note how, although Sloterdijk was the target
of a violent Habermasian attack, his proposed solution, a
"humanist" synthesis of the new scientific Truth and the old

* First published in *lacanian ink* 26 (2005).

horizon of Meaning, although much more refined and ironically-sceptical than the Habermasian "state philosophy," is ultimately separated from it by an almost invisible line (more precisely, it seems to persist in the ambiguity between the Habermasian compromise and the New Age obscurantist synthesis). According to Sloterdijk, "humanism" always involves such a reconciliation, a bridge between the New and the Old: when scientific results undermine the old universe of meaning, one should find a way to reintegrate them into the universe of Meaning, or, rather, to metaphorically expand the old universe of Meaning so that it can "cover" also new scientific propositions. If we fail in this mediating task, we remain stuck in the brutal choice: either a reactionary refusal to accept scientific results, or the shattering loss of the very domain of meaning. Today, we confront the same challenge: "Mathematicians will have to become poets, cyberneticists philosophers of religion, [medical] doctors, composers, information-workers, shamans."[1] Is this solution, however, not that of obscurantism in the precise sense of the attempt to keep meaning and truth harnessed together?

> the simplest definition of God and of religion lies in the idea that truth and meaning are one and the same thing. The death of God is the end of the idea that posits truth and meaning as the same thing. And I would add that the death of Communism also implies the separation between meaning and truth as far as history is concerned. "The meaning of history" has two meanings: on the one hand "orientation," history goes somewhere; and then history has a meaning, which is the history of human emancipation by way of the proletariat, etc. In fact, the entire age of Communism was a period where the conviction that it was possible to take rightful political decisions existed; we were, at that moment, driven by the meaning of history … Then the death of Communism becomes the second death of God but in the territory of history. There is a connection between the two events and the consequence is, so

[1] Peter Sloterdijk, *Nicht gerettet* (Frankfurt: Suhrkamp 1999) 365.

to speak, that we should be aware that to produce truthful effects that are primarily local (be them psychoanalytical, scientific, etc.) is always an effect of local truth, never of global truth … Today we may call "obscurantism" the intention of keeping them harnessed together—meaning and truth.[2]

Badiou is here right in emphasising the gap between meaning and truth—i.e., the non-hermeneutic status of truth—as the minimal difference that separates religious idealism from materialism. This is also the difference between Freud and Jung: while Jung remains within the horizon of meaning, while Freudian interpretation aims at articulating a truth which is no longer grounded in meaning. Badiou is also right in formulating the ultimate alternative that confronts us today, when the impossibility of the conjunction of meaning and truth is imposed on us: either we endorse the "postmodern" stance and renounce altogether the dimension of truth, constraining ourselves to the interplay of multiple meanings, or we engage in the effort to discern a dimension of truth outside meaning— i.e., to put it simply, the dimension of truth as REAL.

However, what rings false is the parallel between the death of God and the death of Communism, implicitly referring to the old boring anti-Communist cliché on Communism as a "secular religion"; and linked to this falsity is also the all too quick acceptance of the "postmodern" notion that, in today's politics, we are limited to "local" truths, since, without a grounding in global meaning, it is no longer possible to formulate an all-encompassing truth. The fact which renders this conclusion problematic is the very fact of capitalist globalisation—what is capitalist globalisation? Capitalism is the first socio-economic order which de-totalises meaning: it is not global at the level of meaning (there is no global "capitalist world view," no "capitalist civilisation" proper—the fundamental lesson of globalisation is precisely that capitalism can accommodate itself to all civilisations, from Christian to Hindu and Buddhist); its

[2] "A Conversation with Alain Badiou," *lacanian ink* 23 (2004): 100-101.

global dimension can only be formulated at the level of truth-without-meaning, as the "real" of the global market mechanism. Consequently, insofar as capitalism already enacts the rupture between meaning and truth, it can be opposed at two levels: either at the level of meaning (conservative reactions to re-enframe capitalism into some social field of meaning, to contain its self-propelling movement within the confines of a system of shared "values" which cement a "community" in its "organic unity"), or to question the real of capitalism with regard to its truth-outside-meaning (what, basically, Marx did). Of course, the predominant religious strategy today is that of trying to contain the scientific real within the confines of meaning—it is as an answer to the scientific real (materialised in the biogenetic threats) that religion is finding its new raison d'être:

Far from being effaced by science, religion, and even the syndicate of religions, in the process of formation, is progressing every day. Lacan said that ecumenism was for the poor of spirit. There is a marvellous agreement on these questions between the secular and all the religious authorities, in which they tell themselves they should agree somewhere in order to make echoes equally marvellous, even saying that finally the secular is a religion like the others. We see this because it is revealed in effect that the discourse of science has partly connected with the death drive. Religion is planted in the position of unconditional defence of the living, of life in mankind, as guardian of life, making life an absolute. And that extends to the protection of human nature … This is … what gives a future to religion through meaning, namely by erecting barriers—to cloning, to the exploitation of human cells—and to inscribe science in a tempered progress. We see a marvellous effort, a new youthful vigour of religion in its effort to flood the real with meaning.[3]

---

[3] Jacques-Alain Miller, "Religion, Psychoanalysis," *lacanian ink* 23 (2004): 18-19.

So when the Pope opposes the Christian "culture of Life" to the modern "culture of Death," he is not merely exploiting in a hyperbolic way the different attitudes towards abortion. His statements are to be taken much more literally and, at the same time, universally: it is not only that the Church harbours "good news," the trust in our future, the Hope that guarantees the Meaning of Life; the couple culture of Life / culture of Death has to be related to the Freudian opposition of Life and Death drives. "Life" stands for the rule of the "pleasure principle," for the homeostatic stability of pleasures protected from the stressful shocks of excessive jouissance, so that the Pope's wager is that, paradoxically, not only is religious spirituality not opposed to earthly pleasures, but it is ONLY this spirituality that can provide the frame for a full and satisfied pleasurable life. "Death," on the contrary, stands for the domain "beyond the pleasure principle," for all the excesses through which the Real disturbs the homeostasis of life, from the excessive sexual jouissance up to the scientific Real which generates artificial monsters ... This simple, but salient, diagnosis ends up in a surprising paraphrase of Heidegger, defining the analyst as the "shepherd of the real." However, it leaves some key questions open. Is the death drive for which science stands, which it mobilises in its activity, not simultaneously an EXCESS OF OBSCENE LIFE, of life as real, exempted from and external to meaning (life that we find embodied in Kafka's "odradek" as well as in the "alien" from the film of the same name)? One should not forget that death drive is a Freudian name for immortality, for a pressure, a compulsion, which insists beyond death (and let us also not forget that immortality is also implicitly promised by science). One should therefore assert also a gap between life and meaning, homologous to that between truth and meaning—life and meaning in no way fully overlap.

Are we entering a post-human era?
The problem with today's superego injunction to enjoy is that, in contrast to previous modes of ideological interpellation, it opens up no "world" proper—it just refers to an obscure Unnameable. In this sense—and in this sense only—we effectively live in a "post-ideological universe": what addresses us is a direct "desublimated" call of jouissance, no longer coated in an ideological narrative proper. In what, more precisely, does this "worldlessness" consist? As Lacan points out in his *Seminar XX: Encore,* jouissance involves a logic strictly homologous to that of the ontological proof of the existence of God. In the classic version of this proof, my awareness of myself as a finite, limited, being immediately gives birth to the notion of an infinite, perfect, being, and since this being is perfect, its very notion contains its existence; in the same way, our experience of jouissance accessible to us as finite, located, partial, "castrated," immediately gives birth to the notion of a full, achieved, unlimited jouissance whose existence is necessarily presupposed by the subject who imputes it to another subject, his/her "subject supposed to enjoy."

Our first reaction here is, of course, that this absolute jouissance is a myth, that it never effectively existed, that its status is purely differential, i.e., that it exists only as a negative point of reference with regard to which every effectively experienced jouissance falls short ("pleasurable as this is, it is not THAT!"). However, the recent advances of brain studies open up another approach: one can (no longer only) imagine the situation in which pain (or pleasure) is not generated through sensory perceptions, but through a direct excitation of the appropriate neuronal centres (by means of drugs or electrical impulses)—what the subject will experience in this case will be "pure" pain, pain "as such," the REAL of pain, or, to put it in precise Kantian terms, the non-schematised pain, pain which is not yet rooted in the experience of reality constituted by transcendental categories.

In order to grasp properly what takes place here, one has to take a detour through what Lacan called *la jouissance de l'Autre*—what is this mysterious jouissance? Imagine (a real clinical case, though) two love partner who excite each other by verbalising, telling to each other, their innermost sexual fantasies to such a degree that they reach full orgasm without touching, just as the effect of "mere talking." The result of such excess of intimacy is not difficult to guess: after such a radical mutual exposure, they will no longer be able to maintain their amorous link—too much was being said, or, rather, the spoken word, the big Other, was too directly flooded by jouissance, so the two are embarrassed by each other's presence and slowly drift apart, start to avoid each other's presence. THIS, not a full perverse orgy, is the true excess: not "practicing your innermost fantasies instead of just talking about them," but, precisely, TALKING about them, allowing them to invade the medium of the big Other to such an extent that one can literally "fuck with words," that the elementary, constitutive, barrier between language and jouissance breaks down. Measured by this standard, the most extreme "real orgy" is a poor substitute.

And it is this dimension of the jouissance of the Other that is threatened by the prospect of "pure" jouissance. Is such a short-circuit not the basic and most disturbing feature of consuming drugs to generate experience of enjoyment? What drugs promise is a purely autistic jouissance, a jouissance accessible without the detour through the Other (of the symbolic order)—jouissance generated not by phantasmatic representations, but by directly attacking our neuronal pleasure-centres? It is in this precise sense that drugs involve the suspension of symbolic castration, whose most elementary meaning is precisely that jouissance is only accessible through the medium of (as mediated by) symbolic representation. This brutal Real of jouissance is the obverse of the infinite plasticity of imagining, no longer constrained by the rules of reality. Significantly, the experience of drugs encompasses both these extremes: on the one hand, the Real of noumenal (non-schematised) jouissance which by-passes representations; on the other hand, the wild proliferation of fantasising (recall the proverbial reports on how, after taking a drug, you imagine scenes you never thought you were able to access—new dimensions of shapes, colours, smells …).

One should thus learn to discern the lesson of recent bio-technological breakthroughs. In 2003, Japanese telecom carriers have now come up with the world's first mobile phone that enables users to listen to calls inside their heads—by conducting sound through bone. The phone is equipped with a "Sonic Speaker" which transmits sounds through vibrations that move from the skull to the cochlea in the inner ear, instead of relying on the usual method of sound hitting the outer eardrum. With the new handset, the key to better hearing in a noisy situation is thus to plug your ears to prevent outside noise from drowning out bone-conducted sounds. Here we encounter the Lacanian distinction between reality and the Real: this spectral voice which we hear in our interior, although it has no place in external reality, is the Real at its purest.

In a step further, in 2003, at the Centre for Neuroengineering at Duke University, monkeys with brain implants were trained to move a robot arm with their thoughts: a series of electrodes containing tiny wires were implanted into the brains of two monkeys; a computer then recorded signals produced by the monkeys' brains as they manipulated a joystick controlling the robotic arm in exchange for a reward —sips of juice. The joystick was later unplugged and the arm, which was in a separate room, was controlled directly by the brain signals coming from the implants. The monkeys eventually stopped using the joystick, as if they knew their brains were controlling the robot arm. The Duke researchers have now moved onto researching similar implants in humans: in the Summer of 2004, it was reported that they succeeded at temporarily implanting electrodes into the brains of volunteers; the volunteers then played videogames while the electrodes recorded the brain signals—the scientists trained a computer to recognise the brain activity corresponding to the different movements of the joystick. This procedure of "eavesdropping" on the brain's digital crackle with electrodes (where computers use zeros and ones, neurons encode our thoughts in all-or-nothing electrical impulses) and transmitting the signals to a computer that can read the brain's code and then use the signals to control a machine already has an official name: brain-machine interface. Further prospects include not only more complex tasks (say, implanting the electrodes into the language centres of the brain and thus wirelessly transmitting a person's inner voice to a machine, so that one can speak "directly," bypassing voice or writing), but also sending the brain signals to a machine thousands of miles away and thus directing it from far away. And what about sending the signals to somebody standing nearby with electrodes implanted in his hearing centres, so that he can "telepathically" listen to my inner voice?[4] The Orwellian notion of "thought control" will thus acquire a much more literal meaning.

Even Stephen Hawking's proverbial little finger—the minimal link between his mind and the outside reality, the only part of his paralysed body that Hawking can move—will thus no longer be necessary: with my mind, I can DIRECTLY cause objects to move, i.e., it is the brain itself which will directly serve as the remote control machine. In the terms of German Idealism, this means that what Kant called "intellectual intuition (*intelektuelle Anschauung*)"—the closing of the gap between mind and reality, a mind-process which, in a causal way, directly influences reality, this capacity that Kant attributed only to the infinite mind of God—is now potentially available to all of us, i.e., that we are potentially deprived of one of the basic features of our finitude. And since, as we learned from Kant as well as from Freud, this gap of finitude is at the same time the resource of our creativity (the distance between "mere thought" and causal intervention into external reality

---

4 See Carl Zimmer's concise report, "The Ultimate Remote Control," *Newsweek* (14 June, 2004): 73.

enables us to test the hypotheses in our mind and, as Karl Popper put it, let them die instead of ourselves), the direct short-circuit between mind and reality implies the prospect of a radical closure.

The same point can be made in Nietzschean terms—what is effectively Nietzsche's eternal return of the same? Does it stand for a factual repetition, for the repetition of the past which should be willed as it was, or for a Benjaminian repetition, a return-re-actualisation of that which was lost in the past occurrence, of its virtual excess, of its redemptive potential? There are good reasons to read it as the heroic stance of endorsing factual repetition: recall how Nietzsche emphatically points out that, when faced with every event of my life, even the most painful one, I should gather the strength to joyfully will for it to return eternally. If we read the thought of eternal return in this way, then Agamben's evocation of the holocaust as the conclusive argument against the eternal return retains its full weight: who can will it to return eternally? What, however, if we reject the notion of the eternal return of the same as the repetition of the reality of the past, insofar as it relies on an all too primitive notion of the past, on the reduction of the past to the one-dimensional reality of "what really happened," which erases the virtual dimension of the past? If we read the eternal return of the same as the redemptive repetition of a past virtuality? In this case, applied to the nightmare of the holocaust, the Nietzschean eternal return of the same means precisely that one should will the repetition of the potential which was lost through the reality of the holocaust, the potential whose non-actualisation opened up the space for the holocaust to occur.

There is, however, another problem with the eternal return of the same. What would the digital virtualisation of our lives, the shift of our identity from hardware to software, our change from finite mortals to "undead" virtual entities able to persist indefinitely, migrating from one to another material support, in short: the passage from human to posthuman, mean in

Nietzschean terms? Is this posthumanity a version of the eternal return? Is the digital posthuman subject a version (an historical actualisation) of the Nietzschean "overman"? Or is this digital version of posthumanity a version of what Nietzsche called the Last Man? What if it is, rather, the point of indistinction of the two, and, as such, a signal of the limitation of Nietzsche's thought? In other words, is the eternal return rooted in the human finitude (since the gap between virtuality and actuality only persists from the horizon of finitude), or does it stand for our uncoupling from finitude?

When today's subjectivity is celebrated as rootless, migratory, nomadic, hybrid, etc., does not digitalisation provide the ultimate horizon of this migration, that of the fateful shift of hardware into software, i.e., of cutting the link that attaches a mind to its fixed material embodiment (a single individual's brain), and of downloading the entire content of a mind into a computer, with the possibility of the mind turning into a software that can indefinitely migrate from one to another material embodiment and thus acquiring a kind of undeadness. The metempsychosis, the migration of souls, thus becomes a question of technology. The idea is that "we are entering a regime as radically different from our human past as we humans are from the lower animals"[5]: by uploading yourself into a computer, you become "anything you like. You can be big or small; you can be lighter than air; you can walk through walls."[6] In the good old Freudian terms, we thus get rid of the minimum of resistance that defines (our experience of) reality, and enter the domain in which the pleasure principle reigns unconstrained, with no concessions to the reality principle, or, as David Pearce put it in his quite appropriately titled book *The Hedonistic Imperative*:

5 Vernor Vinge, cited in Bill McKibben, *Enough: Staying Human in an Engineered Age* (New York: Henry Holt and Company 2004) 102.
6 J. Storrs Hall, cited in *Enough*, 102.

nanotechnology and genetic engineering will eliminate aversive experience from the living world. Over the next thousand years or so, the biological substrates of suffering will be eradicated completely," since we shall achieve "the neuro-chemical precision engineering of happiness for every sentient organism on the planet.[7]

(Note the Buddhist overtones of this passage!) And, of course, since one of the definitions of being-human is that disposing of shit is a problem, part of this new posthumanity will also be that dirt and shit will disappear:

> a superman must be cleaner than a man. In the future, our plumbing (of the thawed as well as the newborn) will be more hygienic and seemly. Those who choose to will consume only zero-residue foods, with excess water all evaporating via the pores. Alternatively, modified organs may occasionally expel small, dry compact residues.[8]

Next comes the confused functions of our orifices: is the multi-purpose mouth not "awkward and primitive"?—"An alien would find it most remarkable that we had an organ combining the requirements of breathing, ingesting, tasting, chewing, biting, and on occasion fighting, helping to thread needles, yelling, whistling, lecturing, and grimacing"[9]—not to mention kissing, licking and sucking, thioralerotic confusion ... Is the ultimate target here, not the penis itself, with its embarrassing overlap of the highest (insemination) with the lowest (urination)?

Today, with the prospect of the biogenetic manipulation of human physical and psychic features, the notion of "danger" inscribed into modern technology, elaborated by Heidegger, has turned into a common currency. Heidegger emphasises how the true danger is not the physical self-destruction of

---

[7] Cited in *Enough*, 102-103.
[8] Robert Ettinger, cited in *Enough*, 110.
[9] Robert Ettinger, cited in *Enough*, 110.

humanity, the threat that something will go terribly wrong with biogenetic interventions, but, precisely, that NOTHING will go wrong, that genetic manipulations will function smoothly—at this point, the circle will in a way be closed and the specific openness that characterises being-human abolished. That is to say, is the Heideggerian danger (*Gefahr*) not precisely the danger that the ontic will "swallow" the ontological (with the reduction of man, the *Da* (here) of Being, to just another object of science)? Do we not encounter here again the formula of fearing the impossible: what we fear is that what cannot happen (since the ontological dimension is irreducible to the ontic) will nonetheless happen … And the same point is made in more common terms by cultural critics from Fukuyama and Habermas to McKibben, worried about how the latest techno-scientific developments (which potentially make the human species able to redesign and redefine itself) will affect our being-human—the call we hear is best encapsulated by the title of McKibben's book: "enough." Humanity as a collective subject has to put a limit and freely renounce further "progress" in this direction. McKibben endeavours to empirically specify this limit: somatic genetic therapy is still this side of the enough point, one can practice it without leaving behind the world as we've known it, since we just intervene in a body formed in the old "natural" way; germline manipulations lie on the other side, in the world beyond meaning.[10] When we manipulate the psychic and bodily properties of individuals before they are even conceived, we pass the threshold into full-fledged planning, turning individuals into products, preventing them from experiencing themselves as responsible agents who have to educate/form themselves by the effort of focusing their will, thus obtaining the satisfaction of achievement—such individuals no longer relate to themselves as responsible agents … The insufficiency of this reasoning is double. First, as Heidegger would have put it, the survival of being-human by

---

[10] McKibben, *Enough*, 127.

humans cannot depend on an ontic decision by humans. Even if we try to define the limit of the permissible in this way, the true catastrophe has already happened: we already experience ourselves as in principle manipulable, we need only freely renounce ourselves to fully deploy these potentials. But the crucial point is that, not only will our universe of meaning disappear with biogenetic planning, i.e. not only are the utopian descriptions of the digital paradise wrong, since they imply that meaning will persist; the opposite, negative, descriptions of the "meaningless" universe of technological self-manipulation is also the victim of a perspective fallacy, it also measures the future with inadequate present standards. That is to say, the future of technological self-manipulation only appears as "deprived of meaning" if measured by (or, rather, from within the horizon of) the traditional notion of what a meaningful universe is. Who knows what this "posthuman" universe will reveal itself to be "in itself"? What if there is no singular and simple answer, what if the contemporary trends (digitalisation, biogenetic self-manipulation) open themselves up to a multitude of possible symbolisations? What if the utopia—the pervert dream of the passage from hardware to software of a subjectivity freely floating between different embodiments—and the dystopia—the nightmare of humans voluntarily transforming themselves into programmed beings—are just the positive and the negative of the same ideological fantasy? What if it is only and precisely this technological prospect that fully confronts us with the most radical dimension of our finitude?

Jouissance as a Political Category
Today, this ideological manipulation of obscene jouissance entered a new stage: today's politics is more and more directly the politics of jouissance, concerned with the ways of soliciting or controlling and regulating jouissance. Is the entire opposition between the liberal/tolerant West and the fundamentalist Islam

not condensed in the opposition between, on the one side, a woman's right to free sexuality, inclusive of the freedom to display/expose oneself and provoke/disturb man, and, on the other side, the desperate male attempts to eradicate or, at least, keep under control this threat (recall the ridiculous Taliban prohibition of metal heels for women—as if, even if women are entirely covered with cloth, the clicking sound of their heels would still provoke men)? And, of course, both sides ideologically/morally mystify their position: for the liberal West, the right to provocatively expose oneself to male desire is legitimised as the right to freely dispose of one's body and to enjoy it as one wants, while for Islam, the control of feminine sexuality is, of course, legitimised as the defence of woman's dignity against the threat of being reduced to an object of male sexual exploitation.[11] So while, when the French State prohibited girls from wearing veils in school, one can claim that, in this way, they were enabled to dispose of their body, one can also point out how the true traumatic point for the critics of Muslim "fundamentalism" was that there were women who did not participate in the game of making their bodies available for sexual seduction, for the social circulation/exchange involved in it. In one way or another, all other issues relate to this one: gay marriage and their right to adopt children, divorce, abortion … What the two opposite attitudes share is the extreme disciplinary approach, which is in each case differently directed: "fundamentalists" regulate in detail feminine self-presentation in order to prevent sexual provocation; PC feminist liberals impose a no less severe regulation of behaviour aimed at containing different forms of harassment.

[11] The ironic twist of this stance in the case of anti-Israeli attitudes cannot but strike the eye: on the one hand, one of the major arguments against the State of Israel in the popular Arab press, the final "proof" of its perverted nature, is that women also serve in the army; on the other hand, remember the publicly praised role of women suicide-bombers (although two decades ago, the role of women in the PLO was much more visible—an indication of the desecularisation of the PLO).

In some "radical" circles in the US, a proposal to "rethink" the rights of necrophiliacs (those who desire to have sex with dead bodies) recently started to circulate—why should they be deprived of it? So the idea was formulated that, in the same way that people assign permission for their organs to be used for medical purposes in the case of their sudden death, one should also allow them to give permission for their bodies to be made available to necrophiliacs ... Is this proposal not the perfect exemplification of how the PC stance realises Kierkegaard's old insight into how the only good neighbour is a dead neighbour? A dead neighbour—a corpse—is the ideal sexual partner of a "tolerant" subject trying to avoid any harassment: by definition, a corpse cannot be harassed; at the same time, a dead body DOES NOT ENJOY, so the disturbing threat of excess-enjoyment to the subject playing with the corpse is also eliminated ...

However, one should add a qualification here. What we have today is not so much the POLITICS of jouissance but, more precisely, the REGULATION (administration) of jouissance which is *stricto sensu* post-political. Jouissance is in itself limitless, the obscure excess of the unnameable, and the task is to regulate this excess. The clearest sign of the reign of biopolitics is the obsession with the topic of "stress": how to avoid stressful situations, how to "cope" with them. "Stress" is our name for the excessive dimension of life, for a "too-muchness" that must somehow be kept under control. (For this reason, today, more than ever, the gap that separates psychoanalysis from therapy imposes itself in all its brutality: if one wants therapeutic improvement, one will effectively get a much faster and efficient help from a combination of behavioural-cognitivist therapies and chemical treatment (pills).)

The superego imperative to enjoy thus functions as the reversal of Kant's "Du kannst, denn du sollst!" (You can, because you must!)—it relies on a "You must because you can!" That is to say, the superego aspect of today's "non-repressive" hedonism (the constant provocation we are exposed to, enjoining us to go to the end and explore all modes of jouissance) resides in the way permitted jouissance necessarily turns into obligatory jouissance. However, the question here is: does the capitalist injunction to enjoy effectively aim at soliciting jouissance in its excessive character, or are we ultimately rather dealing with a kind of universalised pleasure-principle, with a life dedicated to pleasures? In other words, are the injunctions to have a good time, to acquire self-realisation and self-fulfilment, etc., not precisely injunctions to AVOID the excessive jouissance, to find a kind of homeostatic balance? Are the Dalai-Lama's edicts not edicts about how to maintain a balanced "proper measure" and avoid disturbing extremes? The situation is here more complex: the problem is that, although the immediate and explicit injunction calls for the rule of a pleasure-principle that would maintain homeostasis, the effective functioning of the injunction explodes these constraints into a striving towards excessive enjoyment.

One is tempted to oppose here the post-'68 Leftist drive to jouissance (to reaching the extreme of forms of sexual pleasures that would dissolve all social links and allow me to find a climax in the solipsism of absolute jouissance) to the consummation of the commodified products promising jouissance: the first still stands for a radical, "authentic" even, subjective position, while the second signals a defeat, a surrender to market forces … Is, however, this opposition effectively so clear? Is it not all too easy to denounce jouissance offered on the market as "false," as providing only the empty package-promise with no substance? Is the hole, the void, in the very heart of our pleasures, not the structure of every jouissance? Furthermore, is it, rather, not that the commodified provocations to enjoy which bombard us all the time push us towards, precisely, an autistic-masturbatory, "asocial," jouissance whose supreme case is drug addiction? Are drugs not at the same time the means for the most radical autistic experience of jouissance and a commodity par excellence?

The drive to pure autistic jouissance (through drugs or other trance-inducing means) arose at a precise political moment: when the emancipatory "sequence" of 1968 exhausted its potentials. At this critical point (mid-1970s), the only option left was a kind of direct, brutal, *passage à l'acte*, a push-towards-the-Real, which assumed three main forms: the search for extreme forms of sexual jouissance; Leftist political terrorism (RAF in Germany, Red Brigades in Italy, etc.) whose wager was that, in an epoch in which the masses are totally immersed into a capitalist ideological sleep, the standard critique of ideology is no longer operative, so that only a resort to the raw, unmediated Real of direct violence—*l'action directe*—can awaken the masses); and, finally, the turn towards the Real of an inner experience (Oriental mysticism). What all three share is the withdrawal from concrete socio-political engagement into a direct contact with the Real.

Freud's "naïve" reflections on how the artist renders the embarrassing, disgusting even, nature of intimate fantasising socially palpable by way of wrapping it in a socially acceptable form—i.e., by way of "sublimating" it, of offering the pleasure of the beautiful artistic form as a lure which seduces us into accepting the otherwise repulsive excessive pleasure of intimate fantasising—obtain new actuality in today's era of permissiveness when performance and other artists stand under pressure to directly stage their innermost private fantasies in a form of desublimated nakedness. Such "transgressive" art confronts us directly with jouissance at its most solipsistic, with masturbatory phallic jouissance. And, far from being individualist, such jouissance precisely characterises individuals insofar as they are caught in a "crowd": what Freud called "crowd [Masse]," is precisely NOT an articulated communal network, but a direct conglomerate of solipsistic individuals—as the saying goes, one is by definition lonely in a crowd. The paradox is thus that a crowd is a fundamentally anti-social phenomenon.

How is this predominance of jouissance linked to (grounded in, even) global capitalism? When, in his *Logique des mondes*, Badiou proposes the concept of "point" as designating the moment of pure subjective decision/choice which stabilises a world, as a simple decision in a situation reduced to a choice of Yes or No, he implicitly refers to Lacan's *point de capiton*, of course—and does this not implicate that there is no "world" outside language, no world whose horizon of meaning is not determined by a symbolic order? The passage to truth is therefore the passage from language ("the limits of my language are the limits of my world") to LETTER, to "mathemes" which run diagonally across a multitude of worlds. Postmodern relativism is precisely the thought of the irreducible multitude of worlds each of them sustained by a specific language-game, so that each world "is" the narrative its members are telling themselves about themselves, with no shared terrain, no common language between them; and the problem of truth is precisely how to establish something that, to refer to terms popular in modal logic, remains the same in all possible worlds.

There is a nice Hitchcockian detail in *Finding Nemo*: when the monstrous daughter of the dentist enters her father's office in which there is the aquarium with fish, the music is that of the murder scene from Psycho. The link is more refined than the idea that the girl is a horror to small helpless animals: at the scene's end, Nemo escapes by slipping down a washbasin plughole—this is his passage from the world of the humans to his own life-world (he ends up in the sea close to the building, where he rejoins his father), and we all know the key role of the motif of the hole in which water disappears in Psycho (the fade-out of the water disappearing down this hole to Marion's dead eye, etc.). The hole in the wash basin thus functions as a secret passage-way between the two totally disparate universes, the human one and the one of the fish—this is true multiculturalism, this acknowledgement that the only way to pass to the Other's world is through what, in our world, appears as the shit-exit, as the hole into the dark domain, excluded from our everyday reality, into which excrements disappear. The radical disparity of the two worlds is noted in a series of details—say, when the father-dentist catches the small Nemo in his net, he thinks he has saved Nemo from certain death, failing to perceive that what terrifies Nemo to the extent that he appears on the brink of death is HIS OWN presence ... However, the wager of the notion of Truth is that this obscene-unnameable link, this secret channel between worlds is not enough: there is a genuine "universal" Truth that cuts across the multitude of world.

Why did Badiou start to elaborate upon this topic of world, the "logic of worlds"? What if the impetus came from his deeper insight into capitalism? What if the concept of world was necessitated by the need to think the unique status of the capitalist universe as world-less? Badiou recently claimed that our time is devoid of world[12]—how are we to grasp this strange thesis? Even the Nazis's anti-Semitism opened up a world: by way of describing the present critical situation, naming the enemy ("Jewish conspiracy"), the goal and the means to achieve it, Nazism disclosed reality in a way that allowed its subjects to acquire a global "cognitive mapping," inclusive of the space for their meaningful engagement. Perhaps, it is here that one should locate the "danger" of capitalism: although it is global, encompassing the whole worlds, it sustains a *stricto sensu* "worldless" ideological constellation, depriving the large majority of people of any meaningful "cognitive mapping." The universality of capitalism resides in the fact that capitalism is not a name for a "civilisation," for a specific cultural-symbolic world, but the name for a truly neutral economico-symbolic machine which operates with Asian values as well as with others, so that Europe's worldwide triumph is its defeat, self-obliteration, the cutting of the umbilical link to Europe. The critics of "Eurocentrism" who endeavour to unearth the secret

[12] See Alain Badiou, "The Caesura of Nihilism," lecture delivered at the University of Essex, 10 September, 2003.

European bias of capitalism fall short here: the problem with capitalism is not its secret Eurocentric bias, but the fact that it REALLY IS UNIVERSAL, a neutral matrix of social relations.

What is capitalist globalisation? Capitalism is the first socio-economic order which de-totalises meaning: it is not global at the level of meaning (there is no global "capitalist world view," no "capitalist civilisation" proper—the fundamental lesson of globalisation is precisely that capitalism can accommodate itself to all civilisations, from Christian to Hindu and Buddhist); its global dimension can only be formulated at the level of truth-without-meaning, as the "real" of the global market mechanism. Consequently, insofar as capitalism already enacts the rupture between meaning and truth, it can be opposed at two levels: either at the level of meaning (conservative reactions to re-enframe capitalism into some social field of meaning, to contain its self-propelling movement within the confines of a system of shared "values" which cement a "community" in its "organic unity"), or to question the real of capitalism with regard to its truth-outside-meaning—what, basically, Marx did.

Ben Goertzel

Quantum Minds

Foreseeing the Emergence of a Fundamentally Novel Form of Intelligence from Quantum Computing Technology

All us humans are quite familiar with human minds, and for decades now there has been a lot of talk about AI minds implemented on digital computers (though no one has managed to create one yet, I among others have been actively trying). But there's no reason to believe that human and digital-computer minds exhaust the realm of possibility for intelligent systems. What I'm going to talk about here is a different variety of possible mind—one that far as I know has never been seriously discussed before. I will introduce the notion of *quantum minds*, intelligent systems that make use of the peculiar dynamics of the quantum domain in a fundamental way within their cognitions.

My approach to quantum mind will draw heavily on the emerging discipline of quantum computing.[1] Contemporary quantum computing research focuses on extremely simple systems that don't come close to having the potential for powerful intelligence. But by extrapolating the ideas in quantum computing theory, it's not hard to gather a few inklings regarding what future quantum-computing-based intelligent systems might be like. Of course such an enterprise

---

[1] Jozef Gruska, *Quantum Computing* (London: McGraw-Hill, 1999).

is highly speculative and the conclusions necessarily far from definitive. But it's exciting that we are now at the stage where such speculations can be done in a scientifically grounded rather than entirely fanciful way.

There has been some literature on the relationship between quantum theory and cognition, but nearly all of it has centred on the hypothesis that the human brain makes fundamental use of macroscopic quantum dynamics.[2] I am neutral on this point: neither I nor anyone else currently understands how the human brain works. But what I do contend is that, even if this is the case, the human brain makes only scant use of the possibilities that quantum dynamics offers for expanded intelligence. Much wilder and more exciting possibilities for quantum cognition exist, which contemporary mathematical quantum theory and quantum computing technology allows us to glimpse at least dimly.

What Is This Thing Called "Mind"?

Before proceeding any further, I must pause to clarify what I mean by the notion of "mind" itself. This is a topic I have dealt with extensively in earlier publications and I will only briefly mention the main ideas here. Intelligence, I have defined in as the achievement of complex goals in complex environments.[3] I have also introduced a related notion of "efficiency-scaled intelligence," which measures intelligence per unit of processing power. A mind, then, I define as the set of patterns associated with an intelligent system. This means patterns in the intelligent system, and also patterns emergent between the system and its environment (including patterns emergent between the system and its tools, other intelligent systems, etc.). Quantum minds as I'll describe them here will display very

---

[2] M. Jibu and K. Yasue, *Quantum brain dynamics and consciousness* (Amsterdam: John Benjamins, 1995); Roger Penrose, *Shadows of the Mind* (Oxford: Oxford University Press, 1994).

[3] Ben Goertzel, *The Structure of Intelligence* (Amsterdam: Springer-Verlag, 1993).

different sorts of dynamic patterns than human or digital computer based minds—that is what I mean by saying they'll be "fundamentally different."

Next, in order to concretely explore the notion of quantum cognition, it's useful to make a somewhat finer-grained analysis of the structure and dynamics of minds in general. Any such analysis can only be considered provisional since our knowledge of the nature of nonhuman minds is very limited at this point, but even a provisional analysis is better than nothing.

One distinction that is common in human psychology and seems fundamentally grounded in the logic of information-processing in general is that of long-term memory versus short-term memory. Long-term memory refers to most things that an intelligent system recalls; short-term memory has gone by many different names (in my own AI work I have used the term "attentional focus") but the main idea is that it consists of those items that an intelligent system has come to pay a particularly large amount of attention to at a particular point in time. How rigid versus fuzzy the distinction between long and short term memory is will depend upon the architecture of the intelligent system in question. Also there is the possibility for intelligent systems to have more than one separate attentional focus. For instance, the Novamente AI architecture that has been the subject of my recent research has a general attentional focus, and then a set of specific attentional foci associated with particular perceptual/motor "interaction channels."[4] We will see here that quantum minds may use fundamentally different methods for storing knowledge in long-term memory, and may also possess types of short-term memory that are not possible for classical minds, alongside more classical types of short-term memory.

---

[4] Moshe Looks and Cassio Pennachin, "Novamente: An Integrative Architecture for Artificial General Intelligence," *Proceedings of AAAI Symposium on Achieving Human-Level Intelligence Through Integrated Systems and Research, Washington DC, 2004.*

Furthermore, in my AI research work, I have found it useful to decompose cognitive operations into two primary categories: probabilistic inference and evolutionary learning. The Novamente AI system is fundamentally based on these two operations; and one may argue that human brain dynamics reflects these two basic properties as well, with Hebbian learning[5] serving as an approximate probabilistic reasoning engine, and Edelman-style Neural Darwinism[6] serving as a neural implementation of evolutionary learning. Here I will explore the possibilities of quantum cognition by exploring how quantum dynamics allows both probabilistic inference and evolutionary learning to be done in fundamentally different ways. These differences, I suggest, are a large part of what will make future quantum minds so very different from anything else yet conceived.

Brief Survey of Quantum Weirdness
In this section, for the benefit of readers without background in quantum physics, I'll spend a little bit of time giving some preliminaries about quantum theory. Bear with me if you're already a quantum expert—after all the familiar concepts, there will be some original ideas at the end!

Quantum theory began relatively unadventurously as a modern incarnation of ancient Greek atomistic theory. The idea of the "quantum" is that there is a minimum size to the stuff that happens in the universe. Specifically, according to quantum physics, there is a quantum of "action"—action in physics is defined as energy multiplied by time, and the quantum is Planck's constant, $6.6260755 * 10^{-34}$ joules-second.

The existence of this minimum quantum of action, however, has some very peculiar consequences. The key point is that, if there is a minimum amount of action one can exert, then there is no way to measure very small things without disturbing

---

5   Donald Hebb, *The Organisation of Behaviour* (Amsterdam: North-Holland, 1948).
6   Gerald Edelman, *Neural Darwinism* (New York: Basic Books, 1987).

them somewhat. If some phenomenon exists on the Planck scale, then measuring it necessarily also involves action on the Planck scale, which will therefore cause a significant perturbation. This means that what happens to a particular quantum system when we're looking will never be all that close to the same as what would have happened if we hadn't looked.

What is really odd about quantum systems, however, is that when *in principle* there's no way to know what happens in a system—because of the limits on observability posed by the minimum quantum of action—then the logic of what happens in the system becomes different. The in-principle knowability affects the system dynamics itself. This was an unexpected discovery, and I think it probably ranks as the most surprising scientific discovery ever made.

One common—but not complete—way to describe the situation is to say that, in the microworld of particles and atoms, an event does not become definite until someone observes it. An unobserved quantum system remains in an uncertain state, a superposition of many different possibilities. Observation causes "collapse" into a definite condition, which is chosen at random from among the possibilities provided. What is peculiar about quantum physics is that the dynamics of systems in uncollapsed form, unobserved, is different from the dynamics of systems in collapsed form, after observation. I.e., it is that definiteness affects dynamics in a concrete way.

As an example of this kind of peculiarity, consider the classic double-slit experiment. A particle passes through one of two slits in a barrier and leaves a mark on a plate on the other side of the barrier, indicating which slit it passed through. If one observes each particle as it passes through the barrier, the marks on the plate will be consistent with one's observations: "Fifteen hundred through the top slit, six hundred and ninety through the bottom slit," or whatever. But if one does not observe the particles passing through the barrier, then something very strange happens. There are marks on the plate where there shouldn't be any—marks that could not have been made by particles passing through either slit. Instead of passing through the slit like a good particle should, the particle acts as if it were a wave in some mysterious medium, squeezing through the slit and then rapidly diffusing. The key point is whether the particle was looked at or not.

In fact, as the great physicist John Archibald Wheeler—the inventor of the term "black hole" and a leading developer of Einsteinian gravitation theory—pointed out in 1979, this even works if the choice is *delayed*.[7] One then arrives at the phenomenon of the "quantum eraser." In other words, suppose one has a machine record which slit each particle passed through. If after a few hours one destroys the machine's records without having looked at them, and only afterwards looks at the plate, then result is the same as if the information had never existed; the plate shows that the particles behaved like waves. But in the same scenario, if one looks at the machine's information before one erases it, the picture on the plate is quite different: it is consistent with whatever the machine said.

Somehow looking at the particle, measuring it, forces it to make a choice between one of the two alternatives, one of the two slits. This choice is a random one: even knowing all there is to know about the physical system, there is no way to predict the path that each individual particle will take, in the eventuality that it is observed. The reduction from indeterminacy to definiteness occurs at the *point of observation*.

Richard Feynman, one of the physics stars of the century, once said: " He who to tries to understand quantum theory vanishes into a black hole, never to be seen again." Niels Bohr, one of the founding fathers of quantum physics, said in 1927: "Anyone who is not shocked by quantum theory does not understand it." The reason for these declarations of bafflement is clear. If the dynamical equations of quantum theory are taken literally, nothing is ever in a definite state; everything is always suspended in a superposition of various possibilities. But yet

---

[7] John Wheeler, *Frontiers of Time* (Amsterdam: North-Holland, 1989).

that's not what we see in the world around us—neither in the physics lab nor in everyday life. When then does the superposed world become the actual world? When it is recorded by a machine? When it is recorded by a person? What about an intelligent machine ... or an observant chimpanzee, dog, mouse, or ant?

An added, related peculiarity is provided by the phenomenon of nonlocality. The classic example of this involves two particles that are at one point joined together, but are then shot off in different directions until they're far distant. One supposes that the particles are, for instance, electrons, each of which has a property called "spin" that takes one of two values: either Up or Down. One may know, since the two particles were initially joined together, that only one of the particles may have spin Up, the other having spin Down. But which is Up, which is Down? This is random. There's no way to predict this.

Now, when you observe one of the particles, it automatically tells you something about the other particle—no matter how far away the other one is. If the first particle is observed to have spin Up, then the other particle is known to have spin Down, even if it's 10 quadrillion light years away. But the funny thing is that, because of the critical role of observation in quantum measurement, this act of observation in some sense causes a physical change. By observing the one particle to have spin Up, the state of the other, far-distant particle is then in a way caused to have spin Down. Its state is caused to collapse from uncertainty into definiteness.

When Einstein, Podolsky and Rosen discovered this phenomenon in the 1930's they thought they had proved quantum theory false. It seemed to contradict Einstein's special relativity theory, which says that no information can travel faster than light speed. But there's no contradiction, because it's not classical information that's travelling instantaneously, it's just bizarre counterintuitive quantum collapse-into-definiteness. Although Einstein was himself a pioneer of quantum theory, he never liked its indeterminacy: he said, famously "God doesn't play dice." But it turns out that the universe at a very basic level does play dice—and this dice-playing is not only empirically verifiable, but useful as the foundation for a new generation of computing technology.

And, just as critically, it turns out that this dice-playing has far weirder consequences than one would naively think dice-playing would have. Randomness is one thing, but the observation-dependency we see in the quantum world is something else entirely, and in fact goes beyond playing dice. To me, the odd thing isn't that God plays dice, it's that God makes the dice obey different rules when we're not looking at them versus when we are. I'll return to this point a little later.

Quantum Theory and the Human Mind/Brain

The role of observation in quantum theory has caused some theorists to associate quantum theory with consciousness. This idea goes back to the 60's and quantum pioneer Eugene Wigner, and has more recently been adopted by a veritable army of New Age thinkers.[8] But the problem with this would-be "quantum theory of consciousness" is that—so far, at any rate—it fails to connect in a sufficiently thorough way with the *biology* and *psychology* of consciousness.

It's true that in quantum physics, consciousness often appears as *the agent which forces a choice*. And correspondingly, in psychology, consciousness is often psychologically associated with choice or decision. In many cases we only become conscious of something when appropriate unconscious processes judge that some sort of complex decision in its regard is required. But even so, one cannot plausibly define human consciousness as the collapse of the quantum wave function. A good theory of consciousness must have something to say about the psychology of attention, about the neural processes

---

[8] Eugene P. Wigner, *The Scientist Speculates*, ed. I.J. Good (London: Heinemann, 1962).

underlying the subjectively perceived world, and above all about the experience of being a conscious person. So far the idea of quantum observation as the essence of consciousness fails this test by a long shot.

Quantum consciousness advocates have long sought to establish a crucial role for quantum phenomena in the human brain. This is not as outlandish as it may seem; while quantum theory is generally considered a theory of the very small, it is not firmly restricted to the microworld. There are some well-known macroscopic systems that display elementary-particle-style quantum weirdness; for example, SQUIDs, Superconducting Quantum Interference Devices, which are little supercooled rings used in some medical devices.[9] A SQUID is around the size of a wedding ring, but its electromagnetic properties are just as indeterminate, and just as able to participate in peculiar nonlocality phenomena, as the spin of an electron.

Is the brain a macrosopic quantum device, like a SQUID? It's not impossible. If it's true, then all of contemporary cognitive neuroscience potentially goes out the window. Neuroscientists now commonly think in terms of "neural networks." The brain cells called neurons pass electricity amongst each other along connections called synapses, and this constant to-and-fro of electricity seems to give rise to the dynamics of mind. Thoughts and feelings are considered as patterns of electrical flow, and synaptic conductance. But if the brain is a macroscopic quantum system, all this electrodynamics may be epiphenomenal—the high-level consequence of low-level quantum-consciousness-based cognitive magic.

It's a wonderful story; at present, however, there's basically no evidence that the brain's high-level dynamics display quantum properties. The Japanese physicists Jibu and Yasue, in their book *Quantum Brain Dynamics and Consciousness* (1995), put forth a seductive hypothesis regarding quantum effects in

---

[9] J.C. Gallop, *SQUIDs, the Josephson Effect and Superconducting Electronics* (New York: Adam Hilger, 1991).

water megamolecules floating between neurons. But the jury's still out; in fact, from the point of view of the scientific mainstream, there's not even enough cause yet to convene the jury in the first place. We don't currently have enough evidence to verify or refute such theories.

It's quite possible that there are quantum effects in the brain, but without the dramatic consequences that some theorists associate with them. Perhaps the quantum effects aid and augment the neural network dynamics traditionally studied; perhaps they're just one among many factors that go into our experience of consciousness. Or perhaps the sceptics are right, and the brain is no more a quantum system than an automobile—which is also made out of tiny particles obeying the laws of quantum physics.

Quantum Computing and its Limits

Next—and more pertinently to the main theme of the current essay—there is a healthy field of research aimed at bringing the peculiarities of quantum physics to bear on computing technology. Quantum computing is not yet commercial technology, but it's getting there. The first quantum computers will be relatively simple, specialised machines; but their successors will be more general and powerful, and quite possibly we'll see a rate of improvement just as impressive as we've seen in the traditional computing industry.

It seems clear that, purely based on superior miniaturisation, quantum computers will be much more powerful than conventional ones. The capability of exploiting quantum nonlocality and so forth computing is even more exciting. However, physics theory places some interesting limits on just how profoundly superior quantum computers can become. Both the strengths and limitations of quantum computers are worthy of careful attention.

For a while, some theorists thought that quantum computers might be able to compute "incomputable" things—things that ordinary digital computers just can't compute. This turns out not to be the case. But even so, there are many things they can compute *faster* than ordinary computers. And in computer science, very frequently, speed makes all the difference.

What does "incomputable" mean? Something is incomputable if it can't be represented in terms of a finite-sized computer programme. For instance, the number $\pi=3.1415926235$ ... is *not* incomputable. Even though it goes on forever, and never repeats itself, there is a simple computer programme that will generate it. True, this computer programme can never generate *all* of π, because to do so it would have to run on literally *forever*—it can only generate each new digit at a finite speed. But still, there is a programme with the property that, *if* you let it run forever, then it *would* generate all of π, and because of this the number π is not considered incomputable. What's fascinating about π is that even though it goes on forever and doesn't repeat itself, in a sense it only contains a finite amount of information—because it can be compactly represented by the computer programme that generates it.

But it turns out that, unlike π, almost all of the numbers on the number line *are* incomputable. They have infinite information; they can't be stored in, or produced by, any digital computer programme. Although they're the majority case, these are strange numbers, because it's impossible to ever give an example of one of them. For, if one could give an example of such a number, by the very act of giving the example one would be giving a finite exact description of that number—but how can one give a finite description of a number that has infinite information and hence by definition has no finite exact description?

Mathematicians have proved that these incomputable numbers "exist" in an indirect way, by showing that the set of all numbers on the number line is a *bigger kind of infinity* than the set of all computers.[10] Because of the strangeness of these

---

[10] In the lingo of set theory, the set of computers has cardinality aleph-zero; the set of real numbers has cardinality aleph-one.

ideas, some mathematicians think that the idea of a continuous number line should be discarded, and that mathematics should concern itself only with computable numbers, numbers that have some finite description that can be embodied in a computer programme.

Incomputable numbers have a lot to do with randomness. The digits of π are random in a sense, but yet in another sense they're non-random, because you can predict them if you know the formula. The digits of an incomputable number are random in a much stronger sense: there's no formula or computer programme that will allow you to predict exactly what they're going to be.

Because of this relationship with randomness, some scientists thought that quantum theory and incomputability might be connected. They thought that quantum randomness might somehow allow quantum computers to compute these mysterious, seemingly ineffable incomputable numbers. This notion was particularly appealing because of the conceptual resonance between incomputability and consciousness. Incomputable numbers exist, but you can never grasp onto them—they're elusive in the same vague sense that consciousness is. Perhaps quantum randomness, incomputability and consciousness are facets of the same underlying mystery?

But, while it may be that in some sense these things all reflect the same mystery, it is *not* true that quantum computers can compute incomputable numbers. In the mid-1980's, physicist David Deutsch proved mathematically that a quantum computer can't compute anything special, beyond what an ordinary computer can do. The mysterious incomputable numbers, that some mathematicians don't believe in, are also incomputable for quantum computers. Deutsch was not the first to study quantum computing—there was earlier work by legendary physicist Richard Feynman, Paul Benioff of AT&T Bell Labs, and William H. Bennett of IBM Research, among others. But Deutsch's paper set the field of quantum computing on a significantly more solid footing, mathematically and conceptually.

But if quantum computers can't compute anything new beyond what ordinary digital computers can then what good are they? Well, one other thing Deutsch discovered was that, in some cases, quantum computers can solve problems much faster than ordinary computers. They'll come up with the same answer, but their indeterminate nature allows them, in a sense, to explore multiple pathways to an answer at once, hence arriving at the right answer faster. The trick is that they can't be *guaranteed* to get to the right answer faster. In the worst case scenario, they'll take as long as an ordinary computer. But *on average*, they'll be vastly faster.

To understand the power of this, think about contemporary systems for encrypting information, for secure transmission over the Internet. The encryption algorithms in use today are based on factorisation — to crack one of them, you'd need to be able to divide a very large number into its component factors. But factoring large numbers is an intractable problem for ordinary computers today. On the other hand, it's known in theory how, with a quantum computer, one can factor large numbers rapidly, on average. When these devices are built, we'll have to find different ways of creating codes … and fortunately, quantum computing also provides some of these.

Ordinary computers are based on bits — elementary pieces of information, which always take one of the two values 0 or 1. All traditional computer programmes internally represent information as long sequences of bits. A word processing file, a computer programme itself, the Windows operating system — all are represented as sequences of 0's and 1's, where each 0 or 1 is represented physically by the absence or presence of electrical charge at a certain position in computer memory, the absence or presence of magnetic charge at a certain position on a hard drive, etc. Quantum computers are based instead on what are called "qubits." A qubit may be most simply considered as the spin state of a particle like an electron. An electron can have spin Up or spin Down, or, it can have a superposition of Up and Down spin—spin, say, half Up and half Down; or three quarters Up and one quarter Down. A qubit contains more information than a bit—but in a strange sense, not in the same sense in which two bits contain more information than a bit.

Now, quantum theory is not the ultimate theory of the universe. The big thorn in the side of modern physics is the apparent irreconcilability of quantum physics with Einstein's general-relativistic theory of gravitation. Quantum theory talks about indeterminate waves; general relativity talks about curved spacetime; and no one knows how to translate between the two languages with complete accuracy. Mathematician Roger Penrose and a few others have speculated that the ultimate unified theory of quantum gravitation will yield a new kind of computing—quantum gravity computing—that *will* allow the computation of traditionally incomputable numbers. Of course this can't be ruled out. No one knows what a quantum gravity bit would look like, nor how they would interact. However, the vast majority of physicists and computer scientists are rightly sceptical of Penrose's conjecture ... it doesn't take a terribly sensitive nose to detect a scent of wishful thinking here.

Quantum Evolutionary Computing
One important aspect of human and AI cognition, I have argued, is evolutionary learning—the creation of novel concepts and procedures via "guided trial and error" processes analogous to evolution by natural selection. It is interesting to explore how this may take place within quantum computers.

In examples like factoring and searching, one is coaxing a quantum computer to behave with the inexorable precision of a standard digital computer. In *evolutionary* quantum computing, on the other hand, one tries to infuse quantum computing with some of the creative imprecision of living systems (which of course, at the molecular level, are complex quantum systems in their own right).[11]

Evolutionary quantum computing is an extension to the quantum domain of a technique in conventional computer science called "evolutionary programming," in which one creates a computer programme solving a given problem by simulating natural selection.[12] One creates a population of candidate programmes, and evaluates how well each of them does at solving the problem. One takes the better programmes from the population and combines them with each other, in the manner of the DNA crossover operations by which, in sexually reproducing species, a mother and a father combine to yield a child. The population of programmes evolves over time, by the dynamic of "survival of the fittest programmes," where fitness is defined by efficacy at solving the problem at hand. This is a very effective approach to a variety of computer science problems. Novamente currently uses a related but more sophisticated technique called the Bayesian Optimisation Algorithm, which develops the philosophy of evolutionary programming in a direction influenced by probability theory.[13]

The beauty of evolutionary computing in the quantum domain is that it provides a partial way of getting around the decoherence problem that plagues modern quantum computing (which is that, in most cases, after one sets up a quantum computing system, its components tend to "decohere" and hence lose their wonderful quantum weirdness). In theory, one can evolve a set of quantum "programmes" solving a target problem *without ever looking inside the programmes to see how they work*. All one has to observe is how well they solve the target problem. Observing a quantum system is one thing that causes it to decohere, because when you observe it, its wave function

[11] Ben Goertzel, "Evolutionary Quantum Computing," *Dynamical Psychology* 3 (1997).

[12] John Koza, *Genetic Programming* (Addison-Wesley, 1988).

[13] Martin Pelikan, *The Bayesian Optimisation Algorithm: From Single-Level to Hierarchy*, PhD Thesis (University of Illinois at Champaign-Urbana, 2002).

gets smeared up with yours—the famous observer/observed interaction. The ability to create quantum computer programmes without observing them along the way—because, to create programmes in an evolutionary manner, one only has to observe their behaviour—may be very powerful, as quantum computing progresses.

If quantum theory does play a role in the brain, it is probably more in the evolutionary-quantum-computing style than in the manner of quantum algorithms for factoring and searching. Nobel laureate Gerald Edelman and others have argued that the brain is an evolving system, with different "maps" of neural connectivity competing with each other to serve various cognitive, perceptive and active functions. If neural subnetworks in the brain are really molecular quantum computing systems, then the brain may be an evolving quantum computer. Who knows? At the present time, evolutionary quantum computing is still in the domain of theory—just like Schor's codebreaking quantum computers, and all other quantum computers except extremely simple examples.

But as I noted above, it seems to me most likely that, even if the human brain does use quantum effects on a macroscopic scale, it uses them in a not very powerful way. Let's face it, the brain isn't all that brilliant. A cognitive system with really flexible access to the quantum domain would be orders of magnitude cleverer than the human brain, and would also have a fundamental understanding of the microworld that we lack. It would reason fluently with complex as well as real probabilities, and would be able to search huge spaces of possibilities in parallel. True, it would still be nothing more than a set of patterns associated with an intelligent system—but the metapatterns structuring this set of patterns would be quite different than in our purely-classical-physics-based minds.

Hugo de Garis has written a series of papers exploring the notion of quantum evolutionary computing in detail, focusing on the notion of quantum neural networks.[14] He has spelled out in detail how one could construct a quantum neural network and evolve it the quantum way, allowing different sets of inter-neuron weights to be experimented with in different possible universes. Based on the particular set of numerical parameters he explores, he concludes that the quantum evolutionary process would give a 100 times speedup over the classical evolutionary process. This may seem not much but, on the other hand, how much smarter would you be if you could think 100 times faster? And de Garis's calculations, while fascinating, are relatively simplistic—there is no doubt that massively greater speedups could be obtained via more sophisticated architectures.

Quantum Associative Memory

Relatedly, Mitja Perus has explored the relevance of quantum dynamics for memory processes.[15] He has taken a standard neural network model of memory, the Hopfield network, and modified it to make use of quantum dynamics.

A standard Hopfield network consists of a set of formal neurons (simplified mathematical models of brain cells) interconnected with each other. Each neuron may fire or not at any given point in time, and when it fires it passes charge to other neurons along its connections to them. The connections are weighted, and it's the weights of connections between the neurons that differentiate different neural networks from each other. These weights can be used to encode memories, and a single neural network can encode a lot of different memories

---

[14] Hugo de Garis, Ravichandra Sriram, and Zijun Zhang, "Quantum Generation of Neural Networks," *International Joint Conference on Neural Networks*, Portland, Oregon, USA, 20-24 July, 2003; Hugo de Garis, Ravichandra Sriram, and Zijun Zhang, "Quantum Computation vs. Evolutionary Computation: Could Evolutionary Computation Become Obsolete?" *Congress on Evolutionary Computation*, Canberra, Australia, 8-12 December, 2003.

[15] Mitja Perus, Horst Bischof, Tarik Hadzibeganovic, "A Natural Quantum Neural-Like Network," *Neuroquantology* (September 2005).

this way—but what's interesting is that no one memory is encoded in any one neuron, nor even in any small group of neurons. Rather, each memory is encoded as a pattern of activity across the whole neural network, or a large portion thereof. Memory is "holistic"; adaptation of connection weights on the local level leads to intelligent memory behaviour on the global level.

And when a Hopfield network is presented with a stimulus that only partially overlaps with something in its memory, the neurons will iteratively fire in such a way that causes the network to relax into a configuration corresponding to some pattern the network has previously remembered. If the network has remembered the images of 100 peoples' faces, and is then shown an image consisting of part of one of these faces, or a similar person's face, it will automatically iterate into a state of activity corresponding to the "best match" to its input.

Improvising on this standard approach, Perus describes a scheme for encoding information in a quantum Hopfield-like network. In the lingo of quantum theory, each memory is encoded in an eigenfunction, and retrieval is done using quantum holography. Reading out memory then involves collapse of the wave function.

Less technically, what this means is that, in the quantum Hopfield net, information is stored even more holistically than in an ordinary Hopfield net. Not only is each memory spread spatially over the whole network, it's spread across multiple parallel universes as well. Different memories don't just physically overlap, they're quantum-entangled. This gives even more effective performance than ordinary Hopfield nets—more memories stored with a given number of neurons. However, remembering a memory stored in the quantum Hopfield net involves causing a collapse of the wave function—the recollection of a memory involves the macroscopic registration of the memory.

The bottom line: just as evolutionary quantum computing allows faster evolutionary learning, quantum Hopfield nets allow more compact storage of information. And this greater time and space efficiency is not purchased via mere "tricks," it's purchased via distributing learning and memory across multiple parallel universes.

One hypothesis is that the human brain actually uses these sorts of mechanisms. But as I noted above, my suspicion is that this is either false, or true only in a very limited sense. I suspect that the subjective experience of a mind that heavily uses multiple-universe computation for learning and memory will be very difficult for us humans to relate to—even though the greater time and space efficiency that comes along with this different experience is easy for us to understand.

Quantum Probability Theory

Quantum theory, due to its generally human-baffling nature, has generated a wide variety of different "interpretations"— attempts to reformulate and explain the mathematics of quantum physics in terms more familiar and comprehensible to the human mind. Among these, one of my favourites is "quantum probability theory," a radical notion developed in a series of papers by the physicist Saul Youssef.[16]

In ordinary probability theory, one assigns probabilities to events and then manipulates these probabilities using special arithmetical rules. Probabilities are numbers between 0 and 1, as in "there's a .5 chance of rain tomorrow" or "there's a .9 chance that Ben will say something obnoxious in the next 55 minutes." Probabilistic reasoning plays a large role in the Novamente AI system, and in a lot of other current AI work as well.

Ordinarily probabilities are real numbers, but one can also develop an alternate probability theory, which is also

[16] Saul Youssef, "Quantum Mechanics as an Exotic Probability Theory," *Proceedings of the Fifteenth International Workshop on Maximum Entropy and Bayesian Methods*, ed. K.M. Hanson and R.N. Silver (Santa Fe: St John's College, 1995). http://xxx.lanl.gov/abs/quant-ph/9509004

completely mathematically consistent, in which probabilities are complex numbers.[17] So we might say "there's a .5 + .6i chance that the electron will pass through this portion of the diffraction grating." This seems intuitively rather peculiar—but Youssef has shown that, if we consider probabilities as complex numbers, then after some fairly natural mathematical manipulations, the basic laws of quantum theory fall out as natural consequences.

Quantum probability theory provides a beautiful crystallisation of the true weirdness—from a human-intuition perspective—of quantum reality. One must reason about the probabilities of observed phenomena using real probabilities. But, one must reason about the probabilities of unobserved phenomena using complex probabilities. Now, of course, one can never verify directly that these unobserved phenomena are actually obeying the conclusions of complex-probability inference. But assuming this allows one to make very simple explanations of the real-probability-tables one creates from tabulating the results of observations. So the simplest known explanation of the real probabilities one observes via one's laboratory equipment, is that when one isn't looking, the world is acting in a way that can only be predicted via complex probabilities! Somehow, complex probabilities are the logic of the unknowable, whereas real probabilities are the logic of the knowable.

Youssef's mathematics also leaves room for yet more exotic probability theories—involving not just the complex numbers, but abstract "numbers" drawn from higher algebras called quaternions and octonions. As Geoffrey Dixon and others have observed, the octonionic algebra has all sorts of subtle

---

[17] If you're not familiar with complex numbers, it would be too much of a digression for me to introduce them here, but you really should get a primer. There are plenty of good online tutorials, such as http://www.clarku.edu/~djoyce/complex/. The basic idea is to introduce a new "number" called i, which represents the square root of negative one. This simple idea lets you solve all polynomial equations and leads to all manner of amazingly beautiful mathematics.

relationships with modern physics, including the Standard Model of strong and electroweak forces as well as general-relativistic gravitation.[18] It seems quite possible that octonionic probabilities might be part of the key to the long-quested unified model of quantum theory and general relativity.

A fascinating question to ponder is: What happens to probabilistic reasoning when one introduces complex, quantum probabilities?

One may, perhaps, view the distinction between classical and quantum minds, as the distinction between minds that reason using real-number probabilities only, and minds that reason using both real and complex number probabilities.

Of course, real number probabilities are a subset of complex number probabilities; but if one knows one is dealing with real number probabilities only, one can make a lot of simplifications, so that a mind specialised for reasoning about elementary particles using quantum probabilities wouldn't necessarily be good at reasoning about macroscopic systems like baseballs and budgerigars using real probabilities.

The human mind is clearly specialised for real probabilities. Current digital-computer AI designs are similarly specialised. But one of the many flexibilities associated with a digital software implementation is the ability to shift between different underlying reasoning logics. I have thought this issue through in some detail in the context of my own Novamente AI design. Creating a Novamente that reasoned using quantum probabilities rather than real ones would require only small changes to the source code. In fact, if a Novamente system were presented with a lot of sensory data from the quantum domain, it would quite likely modify its inference code to make use of quantum probabilities—a large change in conceptual perspective, but not in terms of software code.

But what does reasoning using complex probabilities mean? This is hard for the human mind to grasp, but some aspects

---

[18] Geoffrey Dixon, *Division Algebras: Octonions, Quaternions, Complex Numbers, and the Algebraic Design of Physics* (Boston: Kluwer, 1994).

may be understood. For instance, in ordinary probability theory, if one has

P(X or Y) = P(X)

(read this "the probability of 'either X or Y' equals the probability of X") then this implies that Y either never happens or is a subcase of Y, so it implies that either Y=X or P(Y) < P(X). For instance one might have

P((a person is between age 20 and 30) or (a person is between age 25 and 26)) = P(a person is between age 20 and 30)

On the other hand, in quantum probability theory, one can have P(X or Y) = P(X) even if Y is neither the same as X nor in any case "less likely than" Y. For instance, if P(X) = 1 and P(Y) = i and X and Y are independent then one has

P(X or Y) = P(X) + P(Y) - P(X) P(Y) = 1 + i − 1*i = 1 = P(X)

This simple calculation illustrates the different meaning that "or" has in quantum probability theory. The whole concept of "alternatives" doesn't mean the same thing in quantum probability theory as in ordinary probability theory, because quantum *or*-ness embodies the possibility of "synergetic" quantum effects between the alternatives. In the simple calculation given above what's happening between X and Y is a kind of "destructive interference" where the additional contribution of Y to "X or Y" is being cancelled out.

Here we see something a little different than in the cases of evolutionary quantum computing or quantum Hopfield memories. In those cases the emphasis of the discussion was on the greater efficiency supplied by quantum computing, and the surreal multiple-universes nature of the computing was viewed as the means to an end. In this case the emphasis is on the different inference rules implicit in quantum dynamics. However, once the results of quantum probabilistic inference are collapsed and turned into macroscopic measurements, they will inevitably result in computations that follow classical probability theory—the difference, as always, being that some computations can be done vastly more quickly via the utilisation of quantum effects.

A New Kind of Mind
So what can we say about the nature of quantum minds? I've discussed quantum learning, memory and reasoning—and in each case we see two fundamental aspects:

- Much more efficient operation than is possible for classical systems
- Distribution of learning, reasoning or memory across multiple universes

But what will be the subjective experience of a quantum mind? Clearly its mind will run much faster than ours, which will make some difference to its experience. But this probably won't be the most critical aspect.

More interestingly, a quantum mind will experience directly quantum coupling with its environment, which may mean that it doesn't feel as distinct from its environment as we do. And the different subcomponents within it will also experience nonlocal quantum coupling with each other—meaning that quantum experience may have an even greater sense of holistic unity than our own experience. It may be very difficult for a quantum mind to conceive of one part of its mind as separate from the others—because its reasoning, learning and memory relies on the interpenetration of the different parts of the mind. Then there may be a direct experience of collapse, when the quantum interpenetration gives way to macroscopic definiteness, and the multiple universes collapse to one. Collapse has to do with statistical correlation with the environment, so the experience of collapse is really to do with the transition between nonlocal quantum correlation with the microscopic environment to statistically, classical probabilistic correlation with the macroscopic environment.

While these speculations are interesting, there is no way we can really know if they're correct. The key point I want to make is the strong possibility of the existence of quantum minds that possess a type of cognition completely different from our own. I see little credibility in claims that the human brain is a macroscopic quantum system in a strong sense, but I do think that macroscopic quantum cognitive systems are possible and will be both powerful and fascinating. Constructing such systems should be one of the major goals of 21st century science.

Ivan M. Havel

At Home in Vesmír

1. Is Scientific Enquiry into Consciousness Possible?
There are two kinds of truths. Those that we all agree on and those in which someone unshakingly believes. I even dare to say, that the more someone is certain about his truth the less it conforms with even his own definition of truth as such.

What exactly does it mean "to be certain about one's own truth"? Here I refer to the certainty from within, which is immediate, unproblematic and non-hesitant. It could be anything, from the obsessive delusions of a paranoid to the trust in one's own experience, which is a life's privilege and necessity for all of us. Of course, we all have our rock-solid beliefs and deeply imbedded fixed ideas (no mind can exist without them) and the reader probably expects me now to begin musings on the divide between tolerance and arrogance. I won't; let us try something different. I would like to ask the reader to kindly chose one of his or her own fixed truths and use it to test himself or herself regarding to what it really means

* The following seven essays originally appeared in the Czech scientific journal *Vesmír* (The Universe) and were included in my book "Otevřené oči a zvednuté obočí" (Prague: Vesmír, 1997). The English version of these essays, translated by Josef P. Skala with the generous assistance of Dr Jennifer Simons, appears here for the first time.

to be certain about something. Quite seriously: grab that truth by your consciousness and, entirely disregarding what it is about, concentrate fully only on the way you experience it. Can one actually do this? Is it possible to analyse one's own certainty without spoiling it? In any case, what certainly is valid, is the notion that my certainty about my own truth is entirely different from my perception of the certainties of others.

Let us illustrate this by a simpler example: While I know very well (or, more precisely, I remember) how it feels when *I have* a headache, I cannot imagine a headache felt by *somebody else* using any means other than remembering again my own aching head. There is, however, another difference: when I am actually experiencing a headache (fortunately not the case right now), the ache felt in my head is straight-forward and unproblematic, and I don't really see any need to objectively test the possibility that I may be mistaken about it. Could I be mistaken? Even if all the neurologists on Earth would insist that I do not have a headache, the matter would not change — I know that I have a headache, and my consciousness does not fool me because my consciousness is me. Something entirely different is, however, your headache, my dear reader (my apologies — it is only an example). Should you complain about your headache to me, I may chose to either believe you or not. It would even make sense to consult neurologists for their "objective" advice about your head (after all they may know what's happening in there if it really hurts).

How is it then? In addition to the realities of the outside world which lend themselves to objective scientific enquiry, there exist worlds of our inner experiences, aches, truths and certainties about those truths — worlds which could only be perceived by our own consciousness. The least mysterious worlds, in a sense, because the closest and the most intimate ones.

We all know that methods of measuring, observing and imaging by the human brain are being improved upon with each passing day; shouldn't we then consider the physical / chemical / biological processes known to occur in the brain to be equal with the events occurring in the consciousness? That is an opinion adopted by some. Never, insist others, neither a sign of equality nor a sign of inequality could be used—nothing which happens in the mind exists in reality, all of it is just scientifically uninteresting "optical" delusions accompanying the brain processes. But it does exist, others suggest, and that what is really doubtful are the brain processes themselves, because, let us face it, isn't even scientific enquiry into those processes itself really just a fabrication? Both really do exist, propose others still, but they are two separate kingdoms which communicate with each other via some mystical means. There even exist, in fact, many other opinions.

In this context it is interesting to note the ever-increasing number of publications in the field of cognitive sciences (comprising psychology, artificial intelligence, neurosciences, linguistics, philosophy of the mind, etc.) which in one way or another address the problem of consciousness. Even modern physics is beginning to pay attention to it. Is then the objective enquiry into the inner universe of the mind possible? Could there really be a sound scientific enquiry into our consciousness?

D.C. Dennett, a well-known American philosopher working in the field of cognitive science, suggests that such an enquiry is indeed possible. In his book, with the boastful title "Consciousness Explained,"[1] he proposes the following methodological approach: to analyse the testimony of others about the experiences in their mind. Granted—we would never be able to verify their testimonies. It would not make sense to even attempt any such verification inasmuch as it does not make any sense to consider verification of what has been described in novels, fairy tales and myths. In spite of that, proposes Dennett, it is possible to theorise objectively about

---

[1] D.C. Dennett, *Consciousness Explained* (Boston: Little, Brown and Co., 1991).

consciousness as well as it is possible to objectively interpret and analyse the content of novels, fairy tales and myths.

Well then, let us allow ourselves to be curious about the contributions of this new science.

2. When the Mind Quarrelled with the Body

There has been a long and relentless debate among scholars and thinkers on the question of whether or not there is a substantial difference between the mind and the body, and if so, whether the mind and the body influence each other, and if so, in what way. If it were true that the more competing theories we have the better off we are, we would surely be in great shape.

The situation is, however, quite confusing. The confusion crept in principally because the words we use to refer to the mind are used in at least four different meanings: in reference to our inner and immediate experience, in reference to the behaviour of others, in reference to processes going on in the nerve tissues of our brain, and in reference to artificial systems, e.g. computers. Furthermore, it is possible to view the mind-body problem *ontologically* (how something is), *epistemologically* (how we learn about it), or *analytically* (how we discuss it).

There is a persistent tendency in Western philosophy, established psychology, and brain sciences to reduce, eliminate, depreciate or in some other way suppress the concepts of mind, soul, spirit and psyche, and to oppose any notion that these concepts could pertain to anything other than to strictly material nature. Science wants to explain things; the most preferred explanation is a reference to causal connections. Physics provides an excellent example; its reduction of everything to its basic physical phenomena exemplifies scientific goals. The primitive variety of reductionism (a reduction of everything to a whirl of atoms) is nevertheless already retreating, if only because modern physics itself has its own problems: the microworld behaves strangely to say the least, and non-linear dynamics introduces chaos even into the macroworld. Reductionism experiences a crisis even within physics itself.

A well-known physicist Silvan Schweber pointed out a hierarchical stratification of the physical universe into separate levels represented each by its own idiosyncratic concepts and principles which are not reducible to neighbouring levels.[2] Interrelationships between the distinct levels exhibit emergent (i.e. non-causal) nature.

A majority of today's materialistic or physicalistic theories of the mind, whether they happen to be reductionistic or not, are based on an implied (often non-verbalised) notion that thinking occurs at a single and sufficiently complex level, well "above" the basic level of neurophysiological and biochemical processes. What remains to be uncovered by these theories is the nature of the relationship between these levels (whether it is causal, non-causal, emergent, deterministic, statistical, bottom-up or top-down, direct or indirect).

I don't believe that the above concept is correct, or, to be more precise, that it is the only one possible—there certainly are many other possible (and also materialistic) theories. Why should we chose the level of neural processes to be the truly basic one? Why should we place it either "under" or "above" the level of mind within some assumed hierarchy? Both these levels could perhaps be independently and differently related to yet another, deeper level. There are increasing numbers of scientists who support a hypothesis that such a deeper level could be a level where quantum physics already applies.[3]

Further still, one may argue about whether any sharp division of levels used in our concept of body and mind does in fact exist at all. It is my personal opinion that in order to

---

[2] See S.S. Schweber, "Physics, community and the crisis in physical theory," *Physics Today* (November 1993): 34–40.

[3] See e.g. H.P. Stapp, *Mind, Matter, and Quantum Mechanics* (Amsterdam: Springer-Verlag, 1993); R. Penrose, *The Emperor's New Mind* (Oxford: Oxford University Press, 1989); and *Shadows of the Mind* (Oxford: Oxford University Press, 1994); and J. Eccles, *How the Self Controls its Brain* (Amsterdam, Springer-Verlag, 1994).

understand life (and even more so when trying to understand the mind) it is unwise to attach ourselves to a particular single level. Doing so may be adequate, or even desirable, when trying to comprehend the physical world (see the above mentioned stratification of the physical universe into separate levels). The very existence and harmony of a variety of interacting processes on many levels—that of molecules, cells, organs, organisms, societies, ecosystems—is after all the principal characteristic which distinguishes living organisms (and brains) from physical systems (and machines). If it were possible to label such an approach "physicalistic," it would result in a new concept of the mind. A concept described in terms of an emergent phenomenon of a higher order: no longer only a phenomenon restricted to a single level and supported by processes occupying a lower level (worse yet, a phenomenon which could be reduced down to be no more than a combination of those lower-level processes) but a phenomenon emerging from a global (and far from causal only) interaction of the entire hierarchy of different levels.

We have very little natural experience with such a concept; consequently it is difficult to discuss it and even think about it. Yet!

3. On "How Something Is"

There exist innocent questions such as "What is a house?" or "What is a rosebeetle?" or perhaps "What is science?" "What is a game?" even "What is that?" (the last question requires us to point a finger). It would appear that such questions do not really presume anything by themselves; nothing more seems to be reflected by such questions than the fact of a somewhat elementary ignorance.

It is not entirely so. All of the above questions, and all of the similar ones, could not exist in the absence of the most common, and at the same time, the most treacherous little word: "is." Consequently, simply because they exist at all, they do make one assumption (at least under normal circumstances): they assume that something in fact "is," or that its existence is at least thinkable. We therefore deal with something, which we can either name (house, rosebeetle, science, game) or can point a finger at. A thing which is worthy of an enquiry.

A question "What is that ...?" may elicit a variety of different answers. Most frequently an answer will teach us the composition of the thing we enquire about, what it comprises, what is it good for, how it could be otherwise called, possibly how it can be distinguished from something which it is not. Only the "is" part of the question is usually, and undeservedly, forgotten. Because of that, we in fact never get (and actually never expect) an answer to an essential part of our question: *how* something is, what is its modus of being.

We do not experience much of a problem when asking questions about things; a house for example. A house has a matter, form, sometimes even meaning. Other attributes, such as the fact that it has its origins, that it will last a certain time and that it does undergo changes, seem to play an inferior role. Let us chose, however, a different example—say the game. What is a game, such as chess? Is it a thing? You would be surprised how many "things" are around us which are not things at all!

Let us start with an important distinction (which in every-day talk becomes clear from the context): a game—let us imagine chess—as determined by a set of rules on how to play it (and, in addition, perhaps by theories on how to play it well) differs substantially from a particular and unique game (match) of chess, which can be described as a longer or shorter sequence of moves complying with the rules.

Another distinction: an abstract chess game (match) is one thing, and its actualisation in a real time and space, and with concrete players under specific circumstances, is yet another thing. Similarly, it is possible to distinguish a game defined as a set of rules (and theories) from the identical game perceived in its historical context as something which appeared at a certain time, had evolved and could continue evolving as a historic or diachronic[4] entity (by changing its theories and even rules). We have thus four components:

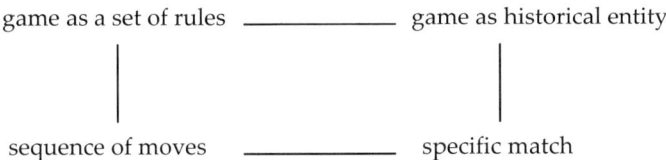

game as a set of rules ———————— game as historical entity

sequence of moves ———————— specific match

When talking generally about a game in terms of its existence, and when enquiring about *how* it is, *what* is the nature of its being, we have to pay attention to all of these four parts. The two on the right refer to the actual realisation of the thing (in time and space), the two on the left determine formal and timeless characteristics of a game.

Of interest is also the relationship between the upper and lower parts of the above diagram. A completely different time scale applies to a game perceived as a historical process as compared to a game perceived as a specific match. The former is measured in years and centuries, the latter in minutes and hours. There is, nevertheless, a bi-directional interaction between the two levels: specific matches obey the theories and rules prevailing at the respective historical moment and, reciprocally, the rules and theory evolve over longer periods of time as a consequence of (many) specific matches. Because of these inter-relationships we have to recognise our distinction of different components only as a heuristic tool. They are in fact only different facets or manifestations of the same entity, a "thing" which lacks the simplicity of beings, of things we can actually touch.

I have chosen the game as an example only. An identical situation is encountered in the case of many other entities which always express themselves at two levels—a coarser one

---

[4] The term "diachronic" was used in linguistics by F. de Saussure, *Course in General Linguistics* (1916), see especially part I, chapter 3.

which is less precise and corresponds to larger scales of time and space, and a more precise fine level which corresponds to smaller scales. Several examples: natural language (versus specific utterances), biological species (versus living individuals), science (versus scientific discoveries), memory (versus recollections), influenza epidemic (versus flu occurrences), a fashion of long skirts (versus long skirts), artistic style (versus works of art), law (versus legal acts), political system (versus governments). On the lower and finer level we encounter specific, concrete and usually isolated occurrences or expressions of the entity in question, whereas at the higher level the entity itself exhibits a latent, non-material but lasting existence, stored in the properties, knowledge or abilities of a substrate.

It is by virtue of such a continuous nature of being that we may consider the occurrences at the finer level to be expressions of a certain single entity and therefore be able to even assign a name common to them.

4. What is it Like to be a Monkey?

> I was soaring by skilfully using the air currents and subtle changes of the position of my wings [...] Minutes later, I found myself a frog and started propelling myself with long kicks.
> —Recording of an experience under the influence of LSD[5]

An occasional dream-flight (which, surprisingly enough, I still manage from time to time) is unfortunately not enough to quench my curiosity to know how an animal (an eagle or monkey, for instance) perceives its own self. To truly know, one would need to actually live through such an existence in its entirety, to live the animal's experience of self. That experiment does not seem, however, to make much logical sense: such a

5 S. Grof, *The Adventure of Self-Discovery* (Albany: State University of New York Press, 1988) 52f.

metamorphosis would mean that I cease to be myself and would truly become a bird or a monkey; this animal would certainly and immediately terminate my experiment.

Whether such a question is at all meaningful provides a good theme for philosophers.[6] (Also included is the question of how to interpret testimonies of those who in psychedelic trance became eagles, tigers, snakes or frogs. Do their recollections reflect a transpersonal memory trace from our evolutionary past, a true transmigration, a wild fantasy, a simple fabulation or dream?) If you think about it, it is not really possible to actually experience even your spouse's migraine headache.

So far I have talked about truly experiencing rather than about how something may appear externally to an observer. The latter becomes a subject of empirical science, particularly when the *if* (something exists) replaces the *how* (does it exist). In other words, instead of "what is it like" we ask whether "something like that does truly exist at all."

There are experimental research efforts which try to ascertain whether monkeys (or rats) posses an individual "self" or not. A dot was painted on a chimpanzee's forehead while it was asleep and the animal was then tested as to whether or not it touched the spot more frequently when provided with a mirror. The hypothesis was that if chimpanzees consider their mirror image to be themselves, they must have a self-realisation, or a perception of their own "selves."[7] It is interesting to note how much this hypothesis is indebted to human behaviour towards mirrors.

While standing in front of a mirror in the morning, I never doubt that the image is indeed me. But wait—try to stand in-between two or several mirrors. The people in mirrors, who look like you but who always turn their head in a direction different from the one you intended, are suddenly somewhat foreign to you. Even if the poor monkey facing a mirror were

[6] See T. Nagel, "What is it like to be a Bat?" *Mortal Questions* (Cambridge: Cambridge University Press, 1979) 165–180.

[7] G.G. Gallup, "Chimpanzees: Self-recognition," *Science* 167 (1970): 86–87.

capable of the deepest self-reflection and possessed the keenest sense of its self, it would probably be greatly confused as to which of its eight hands should touch a spot on which of its two foreheads.

Other authors derive self-consciousness from the ability to identify with others, as reflected for example by imitating others. I am not sure I believe that one either. If evolution were truly as clever as we assume it was, wouldn't it provide us and monkeys (and perhaps even lower animals) with the ability to imitate our peers whenever it becomes advantageous (e.g. energy-saving, faster and thus selectively more efficient than relying on original research and continuous inventions) for us to do so? I also think that such copy-cat behaviour could easily occur without any need to first empathise and identify with the model and then with oneself.

Let us think—are there not situations in which we imitate others somewhat subconsciously without even perceiving ourselves as the imitators and the others as the imitated without even knowing why do we do it? We frequently assume gestures, body movements, accents and clothing styles of other people unintentionally, without thinking. Something out there urges us to keep up with the fads. There are other behaviours which seem to be equally infectious—yawning, laughter, fear. I suppose that even a certain degree of empathy might exist independent of self-consciousness: we push through a crowd while subconsciously anticipating the intentions of those around us.

Hence not only the admiration of ourselves in a mirror, but also our imitation of others could be behavioural patterns independent of self-reflection (even self-consciousness). We have a tendency to assume otherwise, simply because we are spoiled by reason.

The principal danger, and simultaneously a great temptation, experienced while examining minds of animals is the unavoidable anthropomorphism. By asking "Do they have a mind?" we most likely mean "Are they like us?" We keep forgetting that there are several dozen other legitimate components, aspects, dimensions, facets and degrees of consciousness and self-perception. We are aware of some, suspect of some and completely ignorant of others.

Let us draw one possible (and anthropomorphic in nature) scale of consciousness: the lowest degree is a minuscule feeling of distinction between something pleasant and something unpleasant (without any knowledge of what it might be), the next degree is realisation of the extent of one's own body (which part hurts and which does not), next is the awareness of one's identity (requiring memory), then a perception of self as one among others (belonging), conscious worry about one's future (requiring imagination), recognition of the same phenomenon in others, awareness of one's mortality, awareness of one's consciousness (self-reflection), individual conscience, collective consciousness, collective conscience etc., etc. Who knows what I have omitted and how far such a scale can reach.

I am absolutely sure that my donkey David and my tomcat Yin have some consciousness. *What* sort of consciousness and *how* it might feel I will never be able to tell.

5. What is a Rosebeetle?

That's the beetle, the beetle
that's true the beetle that's not
—Jiří Kuběna[8]

As a boy I used to be a keen beetle collector. I hunted them in hundreds, pinned them down or glued the small ones onto paper labels. I got hold of Klapálek's Atlas and Javorek's Handbook, determined which family, genus and species they belong to and sorted them accordingly. I gave my hobby up only at the age when one begins to hesitate before killing a helpless creature. I found the process of determining and

---

[8] Jiří Kuběna (1936-), Moravian poet.

sorting to be interesting in itself. It was, in fact, the second phase of hunting—first to hunt a beetle, then to hunt for its name. It has never been clear to me, and I am afraid not to biologists either, what exactly a species is. Let us take, for example, the common rosebeetle, *Cetonia aurata* L. We all know it, it is a beetle, which

> with its green colour and gold or copper-like lustre pleasingly invites our glance when discovered on the bloom of a rose,

according to the old Obenberger's *Natural History of Insects*.[9] There is, however, a large variety of rosebeetles—how does the one we look at differ from all the others? The green colour and the gold or copper-like lustre are not its principal characteristics. Neither are the leaf-like widening of its antennae, its digger's legs and its habitation on roses. All of those are characteristics of individuals which merely help in sorting them out into different groups, sub-groups, super-groups (such groups are generally called taxonomic units or taxons).

The most basic and most important taxonomic unit is the *species*. According to biologists an important distinction of species as taxons is the fact that individuals of the same species are capable of mating and producing viable and fertile offspring, whereas individuals of different species are not (provided that mating is physically possible). Furthermore the sex of the individuals should also be taken into consideration, however for our purposes a simple assumption that there are always two parents will suffice. Two aspects of the above distinction are of interest. First, in contrast to e.g. colour, lustre and shape of antennae, it is a characteristic somewhat "more objective" and less dependent on what we see and notice. Secondly, it is no longer a characteristic which can be applied to

---

[9] J. Obenberger, *Zoologie III-Hmyz (entomologie). Velký ilustrovaný přírodopis všech tří říší* (Zoology III-Insects (Entomology). Great Illustrated Natural History of Three Kingdoms), ed. J. Janda (Praha, 1933) 296.

a single individual but rather to an entire group: in order to be precise in our definition of a species in terms of a group of individuals, we would have to first examine each and every individual! (Fortunately nature shows its kind face to systematic biologists: individuals of the same species look usually more or less similar to each other.)

The above characteristics of a species do not provide a complete definition by themselves, should we prefer to be exact. It is, for example, impossible to guarantee the applicability of the reproductive criterion throughout the entire species—e.g. it is quite possible to imagine that one individual can successfully mate with the second, the second with the third, etc., but the first individual could not successfully mate with the last on the mating chain (they may even belong to separate biotypes). On the other side of the coin, even inter-species mating can occasionally succeed. The situation becomes much more blurry in lower organisms, not to mention viruses.[10]

In their striving for exactness the modern biologists turn to molecules which carry genetic information. How elegant it would be to define a species in terms of a sequence of nucleotides in a strand of DNA! Exactness which matches that of chemistry in its definitions of chemical compounds, but even that is of no help! When talking about biological species, of viruses for example, we have to acknowledge the fact that an unavoidable proportion of any proper population consists of mutants, i.e. of individuals with minor or major errors in their genetic code. I say "errors" just because of my inertia—in fact, they are not errors but variations—variations which in fact may, under adverse conditions, even save the entire population or species from extinction.

This seems an appropriate place to introduce the term "quasispecies" coined by the German biochemist Manfred

---

[10] Concerning the concept of a species as the basic taxonomic unit see e.g. M. Ereshevsky, *The Units of Evolution: Essays on the Nature of Evolution* (Cambridge, Mass.: MIT Press, 1992).

Eigen.[11] I shall mention only one aspect of this concept. Namely, the way in which the term can be exactly described by statistical geometry which, in addition provides us with a possibility to form the term's intuitive geometrical image. The only prerequisite is a certain abstraction of the term "space" which differs from the common Eucleidean space. On one hand we shall only consider a "discrete" set of points (rather than a continuum), on the other hand we shall define the distance between these points differently than it is usually done in our three-dimensional world.

Individuals are genetically characterised by their DNA sequences (*genomes*)—sequences of nucleotides of four types called *bases*. These sequences may be relatively very long and therefore the number of all possible variants is astronomical—even if finite (we consider all formally possible alternatives, disregarding their biological feasibility). For example, the number of sequences of length $n = 10$ is 4^{10}, i.e. about one million (to compare: the length of the nucleotid sequence of the HIV virus is $n = {\sim}10{,}000$) To make our further discussion simpler, let us presume that there are only two types of nucleotides (giving 2^n possible sequences).

Our abstract "space," called *sequential space*, will have exactly 2^n points; each point would represent one specific sequence. The "distance" between these points will be defined as the number of places in which the two sequences differ from each other. Each point would therefore have exactly $3n$ of immediate neighbours, i.e. of points at the distance of 1.

The points of sequential space represent all combinatorially possible nucleotide sequences. Only a tiny part of the space is occupied by living creatures, and even tinier part by sequences that represent mutations of one chosen sequence. Consider a population in which different mutants appear at a frequency determined by their ability to reproduce in a stable state. Points

[11] See M. Eigen, "Viral Quasispecies," *Scientific American* (July 1993): 42–49; and S.A. Kauffman, *The Origins of Order: Self-Organisation and Selection in Evolution* (Oxford: Oxford University Press, 1993) 358ff.

corresponding to these mutants form an irregular "cloud" surrounding the point representing the initial chosen sequence; each point within the cloud is also assigned a certain weight— i.e. the relative frequency of the respective mutant within the whole population. The weight distribution pattern would exhibit characteristics of a probability distribution with higher values typically located near the selected sequence, lower at the cloud periphery. Formally, a *quasi-species* is nothing else than such a cloud with the related probability distribution. It suffices to talk about the probability distribution only—the shape of the cloud is determined by its non-zero values.

If it were not for the conservation (preservation) effect of the selection pressure, the points representing the mutants would behave like an ideal gas—they would spread out evenly throughout the entire sequential space at an extremely low density.

A change in the external environment or in the parameters of reproduction will be reflected by changes in the probability distribution inclusive of the shape and size of the cloud within the sequential space. A quasispecies can therefore evolve; that raises questions about its identity and individuality. To define a species (of organisms, molecules or anything else) *extensionally* (i.e. by listing all its members) is as useless as to define a walker by listing all people who walk. We have tried some other types of definitions at the beginning of this article and were equally unsuccessful.

It was mathematical statistics and geometry's power of imagination which finally helped us out of a tight spot. Why could not a species be perceived as such a "cloud" of points exhibiting non-null values of probability within some multidimensional space? Each point is one of the possibilities. The cloud is malleable—it behaves like a strange amoeba whose shape, position and density change dynamically in accord with changes in external conditions, variability and tolerance of its own errors. Within a long enough time, the cloud may change into something entirely different, it may shift, may break up into several new clouds, or even disperse and disappear completely.

It is almost like the cloud itself were an organism, "living" in that strange multidimensional space. And that is the *Cetonia aurata* L. It does not sit on a rose. That object on the bloom of a rose, which pleasingly invites our glance, is something which, during its lifetime, provides a non-zero value of probability for one specific point somewhere within the cloud.

6. *Support Your Species*

Being only human, we should not be surprised that we find it difficult to reconcile ourselves with thoughts, theories and even scientific disciplines dealing with the question of how it ever happened that we, humans have appeared on Earth. This is especially the case for the theories of evolution which have been loudly debated for almost a century and a half, sometimes at an emotional pitch rarely seen in other disciplines. The most prominent is the Darwinian theory based on the notion of blind drifting among possibilities. There is no logical bottle-neck in that theory; nevertheless, perhaps because we are too proud of our own attributes, many of us find it difficult to believe that we are nothing more than a product of a blind and inane accident. For the same reasons, others consider it impossible to believe that the world on its own, without our help, could manage anything other than blind and inane accidents.

If that is the case, our conceit would best be served by the despised theory of Lamarck. It gives us, an evolving species, the right to actively influence our own evolution. The fact that so far we have failed to come up with any plausible biological mechanism of such participation does not argue against the hypothesis itself; it only argues against the certainty of its validity.

Very helpful in this context is an effect, called *Baldwin's*, which provides each of us a trick with which to participate in our own evolution (read: the evolution of our species).[12] Simply put, we can do it in a roundabout way. Since I know that it is not that simple to improve my genetic code, I may at least try to improve myself. I should learn something which I was not born with. Something that would allow me to live a better and healthier life, and to produce more offspring under the prevailing circumstances. If successful, I would obviously not change my genetic code (my concrete genome) but would simply multiply the number of its bearers. And that's the trick—my particular genome would be more numerous and therefore stronger within the population. Other variants of the genome within the same population, lacking an ability to change, or more specifically an ability to improve (within our narrow interpretation of the term improve—to better oneself), will drop out of the competition sooner or later.

In fact, no improvement as such is necessary to actually occur; just a potential for improvement suffices. A genome variant exhibiting a potential for success is better off within a given population than a variant lacking it, regardless of whether the success has actually been achieved by a given individual. It is obvious, however, that individuals who explore their potential systematically rather than sporadically will form the principal part of the population which lives longer and is blessed with more descendants. To systematically better oneself means to learn.

If the ability to learn resides in a genome, its preferential expression is of no surprise to any true Darwinist. Let us turn our attention to a certain interesting consequence. Mutations, random and blind (say), obviously must occur most frequently among the most numerous group of individuals. In our case, they would be individuals with a genetically based potential to learn something concrete and useful. The surrounding genetic space will be relatively densely filled with mutations and it is

[12] J.M. Baldwin, "A New Factor in Evolution," *American Naturalist* 30 (1896): 441-51, 536–53. See also J. Schull, "Are Species Intelligent?" *Behavioural and Brain Sciences* 3 (1990): 63–108.

only a question of time when mutations supporting precisely the advantageous characteristics will occur. In other words: genomes of inventive and creative individuals offer relatively larger room for mutations, some of which will fix (randomly) the learned and discovered patterns for the benefit of future generations.

Note: such genetic support could hardly occur if not "preceded" by the inventive and creative individuals who acquired beneficial characteristics during their lifetime. If expressed in such a way, it would be difficult to miss a whiff of Lamarckian theory in our notion.

As far as the dispute over whether evolution is blind or directed is concerned, or if you prefer, whether it is governed by randomness or usefulness, we should consider a possibility that the difference rests only with our perspective or viewpoint used. What appears from a great distance (on a large time-scale) to be a directed, goal-orientated and seemingly predetermined evolution of a species, may appear in a close-up (on a small time-scale) as a play of pure and blind coincidences occurring in a large population of individuals.

It is also possible to demonstrate Baldwin's effect by a computer simulation of evolution.[13] Such a computer experiment validates the functionality of the effect—the proof, however, of whether, to what extent, and in combination with what else it has truly been used by Nature, cannot be provided by an experiment. In spite of that, I believe that the inner logic of the principle prevents its dismissal, particularly when certain prerequisites are fulfilled: a large enough collective of individuals, an adequate time span, random variability, information transfer etc.

It is the proper time to emphasise a basic aspect underlying such discussions; a failure to observe this aspect often results in misunderstandings and emotional outbursts. It is always absolutely necessary to distinguish when we consider and

---

[13] See V. Kvasnička, "Opvlyvňuje učenie evolúciu?" (Does Learning Affect Evolution?) *Vesmír* 74/1 (1995): 8–10.

discuss how it has *really happened* (read: the story of life on Earth) and when we question how it *could have* possibly happened. In the former we struggle with a lack of knowledge necessary to test our hypotheses; even worse, we may never know more. In the latter, we are at liberty to formulate a variety of hypothetical theories on the possible "mechanisms" of evolution (let us call it so). It is also possible, in principle, to test the validity of the latter theories (albeit somewhat artificially): by deductions, thought experiments in logical thinking, and to a certain extent by computer simulations. After all, any internally consistent and statistically valid hypothetical mechanism of evolution could have possibly participated in the evolutionary processes on Earth; but again—it could have been over-ridden, masked, or at least contaminated by another internally consistent mechanism.

Inventing and studying such possibilities (regardless of whether they actually did or did not occur on Earth) constitutes a part of theoretical biology and undoubtedly deserves to be called a science.

7. Is Scientific Enquiry into Consciousness Possible?

This title is identical to the title of the first section of this essay. I see no reason why two parts of the same texts should not share a title, particularly since it happens to be a question which I failed to answer then (and naturally I do not promise to answer now). The question seems to be increasingly fashionable: quite a few books were already published—about both consciousness itself and also the problem of whether it may be a subject of legitimate scientific interest. There are several specialised journals,[14] not to mention numerous conferences and symposia which took place as well. Thus it seems that a new discipline has emerged; whether it is a scientific one depends on our definition of consciousness and that of science.

[14] For instance, see the *Journal of Consciousness Studies* and *Consciousness and Cognition* (Academic Press).

Ten years ago a book was published by Francis Crick, the 1962 Nobel prize winner in chemistry, with a very appealing subtitle, "The Scientific Search for the Soul."[15] Principally on the example of visual perception, Crick attempts to promote the hypothesis that in order to understand consciousness it is necessary (and sufficient) to understand the collective gibberish of neurons in the brain. He is not the only one who supports such a hypothesis. There are, however, numerous critical voices aimed either at the hypothesis itself or at the way Crick defends it.[16]

In the first essay we met with the principal problem with which any future science of consciousness, even more so than other disciplines, will have to deal: it is the fact that besides things such as the brain with its neurons (which are, in principle, available to the objective methods of scientific enquiry) there exists the realm of our subjective, inner experience which we know about only because of consciousness and without which it would be impossible to discuss consciousness at all because there would be nothing left to talk about.

I should note that some of the participants in today's heated discussions consider this subject to be a "pseudo-problem." (The exchanges between philosophers John Searle and Daniel Dennett exemplify one of the more heated debates.[17]) Why a "pseudo-problem"? As these discussants say, every cognitive event has to be related to a corresponding activity of some neurons. Why then should we not consider that activity to be identical to consciousness? If no corresponding neural activity exists, consciousness does not exist either (for science, that is).

The more heated the debate among scientists becomes, the easier it is to find the source of confusion in the wrong choice of

---

15 F. Crick, *The Astonishing Hypothesis: The Scientific Search for the Soul* (London: Simon and Schuster, 1994).

16 See, for instance, S. Grossberg, "Opening the Mind's Eye," *American Scientist* (January-February 1995): 79–80.

17 See especially *The New York Review of Books* (December 21, 1995).

words and their meanings; more specifically, in a failure to agree on a unified use of words and phrases within a given context. A scientist or a philosopher simply selects from the range of possibilities a meaning for the term "consciousness" which is appropriate for his intended path between an original question and his desired solution. I can think about at least three such paths.

The first path, which can be called *phenomenal*, simply builds upon our natural and subjective experience. There is no need to prove the existence of such experience because we all have it, at least those of us who happen to be neither sleep-walkers nor robots. I surely am among those who have it. It is possible, however, to talk about this aspect of consciousness only in terms of the first person singular. In no way could it be objectively described because objectivity does not recognise it. And that's the problem I attempted to describe in the previous chapter.

The second path could be called (inaccurately) that of *objectivistic psychology*. Consciousness here enters the realm of scientific studies and even experiments. It is examined when a person does, says, perceives, feels and thinks something consciously and when he does it subconsciously or even unconsciously. This approach deals with "being conscious *of* something" (awareness) rather than with consciousness in general and it makes it possible to address consciousness as referring to the third person singular, as something observable, explorable. Consequently, it is perfectly legitimate to ask whether donkeys or tomcats have consciousness.

The third path is *physiological*. "The language of the brain is the language of neurons" writes Crick due to his belief that by unravelling the secrets of this language all the mysteries of thinking and consciousness will disappear. No question, until now we certainly knew much more (based on the volume of accumulated data) about man at the level of neurons than at the level of his moods. Very little is yet known, however, about the nature of the language used by neurons, about the content of their "conversations" and about anything else that may invade these conversations and interfere with them.[18] Today we can envisage that soon there will exist ethically acceptable methods for examination of the brains of living, healthy humans in addition to damaged brains or animal brains.

I have listed three paths to understanding consciousness and can clearly see that each concerns something different. What I cannot see, however, is whether these paths converge at some point or whether they run parallel and eventually diverge. A certain degree of convergence may be expected for the second and third paths: it is quite possible that the questions asked in the language of objective psychology will be answered in the language of neurophysiology (as skilfully demonstrated by Crick; after all it is the essence of his project). To pose and to answer such questions may be called, however, an "easy" (methodologically speaking) problem.

To call it "easy" is somewhat overstated, granted, but it is done only in reference to problems labelled "hard" (still somewhat optimistically, I think) by the philosopher David Chalmers.[19] In what way do the physical (chemical, biological) processes occurring in my brain create my subjective experience? Why is it that at the light of a certain wavelength are the processes occurring in my optical brain accompanied by my (and specifically my) experience of yellow colour? After all, my brain could direct me to behave identically (inclusive of my exclamation: "What a beautiful yellow colour!") even in the absence of my subjective perception of the colour. Isn't the behaviour of bees and of robots (and probably often even my

---

[18] See P. Jirounek, "O šíření signálů v živých organizmech I & II (On the Propagation of Signals in Living Organisms)," *Vesmír* 75/2, 3, 4 (1996): 65–68, 150–152, 191–193.

[19] D. Chalmers, *The Conscious Mind* (Oxford: Oxford University Press, 1996). See also D. Chalmers, "The puzzle of conscious experience," *Scientific American* (December 1995): 80–86. An extensive exchange concerning Chalmer's concept of "hard problem" appeared in *Journal of Consciousness Studies* 2.3 (1995); 3.1, 3.4 (1996).

own subconscious behaviour) perhaps directed precisely in such a way?

I believe that the confusion of today's discussions almost always rests on improper distinctions between the "hard" and "easy" problems. It may be noted (along with Chalmers), for example, that authors of specialised studies on consciousness usually begin with contemplations on the mysterious and incomprehensible nature of subjectively experienced consciousness and continue, without a trace of hesitation, with their original theories and solutions which (as revealed by a bit more careful reading), are nothing more than a contribution to the field of "easy."

Perhaps one day we will learn, and maybe even simulate, what really occurs in our brain when we feel happy or sad. I doubt, however, that it would make any difference to anybody who himself never laughs or cries.

Louis Armand

Affective Intelligence & the Human Hypothesis

What would it mean if machines could think?

In Arthur C. Clark and Stanley Kubrick's science fiction version of the then-future and now recent-past, *2001: A Space Odyssey*, HAL—an Heuristically programmed ALgorithmic computer possessing a highly advanced "artificial intelligence"—murders the human crew of a spaceship on a mission to Jupiter, a mission somehow linked to the discovery, on the moon, of a form of cosmic (and only nominally *artificial*) intelligence advanced beyond human understanding in the shape of a sinister black monolith. While the film's premise remains slightly exotic, it nevertheless raises important questions about so-called artificial, cosmic and human intelligence, and it does so both in metaphysical and concrete terms, the latter to do primarily with the idea of computability and machines.

In consultation with scientists in universities, industry, and at NASA, Clark and Kubrick (a former Washington Square chess hustler) sought to design their fictional scenario so as to be both plausible and visionary: "Every detail," we are told, "from the design of the spaceship, the timing of the mission and the technical lingo to the typography on the computer

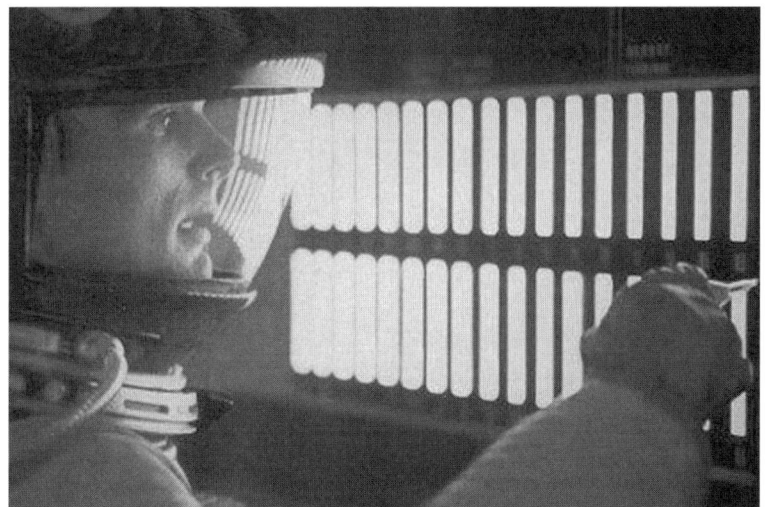

screens and the space stewardesses' hats … was carefully considered in light of the then-current technology and informed predictions."[1] Since that time, several of the characteristics of the HAL 9000 computer have found there way into scientific experimentation and practical application in areas such as the development of chess-playing software, optics, text to speech synthesis, speech recognition, artificial language acquisition, and automatic speech reading. Nevertheless, agreement on the meaning of general intelligence, let alone the idea of "artificial intelligence," remains as much a part of the future today as it was at the time of HAL's conception.

The historical inspiration for HAL and the vast main-frame machines that dominated computing up until the advent of microprocessors and the software revolution in the 1970s, was the Bletchley Park COLOSSUS—Britain's secret code-breaking machine designed and built by Alan Turing along with a team of mathematicians and engineers for the purpose of deciphering the war-time transmissions of the German ENIGMA encryption machines. And while Turing by the 1950s was already

---

[1] David G. Stork, "The Best-Informed Dream: HAL and the Vision of 2001,"*HAL's Legacy: 2001's Computer as Dream and Reality*, ed. D.G. Stork (Cambridge, Mass.: MIT Press, 1997) 2.

A model of the German ENIGMA encryption machine

envisaging the possibility of constructing an "electronic brain," along similar lines to the COLLOSUS, by the time *2001: A Space Odyssey* was released in 1968, computing intelligence had only progressed to the point where programmes like Tom Evans's ANALOGY were able to calculate such things as automated analogies ("figure A is to figure B as C is to ..."), while other programmes like ELIZA sought, in a curious reprise of the "Turing test," to mimic a Rogerian therapist: "In limited dialogues it convinced naïve users that they were conversing with a real person."[2]

In Kubrick's film, the omnipresent HAL not only evinces language comprehension and an otherwise high degree of computative ability, it is also accorded proficiency at both acoustic speech recognition and speech reading, as well as quasi-human capacities of visual recognition (or what very tentatively might be called "perception"), emotional response,

[2] Stork, "The Best-Informed Dream," 9.

and general intelligence. In short HAL is accorded *literacy* in the sense of being able to analyse and "produce" images of both its external and "cognitive" worlds. But HAL is, of course, barely an hypothesis. As computer scientists like Marvin Minsky and Murray Campbell have demonstrated, the actual science of constructing an HAL 9000 computer remains "science fiction" due, in large part, to the lack of an effective understanding of what it is that constitutes general intelligence—or indeed, any agreement on what it means when we speak of "intelligence" as such. The field of "artificial intelligence" (AI), founded at the now famous Dartmouth conference in 1956 by Claude Shannon, Marvin Minsky, John McCarthy and others,[3] has in certain important respects progressed little beyond the foundational hypothesis of "machine intelligence" initially conceived of by Turing as a type of binary calculator in the 1930s and whose design logic underlay the prototype of one of the first "actual" computers—the ACE, or Automatic Computing Engine—built at the National Physics Laboratory in London shortly after WWII.

In a well-known article entitled "Computing Machinery and Intelligence" (1950), Turing considered the question of what it would mean for a machine to be intelligent in terms, not of something that might be called *machine intelligence* or which might be investigated—as an object of knowledge—by way of empirical science, but of what it means when we ask questions about intelligence *as such* and pose these questions *in terms of the human-machine problem*. In this sense, Turing was reformulating the challenge to physics posed by Niels Bohr in terms of the "problem" of the observer in relation to observed physical (even virtual) systems. "I propose," writes Turing, "to

---

[3] Cf. John McCarthy, et al., *Dartmouth AI Project Proposal*, 31 August, 1955: "The study is to proceed on the basis of the conjecture that every aspect of learning or any other feature of intelligence can in principle be so precisely described that a machine can be made to simulate it. An attempt will be made to find how to make machines use language, form abstractions and concepts, solve kinds of problems now reserved for humans, and improve themselves."

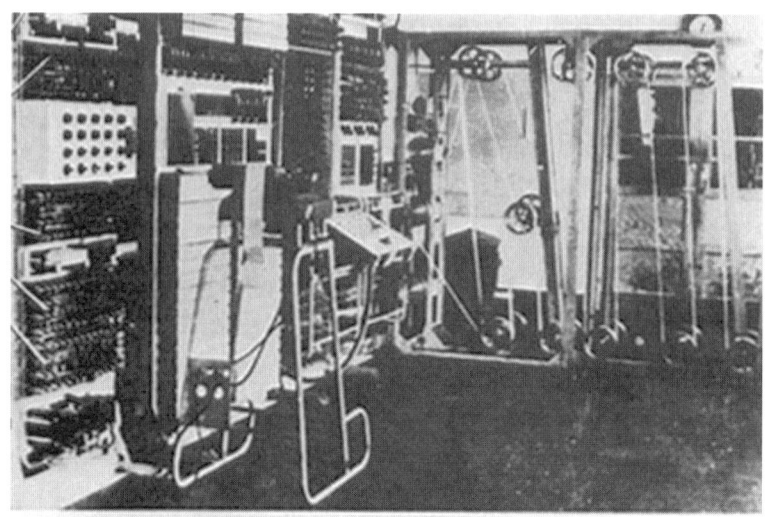

The Bletchley Park COLLOSUS

consider the question 'Can machines think?'" But this reconsideration, Turing explains, "should begin with definitions of the meaning of the terms 'machine' and 'think.'"[4]

In order to arrive at such definitions, Turing proposed what he termed "the imitation game," otherwise known as the Turing test, which sets out criteria for determining if a computer programme may in some way be perceived as having "intelligence." According to Turing, "the new form of the problem can be described in terms of a game which we call the 'imitation game.' It is played with three people, a man (A), a woman (B), and an interrogator (C) who may be of either sex. The interrogator stays in a room apart from the other two. The object of the game for the interrogator is to determine which of the other two is the man and which is the woman. He knows them by labels X and Y, and at the end of the game he says either 'X is A and Y is B' or 'X is B and Y is A.' The interrogator is allowed to put questions to A and B." In order to complicate matters, it is the role of the male respondent to deceive the interrogator, while it is the woman's role to convince.

The premise of the game was that "a successful imitation of a woman's responses by a man would *not* prove anything. Gender depended on facts which were *not* reducible to sequences of symbols." In contrast, Turing "wished to argue that such an imitation principle did apply to 'thinking' or 'intelligence.' If a computer, on the basis of its written replies to questions, could not be distinguished from a human respondent, then 'fair play' would oblige one to say that it must be thinking."[5] Consequently, whereas the original "imitation game" devolved upon a determination of gender-symbolisation, the Turing Test as it is normally understood involves a situation in which "a machine takes the place of (A) in this game"—such that a human being and a digital computer

---

[4] Alan Turing, "Computing Machinery and Intelligence," *Mind* LIX.236 (1950): 433-460.

[5] Andrew Hodges, *Alan Turing: The Enigma* (New York: Simon and Schuster, 1983) 415.

are interrogated under conditions where the interrogator would not know which was which, the communication being entirely by means of electronic textual messages.

Turing argued that if the interrogator could not distinguish between the human and the computer on the basis of their relative responses, any more than in the game involving the male and female respondents, then it would not be unreasonable to consider the computer as being "intelligent." In other words, according to Turing's proposition, a computer-respondent is "intelligent" if the human subject is able to be convinced that its respondent is, like the interrogator, also a human being, and *not* a machine. The negative definition here proceeds on the basis that neither machine nor human, within the parameters of the game, can clearly be distinguished from the other on the basis of assumptions about intelligence and behaviour. As a consequence, Turing effectively locates "intelligence" as a relativistic *interface* phenomenon, rooted in the simulation of any given *criteria of intelligence* measured by the effectiveness of the dialogic illusion—something which has profound implications for how we may then proceed to define "machine," "thought," or even "intelligence."

In Turing's view, it is not so much machines themselves but the *states* of machines that can be regarded as analogous to "states of mind." In other words, Turing's definition of intelligence is an operational one: "The original question, 'Can machines think?' I believe to be too meaningless to deserve discussion. Nevertheless I believe that at the end of the century the use of words and general educated opinion will have altered so much that one will be able to speak of machines thinking without expecting to be contradicted."[6]

One of the many implications of Turing's "test" hypothesis is that intelligence, as something determinate, is regarded as existing (only) insofar as it is recognisable—as such—or insofar as we attach a form of belief to it—in precisely the same way as

[6] Turing, "Computing Machinery and Intelligence," 460.

we attach belief to meaning or to semantic structures. The two—intelligence and meaning—are, for Turing, co-implicated the moment we step beyond "computability" into the speculative realm of universal intelligence, where computability requires there to be an act of recognition (something cannot be computable or incomputable if it cannot first be formulated as a problem). Hence, for Turing, universal intelligence as a concept simply has no meaning other than in terms of a simulation of existing (possible) intellectional attributes. Therefore, if a machine is capable of simulating the attributes of what we establish intelligence to be—either *for us* or *in general*—then, for all intents and purposes, the machine is "intelligent." Or to put it another way, the strictures of verification which we might otherwise wish to apply to an object of scientific enquiry can only extend as far as our *method* of verification—which, as Turing's hypothesis points out, is both extremely rudimentary and indeterminately complex.

In a sense, we should be surprised if the Turing test did not elicit signs of intelligence in this way. Moreover, we need to keep in mind that—above all—Turing's scenario only pertains to the *testing* of (an absent, hidden or hypostatised) intelligence, and not yet to what we might assume to be the deduced *procedures* of intelligence (as we might say "procedures of thought"), assuming that there is such a thing. That is to say, intelligence according to this or any other test hypothesis remains *interpretive* in essence. And just as laboratory chimpanzees and school children learn to ape various procedures and *methodologies* for passing the minimal requirements, or meeting the minimal expectations of their examiners on a routine basis, then the "simulated" intelligence of a machine will not, in effect, have differed at all from the affective intelligence we commonly encounter *in any test scenario*. As we know from the historical effort to determine and justify what are blithely referred to as intelligence quotients, *how* one tests overwhelmingly determines the profile or *type* of results one obtains.

Taken another way, the Turing test might be considered as a reformulation of Wittgenstein's dictum that "the limits of my language are the limits of my world."[7] In this case, the limits of my capacity to imagine, test or recognise "intelligence" marks the limits of what intelligence must effectively *mean for me*. In other words, an idea of intelligence can only extend as far as the horizon of intellection to which it is attached. Put simply, Turing's hypothesis denies that there is any such "thing"—in an objective, verifiable sense—that can be called intelligence, which is not already determined by ideas of *language, limit* and *world*, for example. And let us not forget, in Turing's scenario the machine is programmed *to respond* in a manner that can, at least in principle, be subjected to the *analyst*'s judgement—such that the problem can always be restated as: *if nothing responds to my questions, does it mean there's nothing there*? Henceforth we might say that the analyst here represents a "colophon of doubt," as Jacques Lacan says, and in the suspension of *judgement* corresponding to the test's suspension of verifiability we may identify something like a crisis in subjectivity—that is to say, of a Cartesian subjectivity, in which experience is reduced to a single point of "inaugural certainty" vis-à-vis an implied intelligence of the order of *cogito ergo sum*. "Descartes tells us," we are reminded by Lacan, that *"By virtue of the fact that I doubt, I am sure that I think, and ... by virtue of thinking, I am."*[8]

This leads us to another dilemma identified in Turing's hypothesis, and this has to do with a dependence upon the binary organisation of true/false postulates and the assumption that statements can describe or communicate truth-values. Implicated in the game of identifying truth and falsehood (by way of the mediated "virtuality" of an interlocutor whose truth/falsehood claims are "intentionalised" in order to be

[7] Ludwig Wittgenstein, *Tractatus Logico-Philosophicus*, ed. C.K. Ogden, intro. Bertram Russell (London: Routledge & Kegan Paul, 1922) 5.6.

[8] Jacques Lacan, "Of the Subject of Certainty," *The Four Fundamental Concepts of Psychoanalysis*, trans. Alan Sheridan (New York: Vintage, 1998) 35.

misleading, arbitrary, beguiling and so on) is the assumed possibility of *identifying* intelligence or unintelligence *as such*, an activity that ultimately comes to rest upon a notion of "plausibility," the structure of "attestation" and the "game of witness," as an extension of, or counterpart to, the play of counter-interrogation. Increasingly it is in terms of what we might call the *inhibitory reflex*—or the structural detour that Freud calls "repression"—that the *implications* of intelligence here can be regarded as "manifesting" themselves even, or precisely, where they appear to be most dissimulated, rather than as the (inaccessible) object of verification, judgement or attestation. What Turing's test teaches us, or should teach us, is that it is not in the content of the messages transmitted between the analyst-interrogator and the so-called test subjects (A and B; X or Y) that constitute a measure of intelligence—but the procedural logic of the test itself (as a *conjectural science of the subject*). In other words, the binary vicissitude, the détournement of verifiability, and the artifice of intellection, which—in accordance with this logic—always assumes the form of a rebus or symptom.

The mirroring-effect of Turing's test—by relocating the *analyst* as the subject in a Pavlovian experiment of conditioned responses—suggests that this symptom already points towards a general rupture in the epistemological field: the rupture or gap implied by the Freudian unconscious (the *gap*, as Lacan reminds us, in which the "subject" is constituted as such). To a certain extent, and rather despite himself, Turing develops the implications of this point in an earlier investigation of machine intelligence, characterised by an hypothesis about metonymic recursion: a process of self-substitution and what we might call inflationary or excessive "containment." This hypothesis is called the Turing machine.

In a 1936 article entitled "On Computable Numbers," Turing proposed a hypothetical universal calculating machine (or *universal Turing machine*) capable, in principle, of imitating any and all other calculating machines, including all other "Turing machines."[9] That is to say, the theoretical apparatus called a universal Turing machine is conceived as being capable of "simulating" all possible Turing machines by means of a programmatics in which computing is linked to a general recursiveness (known as the Church-Turing thesis): although today the Turing machine hypothesis has been extended into discussions of stochastic and quantum computing and computability. Being simulatory, the universal Turing machine can be said to function on the basis of a certain illusionism, and it is the possibility of such an illusionary interface between the universal machine and "all other possible machines" (whether Turing, stochastic or quantum "machines") that provides for an understanding of what is termed intelligibility.

For Turing, intelligence, as an effect of recursivity, is linked to symbolisation—or *representability*—and it is a key feature of the Turing machine that it is both capable of producing symbols and of scanning, or *reading*, and analysing them. In other words, the Turing machine operates on the basis of a type of literate technology, capable of not only affecting but of also producing "interpretations." In Turing's original proposal, the machine's function is hypothesised according to a strict set of procedures, of writing, reading—and erasing—binary "marks" (1 or a blank) on a strip of ticker tape. The "markings" on the ticker tape are used to instruct the scanner to either remain stationary or to move left or right, and to inscribe new marks (or erase existing ones)—with the scanner moving left or right only one mark (or set of marks) at a time and then halting. At the end of each movement, the machine enters a different configuration, depending upon the "set of instructions" encoded in the marks on the ticker tape. In this way, the machine is said to effect "acts of *recognition*."

But to speak of acts of recognition presupposes an act of representation, by which the machine is somehow able to

[9] Alan Turing, "On Computable Numbers, with an Application to the Entscheidungsproblem," *Proceedings of the London Mathematical Society* 2.42 (1936): 230-265.

represent to itself—is able to represent *itself* or take itself into account—in order that recognition not remain a "merely figurative" term. In other words, this recognition—if it is to be a basis of "intelligence"—needs to be literalised, in the sense that the machine is able, in a sense, to take into account—and to account for—the process of recognition itself (scanning, inscription, erasure). Yet how can we make sense of such a demand?

We might say that, in the process of inscription and erasure (and in the binary relation of these procedures) the machine effects to produce what might be called an *image*. This image is at once *distinct from* the calculus represented by the individual marks left on the ticker tape, and *affective of* a calculus of recognition (apprehension, intellection)—a calculus that already resembles a primitive form of "cognitive mapping." Further, the machine's capacity to produce images is limited only by the material conditions upon which its machinery depends, and its process of discursive production continues without concern or need of a "subject." Yet although the machine at every point affects the conditions of recognition, we cannot say that there is an ego in the machine—a *deus ex machina* hidden inside the automaton, like the dwarf in Wolfgang von Kempelen's chess-playing "Turk" (1769)—which could magically explain away this phenomenon that we risk calling intelligence.

In the absence of an ego by which it might be "raised to consciousness," this image remains barely a figure—a moment of inertia between material "states" (of inscription/erasure) whose *qualitative difference* it remains as the only legible sign. The question here, however, is not at what point or in what pseudo-subjective configuration inertia can be "made to" signify—in the form of an image or the *difference* of inscription and erasure—but rather what it means to speak of a mechanism of apprehension at all in the absence of an ego, or more precisely of a determinate subjectivity, and what it consequently means to speak of a mechanism "productive " of

Built at the Stanford Research Institute in 1970, "Shakey" (above)—the modern day counterpart of Kempelen's automaton—was the first autonomous robot, remote-controlled by a large computer. It hosted a clever reasoning programme fed very selective spatial data, derived from weak edge-based processing of camera and laser range measurements. On a very good day it could formulate and execute, over a period of hours, plans involving moving from place to place and pushing blocks to achieve a goal.

images. That is to say, of potential "signs." For it is clear that this machine is not merely an *agent* of transmission, but also of a certain *metaphoros* or *translatio*. For the image, after all, bears no relation to any assumed object as an object of apprehension, or of intellection. The image itself is a "virtual," and in its virtuality resides the meaning of what Turing refers to as an *act of recognition*.

Science, whose arbitration, if not agency, is always evoked at moments like these, provides us with various explanatory models for mechanical forms of *recognition*, if not (yet) for *intelligence* as such. Yet science, too, as Turing's test and Kubrick's HAL for different reasons imply, is to a certain extent vested in what, without risk of provocation, we may call the "imaginary." The meaning of such things as intelligence, or perception even, remains something that science must firstly evoke before it is able to invoked it as a paradigm or principle—that is to say, as a *scientific* principle. We always run the risk, as science fiction consistently reveals, of becoming fascinated by "scientific" affects in place of an actual understanding of the terms of the problem at hand—a fascination which is, at root, a blindness already at work within the epistemology of scientific discourse itself. And it is on this level—the level of the *limits* of scientific method, that Turing's test remains somehow controversial, and *not* in the claims it makes, or is made to make, for a "definition" of intelligence.

Even today, when we are surrounded by a new species of automata, from robots to RNAi—the seemingly ubiquitous legacy of HAL, we might say—there is no reason for supposing that this progeny of ours sees in us what we ourselves might wish to see, so to speak, by way of it. An image, that is, of our own idea of invention, the very technē of reason, both recognisable and, in a sense, affecting an act of recognition. An image, that is to say, of its true paternity, in the very image of reason itself. But this would already be to erase the meaning of recognition presupposed in what is commonly understood by the term "intelligence," and indeed by what is meant by reason, or an image as such—since recognition of this order is merely analogical, and belongs to the thinking of man as presumptive *artifex maximus*. Even if, on a certain practical level, we are able to speak today of advanced mechanised or digital optics, imaging systems, infrared tracking, emotion detection and so on—such technics as provide us with quantitative means of describing such things as "pattern recognition" and other more or less comprehensive forms of technical literacy, if not of technical comprehension—we are still unable to do more than locate intelligence in terms of a structural affectivity.

While the pervasiveness of such things as systems of surveillance render the more or less uncritical notion that machines are able to *see* or even *perceive* increasingly commonplace—by *seeing* and *perceiving* we in fact mean the operations of computing programmes in translating optical phenomena into analysable digital code or information (edge and motion detection, face tracking, scene analysis, and so on). Hence one speaks of image "recognition," or "scanning," or "computer literacy."

But this impression that machines *perceive* in an analogous manner to human beings, for instance, leads—among many other things—to notions as that machines are also capable of "making decisions" based on these perceptions: decisions which are in fact based on operations whose appearance is otherwise *analytical* but which we know to be "determined" in advance by structural protocols. That is to say, based upon *affectiveness* just as the idea of recognition remains largely based upon a pathetic fallacy: the wish that our inventions will come, like Frankenstein's "monster," not only to see *like us*, but to *see something in us*. Could this be the meaning of intelligence?

In truth, there is little reason not to accept that a machine, as analytically affective in a manner that is situationally dependent, may be capable of "recognising" what are called pattern formations and, as in chess computers like IBM's Deep Blue, being able to transpose the unfamiliar into a recombination of "familiar" scenarios already stored in a database or "electronic memory." Its capacity to do so would presumably be limited only by the nature of any given programme and the empirical (genetic) limitations set down by its particular manufacture. By adding new scenarios or configurations of scenarios to its database the machine may thus said to "learn." Its operations might then be considered as becoming more subtle and complex in more than merely a statistical sense. It may even be said to "invent" scenarios of its own, so as to effect a type of *experimentality*: to take itself, as we say, into account, or to function auto-poietically. And yet at precisely this point, the machine's operations become increasingly *imaginary*, as both the aporia and interval of an inscription-erasure whose binary coordinates are taken as describing a *ratio of thought*.

Be this as it may, each of these operations, framed by algorithms and computing protocols (case-based, rule-based, or connectionist), remain materially quantitative. To speak, with regards to the machine, of "qualitative judgement" is to metaphorise a set of heuristic, quantitative relations. But what *is* qualitative judgement? In the Turing test hypothesis, where is the qualitative judgement about intelligence located? Is it the *analyst*, for example, who makes the judgement or is it the *analyst* (the very condition of the analyst as the possessor of agency, instrumental intelligence, and therefore—why not?—humanity) who becomes a subject of *being-judged*, or rather of being *placed in question* (not by an ego, but simply by a conspiracy of protocols)?

And if it is impossible to speak to the intelligence question in any qualitative sense, is it even possible to know which one of the variables in the test equation represents the machine, and which the human, or to *know the difference*? And so we move imperceptibly from a machine hypothesis to a human one. Indeed, it would be to overlook the glaringly obvious not to realise that Turing's hypothesis is itself a kind of machine, and that it is an actual machine and not simply a science fiction, whose operations do not simply pose the question of whether or not a machine can be intelligent, so much as they put intelligence itself into question, and with it the very meaning of what we call man.

Donald F. Theall

From the Cyberglobal Chaosmos to the Gutenberg Galaxy: The Prehistory of Cyberelectronic Language(s)

In the 1970s a distinguished Québécois author, multimedia artist, broadcaster, and dramatist produced a short book on the cover of which was an illustration of a figure dressed in the jersey of a Montréal Canadien hockey star, the head of which was a famous bust of Pythagoras. The author, Jacques Languirand, entitled his little book *De McLuhan à Pythagore* (i.e. *From McLuhan to Pythagoras*). I begin at this point, for two reasons—both of which will play roles in my remarks: first, Languirand had designed one of the multi-media productions within the Man and Community theme pavilions at Expo '67 (Montreal) which has been dubbed "McLuhan's Fair"; second and more significantly he was one of the few Québécois cultural figures of the moment who commented in a playful, offbeat book that emphasised McLuhan's leading us back through the complex traditions of the past in order to understand "the tradition of the new." Probably Languirand did so, because existing in the relatively small cultural complex of Montreal orientated to the past of France and Romance

* First published in *Hypermedia Joyce Studies* 3.2 (2003).

Europe as well as to the future of the United States and North America, he was acutely aware of the coming together of the distant past, the immediate past and the future-orientated transformations of the present at the moment when McLuhan emerged.

My title plays against the same motifs which interested Languirand in McLuhan's work, for it points to the historical connections of the understanding of modern media with the long march from the birth of civilisation in the Near East, Egypt and Greece to the period of McLuhan's *Gutenberg Galaxy* (from the Renaissance until the twentieth century), a work which contemporises the medley of science, art and the occult in the world of Pythagorean virtuality. By 1950 with the inception of electric media the *Galaxy* signals a present in which the cybernetic global theatre could be partly anticipated. It also weaves together the ways that the arts, philosophy, theology, occult traditions as proto-science and poetry contributed to understandings that were crucial to the early development of humanistically orientated studies of human communication. Two historic intellectual cultures were central as the historical work of Friedrich Kittler and James Peters confirm: first, liberal scholarship with its emphases on the arts, drama, literature, poetry and the historical and archaeological study of the past; second, the near immediate history of the arts and literature from the inception of electric media in the nineteenth century to major radical and avant-garde movements of the twentieth. I will examine the second of these clusters, the avant-garde, within the context of the first, the classical and ancient as its ground.

While both of these clusters are intrinsic to those fundamental, yet implicit intuitions of McLuhan, which subsequently became a foundation of media ecology as he understood it, that which relates to the immediate past history is crucial. He never fully articulated his fleeting intuitive sense that the long term drift of electric media, from their inception in the mid-nineteenth century on through to the conclusion of the twentieth century, would be to create a totally new integrated language (oral, visual, verbal, tactile, gestural, digital) which might become more primary than speech and certainly would become more primary than print, since he never felt he could confront all its implications and he also knew that his major audiences in business and conservative academia (as distinct from the avant-garde arts and cultural production) would not understand, even if he provided a comprehensive interpretation and critique. Consequently such paradoxes as his appearing to be concerned about the death of the book, while also appearing to speak of new roles for the printed book, realising that there would come to be new automated intermedia productions which would constitute a new kind of book. Nevertheless his intuition was possible because he and many others intuited that the thrust of the past century and a half related to connections between electricity, telegraphy and telepathy pointed towards such integration of modes of statement, as had been hinted at late in the nineteenth century by artists such as Wagner in his conception of the "total work of art," which has been seen in retrospect as a kind of proto-virtual reality.

The rise of the so-called avant-garde, directly connected to these theoretical, mathematical, scientific and technological phenomena, is really a coming to terms with the evolutionary (and therefore also devolutionary) aspects of the growth of cities, the taking command of mechanisation, the impact of electricity and photography and the "shrinking" of the globe. To understand turbulent transformation it was necessary for those creative minds living through the experience to revisit and re-examine the modes of statement and communication. Walter Benjamin, reviewing the development of the history of modernism from Baudelaire through Dadaism and Surrealism and the emergence of "technological modes of reproducibility," dramatised their intense interest in extending the sense of what language meant, while simultaneously associating it with the esoteric traditions of the occult, particularly the Kabala. His ability to bridge the work of Baudelaire, of Brecht, of Kafka, of the surrealists and of new modes of technological production, reproducibility and dissemination arose from his awareness that there existed a spectrum of languages rather than any relatively limited sense of what constituted language.

While Benjamin respected the "language of man" with its propensity towards naming, he still asserted the importance of the language of things which could reach its realisation through painting, sculpture, architecture, design or the new modes of production:

> There is a language of sculpture, of painting, of poetry. Just as the language of poetry is partly, if not solely, founded on the name language of man, it is very conceivable that the language of sculpture or painting is founded on certain kinds of thing language, that in them we find a translation of the language of things into an infinitely higher language, which may still be of the same sphere. We are concerned here with nameless, nonacoustic languages, languages issuing from matter; here we should recall the material community of things in their communication. Moreover, the communication of things is certainly communal in a way that grasps the world as such an unidentified whole.[1]

In this essay "On Language as Such and On the Language of Man," Benjamin notes the future importance of the convergence of languages—the blending of modes of discourse—and points out that the artists of the later nineteenth century and of the early twentieth century are the early stages of a dramatic interface with this—an anticipation of the emergence of cyberspace.

This theme of the blending of modes of discourse runs throughout the history of Dadaism and Surrealism and their aftermath, and represents a major unanticipated contribution which Marcel Duchamp and his associates made to the

---

[1] Walter Benjamin, *Reflections*, trans. Harry Zohn (New York: Schocken, 1986) 330.

evolution of digital art—a contribution noted early in his career by McLuhan, who entitled his first book, *The Mechanical Bride* after Duchamp's *Large Glass,* or *the Bride Stripped Bare by Her Bachelors, Even.* Duchamp and other avant-garde figures became part of the pantheon of McLuhanesque media ecology, partly because they provided him with such techniques as the collage, the visual punning on cultural icons, the use of headlines and telegraphic comic aphorisms and many of his basic strategies in *The Bride,* and works like *The Medium is the Massage, Counterblast, Culture is Our Business* and *Take Today.* But even more because they were offering comic poetic insights in a variety of modes into the directions in which techno-culture was developing. It is probably through these avant-garde artists and poets that McLuhan was able to first intuit a real role for his classical education in understanding the drift of contemporary culture towards a transformation of the book.

To digress for a moment, many media ecologists, such as Walter Ong or McLuhan (even Eric Havelock) have obtained initial insights from the work of poets, and artists which fascinated them. Ong's sensitivity to orality and its complex conflicts with literacy were certainly enhanced by his fascination with Gerard Manley Hopkins, just as Shakespeare's *Lear* and Pope's *Dunciad* provided McLuhan with insights. From *Lear,* as he points out, a sense of "the anguish of the third dimension" as well as "the shift from people being translated from their having roles to having jobs"; from Pope he gleaned how "the mass distributed, printed book [was] leading to a primitivistic and Romantic revival" and how the new emerging collective unconscious was a backwash of private self-statement. From such sources also came insights about the interplay of the visual and the auditory in altering the ratio of the senses.

But the most relevant poetic insights in understanding the processes of change of the actual moment are those of contemporary or near contemporary artists, since their impact extended beyond Ong and McLuhan to other critics and historians of media. The Dadaists and other avant-gardists, including Mallarmé mentioned earlier, became involved with the fluidity of language as manifested in its polysemy. A little known figure in this history of the pun, Jean-Pierre Brisset, who until recent years was a barely remembered figure of French intellectual life, was adopted by Jarry, Duchamp, Apollinaire and others.

Duchamp included Brisset in his "ideal library" with authors such as Mallarmé. As Hans Richter, one of the early Dadaists points out Brisset "attributed to language a sort of divine consciousness … From the sound of speech and from affinities of sound he deduced a deeper divine meaning and on it based his 'Great Law, Key to Words.'" In Brisset's vision and its echoes in Apollinaire, Breton, Duchamp and other Dadaists and Surrealists resides one aspect of the roots of Joyce's *Finnegans Wake*, which became not only a text-book for McLuhan, but for writers on hypertext and VR such as J. David Bolter, Michael Joyce and Darren Tofts. The entire movement of the avant-garde during this period is directed towards the creation of "new languages" which could be various blends of multiplicity of different modes—gestures, sounds, images, words and their movement.

This is certainly part of what was implicit in the symboliste and avant-garde interest in Rimbaud's "alchemy of the word"—an alchemy which about five decades later has been partly co-opted by the post World War II advertising industry. This motif of "alchemy" is specifically linked by Antonin Artaud to his conceptions about the theatre, for in 1938 he links the theatre to multi-modal language and the creation of virtual realities. "The theatre, which is in *no thing*," Artaud says, "but makes use of everything—gestures, sounds, words, screams, light, darkness—rediscovers itself at precisely the point where the mind requires a language to express its manifestations."[2] Later he points out that the theatre is "a mirage" just as the

---

[2] Antonin Artaud, *The Theatre and its Double*, trans. Mary Caroline Richards (London: Calder, 1958) 12. Originally published in France in 1938.

alchemical symbol is and he continues noting the perpetual allusion to the materials and principle of the theatre found in alchemical books, concluding that this expresses an identity between "the purely fictitious and illusory world in which the symbols of alchemy are evolved" and "the world in which the characters, objects, images, and in a general way all that constitutes the *virtual reality* of the theatre develops."[3] With the coming of age of VR in the digital world during the closing decades of the second millennium, it is intriguing, to note such an anticipation of the affiliation of the "theatre" as an inclusive form—a convergence of modes of communication and statement. Furthermore, Artaud concludes his essay by putting the "essential drama" at the "root of all Great Mysteries."[4]

Artaud's corroborating the twentieth century thrust towards the goal of an all encompassing language integrating a wide spectrum of modes of statement, also stresses the poetic as intrinsic to the complexities of cognition and neurology that constitute the realities of mind and the external world. In the first half of the twentieth century avant-garde movements in all of the arts were moving in the same direction—a direction which not too surprisingly anticipated the evolution of a digital world and of cognitive science that would re-establish some new links between the arts, science and technology: Artaud's "Theatre of Alchemy"; Duchamp's envisioning the "alchemy" of Rutherford's theories on radiation and later the splitting of the atom; and Joyce's making Shem the poet in and of *Finnegans Wake*, an "alshemist," whose dream vision plays with complex paronomasia and with scientific and mathematical theories from Helmholtz, Rutherford and Poincaré to Heisenberg, Planck and Gödel.

The simultaneous inter-relationship of all these writers with such motifs as linguistic ambivalence, engineering, science, the occult (such as alchemy) and the intuitive modes of daydream and vision are in many ways rooted in the histories of science

[3] Artaud, *The Theatre and its Double*, 49.
[4] Artaud, *The Theatre and its Double*, 51.

itself and its connections with the histories of memory, statement and the occult. If Duchamp regarded his activity as a mode of engineering, as many other avant-garde artists did, Joyce spoke of himself as "the greatest engineer"—something he found easy to put into juxtaposition with being a musicmaker and a philosophe. Joyce, like Duchamp, regarded himself as enmeshed in the alchemy of the word, which leads to the splitting of the atom and the "etym." Linking language through etymology with atomic science, Joyce predicts the explosions and detonations of the coming world war, simultaneously noting the transformation of language itself in this new world of Rutherford's alchemy.

This linguistic alchemy—a language-orientated modality of chaos—simultaneously lays the groundwork for the ongoing transformations of media, since it underlines the fluidity of modes of communication, linking them with transitions in science and technology. It leads to Joyce's speaking in the *Wake* of "chaosmos"—the world as cosmos transformed in a multi-dimensional earth—which became a key word in later discussions in Eco, Deleuze, Guattari, Baudrillard and many others since complexity and chaos emerged as ruling theoretical principles—a phenomenon reflected throughout popular culture. Simultaneously it lays the groundwork for a growing acceptance of the quest for hypermedia, since it presents the probes which provide the linguistic fluidity and the synaesthetic consciousness that are requisite to understand the accelerating convergence of modes of statement that had earlier been intuited by film makers, photographers, typographers and many others. All of this is grounded within the satiric exposure of the ecological problems of media that permeated the work of avant-gardists, especially Marcel Duchamp, Wyndham Lewis and James Joyce.

I am primarily using the insight gained from such associations as an exemplum of how all the arts—the traditional fine arts; what were then in the 1930s called by Gilbert Seldes the newer "lively arts"; and subsequent pop arts and media—

were with varying degrees of consciousness developing a vision of newly transformed *paraoral* and *paraverbal* languages. (I am coining these terms to indicate that the new, potentially primary language would exist beyond, beside and above existing oral languages.)

A key document in this pre-history is Laszlo Moholy-Nagy's *Vision in Motion*. Along with Wyndham Lewis he was a strong influence on the early McLuhan. Moholy-Nagy invited to the United States to become director of the New Bauhaus ultimately became director of the Chicago Institute of Art. Within his own creative work he had explored a variety of approaches and media: photograms, painting, sculpture, design, industrial design, experimental film and writing. He also articulated the importance of the growing inter-relation of art, technology and science in developing contemporary solutions to living in a global society.

Moholy-Nagy's basis for this project is his assertion that the primary discovery contemporary artists and poets had made is the significance of "vision in motion." In his writings he demonstrated repeatedly that painting, sculpture, architecture, music, film and contemporary poetry and creative writing along with many other artistic developments were all becoming more conscious of the ancient awareness of the arts as aspiring to reproduce "vision in motion." He also stressed that "vision in motion" had a particular relationship with the new space-time world in which everyone in the twentieth century had become immersed, and consequently with the increasing importance of electricity and electronics, all of which he specifically mentions. In this respect, Moholy-Nagy is building on the work of the Dadaists and the Cubists, but particularly Duchamp, whose *Large Glass* was so intrinsically involved with electricity, with new technologies, with the new space-time continuum and the fourth dimension. *Vision in Motion*, is, therefore, an exploration of the possibilities of an assemblage of new languages, which partly reflect his own lifelong practice as an artist, designer and teacher.

Moholy-Nagy in many ways is the pioneering founder of what led through his successors, particularly his student György Kepes, to the MIT visual arts programme and then to the MIT Media lab with its exploration of cyberspace and the World Wide Web. He stressed the importance of linking Joyce's work to the new directions of vision in motion as well as indicating the intimate association of advertising, comics and industrial art with the avant-garde critique of media. As McLuhan realised through his study of and association with Wyndham Lewis, the early avant-garde were involved in an ecologically orientated satiric critique of the rise of new electric modes of communication. Such a critique is not intended to be purely negative, since there is always within it a positive element of what might come to be along with a powerful comic critique. It is from this critique by the early avant-garde as well as from the perceptions of modernist poets and artists that there arose the intellectual satire of media ecology which vitiated the work of McLuhan, and then moved in differing ways into that of such successors Ong, Kroker, Baudrillard, Neil Postman, Bob Dobbs and John Cage. Beyond McLuhan and in his wake there came the pragmatic practices and critical discussions of the exploration of hypertextuality and cyberspace. These practices and discussions are beginning to provide a new ecological perspective to what Ong called "secondary orality" and what McLuhan and later Baudrillard, could see as the next transformation of the idea of the *libris*, which has moved through history from stone and papyrus to manuscripts, printed words, illustrated words and the like. As Baudrillard has pointed out, tactility (and the ratio of all the senses) was always more crucial in the McLuhanesque understanding of media than specific biases toward the acoustic sphere or the visual range. Implicit in that transformation was an acceptance of the "chaosmic" nature of our complex cosmos, which is the context in which the new cyber-electronic language(s) is taking form. Understanding the cyberglobal chaosmos takes us back to the Gutenberg Galaxy (just as McLuhan's work naturally led back to Pythagoras). This enables us to appreciate the complexities involved in exploring the transformations of the modes of statement and their dissemination, while also demonstrating that we have always already been moving towards our parahuman—not *posthuman*—vision of virtuality.

The reason it is important to appreciate the roots of this in the avant-garde movements and the roots of such artistic movements in the poetics and rhetoric of the ancient world is both to return to them for a deeper understanding of the problems of media ecology (or in a play on McLuhan's ratio of the senses—an ecology of sense) and to appreciate the need to attend to and study the mature contemporary artists and poets (particularly playing with the new hypermedia) as a guide to understanding the ecological implications of the future of the Twenty-first century. The examples of anticipation and illumination are legion, arising in visions such as Jean Luis Borges's parabolic stories on "The Library of Babel" and "The Garden of the Forking Paths" or in the cultural productions of Rauschenberg, Cunningham and Cage—but that is a tale for another time and place. What we have looked at today is the importance of realising that there is a musical, choreographic, visual art and poetic presence side by side with the techno-scientific in the emergence of our new cyber-electronic languages (our contemporary thrust for the para-oral and para-verbal) and that the history and current immediacy of that presence is an important aid to media ecologists.

Arthur Bradley

The Letter Giveth

> For the letter killeth, but the Spirit giveth life
> —2 Corinthians 3:6

> Instead of opposing them, as is almost always done, they ought to be thought *together*, as *one and the same possibility*: the machine-like and faith …
> —Jacques Derrida, "Faith and knowledge"

> Technics is the condition as much of science and knowledge as of religious faith …
> —Bernard Stiegler, "Fidelity at the limits of deconstruction and the prosthesis of faith"

It is possible to argue that deconstruction has always been a philosophy of both *faith* and *technics*. As Bernard Stiegler has recently argued, Derrida's thought is at *one and the same time* a "thinking of technics, of tele-technologies, and, as a thinking of tele-technologies, of the 'media' in all its guises" *and* a "thinking of fidelity, of fidelity to the past, of memory and of heritage— that is, fidelity in the Law. And, in this sense, a thinking of faith, of truth and religion."[1]

* I am grateful to Richard Beardsworth, Michael Dillon and delegates at the *Derrida: Negotiating the Legacy* conference at the University of Aberystwyth in January 2005 for their helpful comments on this paper.

1 Bernard Stiegler, "Derrida and Technology; Fidelity at the Limits of Deconstruction and the Prosthesis of Faith," trans. R. Beardsworth in *Jacques*

On the one hand, for example, deconstruction is a discourse on *fidelity*—the trust *and* the trustworthiness—of the classical subject. The deconstruction of subjectivity (whether it takes the form of Husserl's transcendental constituting subject or even Heidegger's authentic *Dasein*)—shows how that subject unwittingly depends upon an *immemorial or absolute past* that has never been present to consciousness and so cannot be recollected as such. This aporia of origin (which is variously thematised under the names of archē-writing, *différance*, passive synthesis and so on) famously forms the condition of possibility of the presence of the subject to itself *without* ever being an object for knowledge or calculation. In the absence of any present ground or foundation, the metaphysics of subjectivity is thus revealed to be nothing more than the profession of an originary *faith or trust* in the subject's own self-constitution that precedes any particular act of faith whether religious or secular: the subject is precisely *that which believes itself to be a* subject.

On the other hand, deconstruction consistently links the aporia that precedes and constitutes the metaphysics of subjectivity through the *vehicle* of a certain (if again concealed) *technē*. The *immemorial* past that constitutes the supposedly self-constituting Husserlian or Heideggerian subject is consistently thought through the *historical or empirical past* of, for example, the *writing* that makes possible ideal objects,[2] or through the originary contamination of the ontological question by *ontic* technologies.[3] This paradoxical situation—whereby the transcendental field of consciousness is always "quasi-transcendentally" constituted by the empirical or worldly force of technology—introduces a radical or "originary" technicity into thinking that is irreducible to any Aristotelian concept of

Derrida and the Future of the Humanities, ed. Tom Conley (Cambridge: Cambridge University Press, 2002) 239.

2 Jacques Derrida, *Speech and Phenomena and Other Essays on Husserl's Theory of Signs,* trans. D. Allison (Evanston: Northwestern University Press, 1973).

3 Jacques Derrida, *Of Spirit: Heidegger and the Question,* trans. G. Bennington and R. Bowlby (Chicago: Chicago University Press, 1989).

technē as instrumentation. In the absence of any unmediated, self-identical—that is to say non-technological—living presence, the subject is once again delivered over to a pre-originary engagement or commitment that makes it possible for it to be a subject: the subject *is that which is subject to, or by means of,* technology.

Yet the relationship between these two distinct lines of enquiry or questioning within deconstruction—faith and technics—remains frustratingly undetermined both within Derrida's work and more generally. It is only necessary here to recall Richard Beardsworth's prediction about two possible futures for deconstruction at the end of his *Derrida and the Political* (1996) in order to grasp the problem. As is well-known, Beardsworth makes an important distinction between what he calls Derrida's early meditations on technology in the essays on Husserl, Saussure and Rousseau and the later work on literature and religion in the works on Levinas, Heidegger and negative theology. Either deconstruction will take its inspiration from Derrida's early work and become a "left-wing" reflection upon technics that opens new points of dialogue with the technosciences, he argues, or it will align itself with the later work and become a "right-wing" generalisation of the religious and negotiate points of contact with religious or literary tradition.[4] If Beardsworth's argument seemed polemical at the time it was written, the massive gulf that exists between contemporary Derrida scholars such as John D. Caputo and Arkady Plotnitsky[5]—to the point where it is hard to believe that they are even writing about the same philosopher—makes it seem almost prophetic today. For Beardsworth, it is too simple to say we can simply *choose* between these two possible futures for deconstruction—the future of deconstruction being above all a question of invention—but nonetheless it seems like a choice has—more or less arbitrarily—been made.

[4] Richard Beardsworth, *Derrida and the Political* (London: Routledge, 1996) 156-7.
[5] Cf. John D. Caputo, *The Prayers and Tears of Jacques Derrida: Religion Without Religion* (Bloomington: Indiana University Press, 1997).

In what follows, I briefly want to explore the relation between Derrida and Stiegler's accounts of the relationship between faith and technics in deconstruction. It is in their respective essays "Faith and knowledge: the two sources of 'religion' within the limits of reason alone"[6] and "Fidelity at the limits of deconstruction and the prosthesis of faith" that we receive the most explicit account of what that relation might look like.[7] As the epigraphs to this essay indicate, both Derrida and Stiegler express a desire to think faith and technics *together*. Yet it is possible to detect a critical and irreducible difference between Derrida and Stiegler's versions of deconstruction within their more general agreement. If both are concerned to articulate an aporetic relation between faith and technics—where neither can exist without the other—the approaches they take diverge significantly. The Derridean account attempts to analyse the aporia between faith and technics in terms of a *philosophical logic* whereas the Stieglerian approach works out that aporia more *genealogically* in terms of the specific temporal passages that it must go through if it is not to be confused with a simple transcendental concept or condition. This paper will assess Derrida and Stiegler's distinct presentations of faith and technics in terms of what we might (with the emphasis being placed on the prefix in both cases) call a *quasi-transcendental* approach on the one hand and a *quasi-genealogical* approach on the other. What, to set the perimeters of the debate, is at stake within the Derrida-Stiegler debate? How do the two thinkers attempt to fulfil their declared promise of thinking faith and technics together? To what extent do Derrida and Stiegler do justice to what we might call the "spirit and the letter" of deconstruction?

---

[6] Jacques Derrida, "Faith and Knowledge: the Two Sources of 'Religion' within the Limits of Reason Alone," trans. S. Weber in *Religion*, eds. J. Derrida and G. Vattimo (London: Polity, 1998).

[7] Stiegler, "Derrida and Technology," 241.

Derrida and Stiegler

Firstly, I would like to briefly set out what seems to me to be the basic difference between Derrida and Stiegler's concepts of deconstruction. It is necessary to explore in a little more detail Derrida's critique of the metaphysics of subjectivity. As we have already begun to see, Derrida's work seeks to articulate an originary point of aporia that precedes and determines the opposition between the transcendental and the empirical upon which the metaphysics of presence seeks to institute itself. Derrida always insists upon the *irreducibility* of this aporia to *either* an empirical time or place *or* a transcendental concept or condition: "What deconstruction is not? Everything! What deconstruction is? Nothing!"[8] If he does give the aporia of origin a series of names throughout his work—from *différance* up to the recent *anacoluthia*—Derrida is insistent that these are not proper names so much as nick-names for the aporia strategically borrowed from the texts he discusses to briefly function as "quasi-transcendental" meta-concepts for the aporetic structure itself.

The early works such as *Of Grammatology*, *Voice and Phenomena* and *Writing and Difference* tend to think the aporia of origin through specific historical, empirical or technical sites like writing whereas later work like *Adieu to Emmanuel Levinas* or *Of Hospitality* prefer to translate that aporia through ethical, political and even religious concepts such as the immemorial promise, originary hospitality to the other or, increasingly, messianic time. This raises the inevitable question of whether these two strikingly different ways of understanding the aporia of origin—which we might crudely call the "technical" and the "religious"—are merely two "equally valid" ways of saying the same thing or whether one might be "better" than the other. What, then, is Stiegler's answer to this question?

---

[8] Jacques Derrida, "Letter to a Japanese Friend," trans. D. Wood and A. Benjamin in *A Derrida Reader: Between the Blinds*, ed. P. Kamuf (New York: Columbia University Press, 1991) 72.

To be sure, Bernard Stiegler sticks closely to Derrida's project of articulating an unthought point of aporia between the transcendental and the empirical from which the essential finitude of western metaphysics can be questioned. It is clear, however, that there is an important difference between Stiegler and Derrida's accounts of deconstruction around the question of how that empirico-transcendental aporia might best be thought. As we will see, Stiegler distances himself from Derrida's attempts to insist upon the irreducibility of the aporia to either the empirical or the transcendental by exclusively and controversially thinking that aporia through the means of *technics*. Stiegler's ongoing project *La technique et le temps* (1994-) identifies an originary and aporetic relation between technics and time that is only subsequently and retrospectively transformed into the metaphysical opposition between the transcendental and the empirical, the infinite and the finite, the immortal and the mortal and so on.[9]

If metaphysics depends upon instituting a hierarchy of the transcendental over the empirical, for example, Stiegler is concerned to show—through a succession of readings of the Platonic opposition between *anamnesis* and *technē*, the Husserlian attempt to protect primary retention from secondary memory and the Heideggerian attempt to separate an ontological temporality from the vulgar concept of time—that the empirical is the *condition* of (im-)possibility *of* the transcendental in the sense, for example, that the inscription and exteriorisation of thought through mnemo-technological support systems (what he calls, in Husserlian terms, "tertiary memory") constitutes the only basis on which any metaphysical project can transcend finitude in the first place.[10] In Stiegler's account, Derrida's attempt to insist upon the irreducibility of

<hr>

[9] Bernard Stiegler, *La Technique et le temps 1: La Faut d'Épiméthée* (Paris: Galilée, 1994); trans. R. Beardsworth and G. Collins (Stanford: Stanford University Press, 1998).

[10] Cf. Mark Hansen, *Embodying Technesis: Technology Beyond Writing* (Ann Arbor: University of Michigan Press, 2000).

the aporia of origin to *either* the transcendental *or* the empirical constitutes a residually metaphysical disavowal of this originary *relation* between technics and time.[11]

Stiegler goes on to argue that Derrida's deconstruction of the empirico-transcendental opposition remains dominated by the metaphysical logic it seeks to call into question on a number of closely-related levels. It is Stiegler's basic position that Derrida's account of deconstruction is in too close proximity to the classic metaphysical logic of the transcendental and the empirical it seeks to deconstruct and merely ends up reproducing that logic under the pretence of overcoming it. To be more precise, Stiegler argues that Derrida's *quasi-transcendental* attempt to insist upon the *absolute irreducibility* of the aporia of origin to the transcendental and the empirical starts to become indistinguishable from a *simple transcendentalism* whereby that aporia seems to exist *outside* history.

If Derrida is right to argue that the aporia of origin is irreducible to some historical event or empirical object in this world, the fact remains that there is no "*other world*" than this one and so the aporia must *necessarily pass through this world* in order to be thinkable at all.[12] Yet it is precisely this passage of the aporia *through* the empirical history of the world that Derrida's work increasingly fails to articulate (particularly when it resorts to a quasi-theological vocabulary of an immemorial promise that has always already been given or a messianic future that will never absolutely arrive) and Stiegler's own work seeks to fill in this empirical deficit or lack. In Stiegler's philosophy, we are offered a *genealogy* of the aporia from the "bottom upwards" which, by tracing its own materialisations in the form of mnemo-technologies, attempts to

---

[11] See Stiegler's *La Technique et le temps* 1 (1994) for the outline of this larger project. The best overall introduction to Stiegler's work is the collection of interviews with Elie During entitled *Philosopher par accident*.

[12] Derrida, "Faith and Knowledge," 57.

correct a perceived transcendental, or "top downwards," bias within Derridean deconstruction.[13]

Faith and Technics

Secondly, I would like to focus in more detail on the Derrida-Stiegler debate on faith and technology. It is in this particular exchange that the complex relationship between the two philosophers can be seen most clearly. As we will see, Derrida and Stiegler seem at first to come to *exactly the same conclusion* about faith and technology—what we call faith is inextricably tied to technics—but this apparent agreement conceals a larger and more important difference of emphasis concerning the precise status of that *technē*. On the one hand, Derrida uses the concept of *technē* as little more than a strategically deployed quasi-transcendental meta-concept that communicates with, yet does not belong to, any simple empirical technology. On the other hand, Stiegler wants to insist upon an "essential" relation *between* that quasi-transcendental technicity and its empirical context.[14] If Derrida would undoubtedly see Stiegler's refusal to countenance a *quasi-transcendental excess* of what he terms the "machine-like" *over* the empirical history of technology[15] as

---

[13] In a well-known review article of the first volume of *La Technique et le temps,* Geoffrey Bennington criticised Stiegler on the grounds that his philosophy contains an illicit positivism that seeks to reduce the aporia of origin to its own empirical history and install technics as its "proper name." Cf. Geoffrey Bennington, "Emergencies," *Oxford Literary Review* 18 (1996): 175-216. It is pointless to deny that there is a danger of positivism in Stiegler's work when he insists so forcefully that the aporia of origin "depends" upon technicity, or that technicity is "essential" to the aporia. Yet the allegation that he simply *equates* technics with the aporia seems to me misplaced because Stiegler acknowledges quite explicitly that there is no essential link between the two and, thus, no positivism of deconstruction: "Deconstructive grammatology cannot for this reason be a positive science" ("Derrida and Technology," 263). In my view, Stiegler's much more subtle position is that although the aporia absolutely *precedes* empiricity it can *only* take place within it: we can speak of these *positivisations* of the aporia without being simply positivist.

[14] Stiegler, "Derrida and technology," 241.

[15] Derrida, "Faith and Knowledge," 47.

indicating a worryingly naïve positivism, Stiegler would reply that Derrida's constant resistance to the possibility of an *essential relation between* the two constitutes a transcendentalist *disavowal* of the technological real. Let me briefly set out their respective positions.

Derrida's essay "Faith and knowledge: the two sources of 'religion' within the limits of reason alone" argues that religion (apparently including the categories of faith, revelation and philosophical theology) and reason (including the categories of critique, science, technoscience, philosophy and even thought in general) share the same aporia of origin.[16] It contends that both religion and reason share what we have already seen to be an immemorial "performative of promising" which calls for an "elementary act of faith."[17] To make any speech act whatsoever, whether rational or religious, whether sincere or dissimulating, requires a primordial promise to speak the truth on the part of the speaker, and an equivalent gesture of trust on the part of the recipient, if it is to assume the status of communication, understanding or knowledge.

Yet according to a logic that will be very familiar to readers of the later Derrida this "messianic memory and promise" that is "older than all religion" contains the necessity of confirmation, repetition and with it "everything technical, automatic, machine-like supposed by iterability."[18] If the promise is not originarily possible without containing the possibility of being repeated and confirmed as such, then the technical becomes the very condition of fidelity: "the technical is the possibility of faith, indeed its very chance."[19] The *empirical relationship* between contemporary religion and technology which Derrida goes on to analyse at length in this essay— whereby religious fundamentalism simultaneously embraces and reacts against contemporary tele-technoscience in a process

16 Derrida, "Faith and Knowledge," 28.
17 Derrida, "Faith and Knowledge," 18.
18 Derrida, "Faith and Knowledge," 47.
19 Derrida, "Faith and Knowledge," 47.

of auto-immunisation—needs to be understood as an expression of this more "originary" *aporia* between faith and technics. This leads Derrida to the apparently Stieglerian conclusion that the very *relation between religion and technology*—which takes the empirical form of an opposition between living spontaneity or plenitude on the one hand and mechanisation, autonomisation and the machine on the other—is *itself originarily technical* albeit in an obviously *quasi-transcendental* sense of that term: "The *relation* between these two motions is ineluctable, *and therefore automatic and machinal.*" For Derrida, to summarise, "Instead of opposing them, as is almost always done, they ought to be thought *together*, as *one and the same possibility*: the machine-like and faith."[20]

Stiegler's essay "Fidelity at the limits of deconstruction and the prosthesis of faith" looks like a simple commentary upon Derrida's text but it is also a subtle and penetrating critique of the latter from a materialist and genealogical perspective. It is Stiegler's position that, for all its insistence upon the "machine-like," Derrida's account of faith and technology remains residually transcendental. As we have already seen, Stiegler is suspicious of an apparent repression or disavowal of technicity within Derrida's presentation of the aporia of origin that leads him to privilege its quasi-transcendental dimension *over* its empirical history. Stiegler is insistent that Derrida's transcendental account of the aporia needs to be supplemented with a genealogy *of what we have seen to make the transcendence of thought possible in the first place,* namely, technics: "the inverting logic of the supplement outlined here requires a history of the supplement, *one which is also a history of technics [les techniques].*"[21] Yet Derrida's stress upon the irreducibility of the aporia to history constitutes a "somewhat surprising declaration of *independence*" that risks excessively transcendentalising that aporia at the expense of the empirico-historical contexts through which it *must* pass if Derrida is right

[20] Derrida, "Faith and Knowledge," 47 emphasis added; 48.
[21] Stiegler, "Derrida and Technology," 248.

to claim, as he surely is, that it does not exist in some transcendental "other world."[22]

If Derrida's account seems to transcendentalise the aporia, Stiegler goes on to offer a finely balanced account of that aporia as suspended *between* the empirical and the transcendental. On the one hand, Stiegler argues that the aporia must refer to what he calls an *absolute past*, an origin that has *never* been present and cannot be presented as such because it is irreducible to empiricity as its condition of possibility. On the other hand, Stiegler contends that the aporia must also refer to what he calls a *relative past*, an historical origin that has *once* been present, because it does not exist *anywhere* else but in this world and can only appear, even as irreducibility, *through* empiricity and technical exteriorisation if we are to know it exists at all.

For Stiegler, to condense his argument somewhat brutally, the absolute past *precedes* any historical knowledge whatsoever as the condition of its *possibility* but, at the same time, the relative past constitutes the condition of *effectivity* of the absolute past because, if it did not pass *through* history, the latter would not just be something that we *know* to be inaccessible, but something *absolutely unknowable*. The problem with Derrida's account is that it privileges the "always already there" of the absolute past and thus misses what Stiegler calls its necessary passage through the relative past that was once "there" in historical time. This is why Derrida's quasi-transcendental account of the *logic* of the aporia in terms of an "originary technicity" needs to be supplemented by Stiegler's account of the *history* of the empirical supplementations in which that logic is (retrospectively) re-constituted if it is not to succumb to the simple transcendentalism it does so much to question. In Stiegler's argument, Derrida's analysis of the *quasi-transcendental* "technicity" that underwrites the determined empirical opposition between faith and technology thus needs to contain an account of its own *technical history* (both the

---

22 Stiegler, "Derrida and Technology," 253.

history *of* technics and history *as* technics) if that "technicity" is not to remain simply an empty philosopheme: *"Technics is the condition as much of science and knowledge as of religious faith."*[23]

The Letter Giveth?

In conclusion, I want to return to the question with which we began, namely, the precise *relation* between deconstruction as a philosophy of *both* faith *and* technology. It is Stiegler's conclusion that the mutually constitutive relation between the absolute past and the relative past is ultimately "a question of faith."[24] As we saw at the beginning of this paper, Derrida's deconstruction of the subject of western metaphysics simultaneously exposes that subject as already delivered over to an originary fidelity or trust in an absolute past on the one hand and an originary engagement with the empirical or historical past of technological supplements such as writing on the other. Yet it is Stiegler's articulation of the *mutually constitutive relation* between the absolute past and the relative past, I would argue, that enables us to fill in the gap *between* Derrida's discrete accounts of faith and technology. What. to summarise, is his position?

To put it in a word, Stiegler argues that fidelity (whether it be religious or secular) lies in the "break [*brisure*]" *between* the absolute past that can *never* become a form of knowledge on the one hand and the relative past that constitutes the *only* medium through which that absolute past is communicated on the other. On the one hand, the absolute past stops the relative past from freezing or reducing everything to a form of present or representable knowledge. On the other hand, the relative past prevents the absolute past from becoming totally irreducible to any form of knowledge whatsoever. Neither absolute nor relative, faith is the *effect* of this necessary *mediation* or *negotiation* between the two pasts and the poles of total

23 Stiegler, "Derrida and Technology," 259.
24 Stiegler, "Derrida and Technology," 256.

knowability and unknowability they respectively represent: "In other words, this "past" that has never gone past, that never stops passing, passes through tertiary memory without passing through it. Quasi-transcendental. But *through* empiricity. Empiricity invested with spirit, with the spirit, for example, of the *letter*: the empirical mark of the trace common to geometry, the *Bible*, the *New Testament* and the *Koran*."[25]

If Corinthians 2:8 insists that "the letter killeth, but the Spirit giveth life," Stiegler's radical response is not simply that the spirit exists *in* the letter but that the letter itself *is* the spirit: *the letter giveth life.* The letter gives life in the sense that it is only because the empirical mark of the "letter" has the ability to preserve intuition, to exceed the essential fallibility of human memory, and be transmissible to future generations, that the transcendental status or "spirit" of either the subject, the Judaeo-Christian god, the ideal object of Husserlian geometry or the absolute past of the aporia described by Derridean deconstruction is possible at all. This life-giving letter constitutes the condition of possibility of transcendence but— by intrinsically connecting it to the very empirical matter it seeks to transcend in the first place—it also forms its condition of impossibility. For Stiegler, it is this (de-)constituting technical structure, simultaneously compelling faith and interrupting it, that forms the basis for the religious violence of which Derrida speaks in "Faith and knowledge": "It is thus that which uproots from the ground, that which does violence to one's home, that which thrusts outwards the intimate, and that which corrodes idiomatic differences. But this violence is also the very possibility of idiomatic differentiation, that which *constitutes* one's home in the first place by opening it to what is other than oneself."[26]

Finally, however, I would like to raise one larger question about the Derrida-Stiegler debate that goes beyond the scope of this question. It is the question of *what constitutes life* itself. As

[25] Stiegler, "Derrida and Technology," 260.
[26] Stiegler, "Derrida and Technology," 260.

we have seen, it is the ostensibly dead, inanimate or spiritless letter that *gives* life. Yet this radical claim immediately begs the question of the *relationship between* life and death, between *zoē* and *technē* or between technology and life. If the transcendence of the subject depends upon an originary faith in the *constitution* of a past that has always already been taken place, yet that past must in turn find itself *re-constituted* in the relative past by writing and other empirical mnemo-technical support systems, then the possibility that arises from this is not simply an essential relation between the transcendental and the empirical but between *technics* and *life* itself. In this sense, the Derrida-Stiegler exchange is nothing less than a debate about the *technical constitution of life itself* or what we might even call *life's technicity*:

The living is what *wants* to live, and, wanting to live, what *believes unconditionally* in life [but] it only believes in life insofar as it is haunted by the dead qua the non-living, by the dead in the sense of those who have lived, and by death as that to which life testifies. This haunting is only possible as the technicity of life.

Simon Critchley & Tom McCarthy

Universal Shylockery

What if Nietzsche were a Jew, and a mean-minded Venetian Jew at that? We'd like to begin with the thought-experiment of imagining *The Merchant of Venice* as a genealogy of morality and imagining Shylock as Nietzsche. What is *The Merchant of Venice* about? What is at stake in this oddly inside-out drama, where a piece of good-old Elizabethan comic Jew-baiting rotates 180 degrees into a devastating study of Christian anti-Semitism only to flip back into what it seemed to deny? Our initial hypothesis is that it is nothing less than an inquiry into the origin of our moral concepts of justice, good and bad, and more particularly guilt, law, mercy and love. It is here that a link with Nietzsche suggests itself, particularly with the Second Essay of *On the Genealogy of Morals*.

א

How do we breed an animal with the right to make promises? For Nietzsche, the human being is an originally forgetful creature, like a young child. To make this originally forgetful creature remember requires physical discipline; it behoves punishment. The teaching of morality was never gentle, it never droppeth from heaven like gentle rain. On the contrary, if something is to be retained in memory, it must be burned in. The origin of memory lies in pain and cruelty: "Man could never do without blood, torture and sacrifices when he felt the need to create a memory for himself."[1] Nietzsche's first, astonishing hypothesis in the Second Essay is that the origin of concepts like responsibility and conscience lies in cruelty—cruelty administered and maintained through a corporal and corporeal regime. Further, as religions are systems of cruelty, all forms of asceticism originate in the same painful place. "Consider the German punishments," Nietzsche proposes—and we all know that there's nothing quite like the German punishments: stoning, breaking on the wheel, piercing with stakes, tearing apart or trampling with horses, boiling in oil, flaying alive, cutting straps from the flesh, smearing the wrongdoer with honey and leaving him to the flies in the blazing sun. As Nietzsche quips, with magnificent understatement, "With the aid of such images and procedures one finally remembers five or six 'I will not's.'"[2] It is on the basis of this burned-in memory of cruelty that good, decent, upright burghers such as ourselves acquired the habit of moral reasoning:

> Ah, reason, seriousness, mastery over affects, the whole sombre thing called reflection, all these prerogatives and showpieces of man: how dearly they have been bought! How much blood and cruelty lie at the bottom of all "good things."[3]

"Dearly bought": let's hold onto that trope of purchasing. In another extraordinary passage of the Second Essay, Nietzsche explains the origin of thinking itself in terms of economic activity:

1 Friedrich Nietzsche, *On the Genealogy of Morals,* trans. W. Kaufmann (New York: Vintage, 1967) 61.
2 Nietzsche, *On the Genealogy of Morals,* 62.
3 Nietzsche, *On the Genealogy of Morals,* 62.

Setting prices, determining values, contriving equivalences, exchanging—these preoccupied the earliest thinking of man to so great an extent that in a sense they *are* thinking (*das Denken ist*).[4]

In the beginning was trade. Human activity begins with exchange, with the to and fro of buying and selling, which are forms of life older than all other social alliances and organisation. It is from here, Nietzsche insists, that human beings arrive at the first moral canon of justice:

"Everything has its price; all things can be paid for"—the oldest and most naïve moral canon of *justice*, the beginning of all "good-naturedness," all "fairness," all "good will," all "objectivity" on earth.[5]

Which brings us to the origin of *das Bewusstsein der Schuld* and *schlechte Gewissen*, the consciousness of guilt and bad conscience. Nietzsche's hypothesis here, and our theme is beginning to come into focus, is that the origin of guilty conscience lies in the relation between a creditor and debtor, *Glaubiger und Schuldner*. The spiritual concept of guilt, *Schuld*, originates in the very material concept of *Schulden*, debts. Guilt in, say, Saint Paul's sense of the essential self-division of the Christian subject, a subject constituted by the guilt that divides it—"for the good that I would, I do not, but the evil that I would not, that I do," *Romans* VII—lies in a fundamentally *contractual* relationship, *Vertragsverhältnis*. The spirituality of Christian guilt is but the airy halo that floats over the materiality of a contract. In other words, morality begins with what Shylock would call a *bond*.

With that in mind, consider the meaning of punishment. The apparently self-evident, universal and even natural idea that

---

4 Nietzsche, *On the Genealogy of Morals*, 70.
5 Nietzsche, *On the Genealogy of Morals*, 70.

punishment is imposed because the criminal knew how to act virtuously, but acted viciously, and is therefore *responsible* for his crime, is a lie. On the contrary, for Nietzsche, punishment is necessary because the victim of the crime believed that the culprit could pay back their crime through their pain. That is, punishment is a corporeal payment for a criminal act and has nothing to do with something as ethereal as responsibility. The point is that the punishment of the criminal gives *pleasure* to the punisher. This, it would seem, is precisely what is in Shylock's mind in Act 4 of *The Merchant of Venice*.

We'll come back to this—but for the moment let's take stock of where we've got thus far: morality points back to contractual relations and these contractual relations point back in turn to merchandise, to mercantile relations of "buying, selling, barter, trade and traffic" (*"Kauf, Verkauf, Tausch, Handel und Wandel"*).[6] The thought here is etymologically contained in the central and essentially contested Christian concept in *The Merchant of Venice*, namely *mercy*. The mercy that cannot be strained, that should season justice, that the Jew should show, and which is even, according to Portia cross-dressed as the young lawyer Balthazar, an attribute of God himself, is derived from *merches*. That is, from the same root as merchant, meaning payment, recompense and revenue. What is *revenu* in talk of mercy is mercantile revenue. Christianity is the spiritualisation of the originally material. *The Merchant of Venice* might be viewed as an essay in the genealogy of morals.

א

Let's look more closely at the play. To describe it as a play about economics is stating the obvious—the bleeding obvious, as Portia might add—but the extent to which its rhetoric is drenched in the diction of the market simply cannot be overstated. Flip through the text to almost any passage and you

<hr />

6 Nietzsche, *On the Genealogy of Morals*, 63.

will find variants on owing, exchanging, bequeathing, expending, accounting and converting applied as the default-vocabulary for all manner of subjects and phenomena one would not normally consider to be "economic": gender, mood, reason and so on. Again and again, the two grand ontological axes, that of spirit—the airy and ethereal, the index of all that's elevated and sublime—and that of matter—the objective, quantifiable and bodied—are hinged together around economic signs, economic mechanisms, economic practises. Take the very first scene: right at the beginning we are told that Antonio's mood, the state of his soul, is index-linked to his merchandise: his mind lies in his bottoms. This is the thesis Salerio advances to explain the enigma of Antonio's melancholia with which the drama begins in Act, line 1: "In sooth, I know not why I am so sad." Were I in your position, Salerio conjectures, even the font of the divine spirit, "the holy edifice of stone," would make me think of all-too solid rocks,

> Which touching but my gentle vessel's side
> Would scatter all her spices on the stream,
> Enrobe the roaring waters with my silks,
> And in a word, but even now worth this,
> And now worth nothing. (I.i.32-36)[7]

The scenario he alarmingly, if well-meaningly, paints binds that most abstract of concepts, value, to a material, even visceral event whose imagery of "ribs," torn sides and spilt innards anticipates the violence Shylock will threaten to wreak on Antonio. And it does so by evoking both ends of the economic scale: that is, by envisaging a dual-movement of surfeit or surplus—abundance, overflowing, splendour—and of loss, of surfeit which *is* loss. The motif is almost immediately reprised by Gratiano, who warns Antonio:

---

[7] All references to *The Merchant of Venice* given in the text with act, scene and line numbers.

You have too much respect upon the world;
They lose it that do buy it with much care. (I.i.74-75)

When excessive expenditure occurs, too much runs into too little. Anyone with basic economic sense could tell you this— but Shakespeare has this economic figure underpin a whole subjective state, a state of being-in-the-world and contemplating it; and here, incidentally, Gratiano's use of the word "care" anticipates the quasi-economic terminology Heidegger will use to describe the way we mortals gather and store the world in thought and language.

Bassanio, the luxurious young man who projects such splendour out into the world (the clothes, the entourage), has also moved to both ends of the economic scale, done deficit and surplus at the same time: he has surpassed himself, expanded his persona beyond its natural bounds,

By something showing a more swelling port
Than my faint means would grant continuance (I.i.124-125)

In so doing, Bassanio has "disabled [his] estate." In short, Bassanio is both leading a lavish lifestyle *and* skint. This bad economic practise is what lies behind his self-projections; it both constitutes and ruins him. The sliding gap that opens up within what we could call his subjectivity, a schism or chasm founded on an economic gap between expense and means, anticipates the many faults that will open up within the play's tectonics: between inside and outside, appearance and reality, word and deed and so on. Bassanio's solution is not to close the gap down again but rather to open up another one, an interval of credit and of credence. And he does this by quite brilliantly invoking the logic of venture capital itself, of speculation, the logic on which Antonio's whole life and livelihood is founded, by invoking the parable of the lost and found arrow. Bassanio says:

In my school days, when I had lost one shaft,
I shot his fellow of the self-same flight
The self-same way, with more advised watch
To find the other forth, and by adventuring both,
I oft found both: I urge this childhood proof
Because what follows is pure innocence.
I owe you much, and (like wilful youth)
That which I owe is lost, but if you please
To shoot another arrow that self way
Which you did shoot the first, I do not doubt,
(As I will watch the aim) or to find both,
Or bring your latter hazard back again,
And thankfully rest debtor for the first. (I.i.140-152)

The real profit, his logic seems to go, lies not in having possession of a commodity in the here-and-now, but rather in buying into a deferred return, investing in an imaginary future. This Freudian *fort-da* credo underpins stock markets to this day. The commodity upon which Bassanio and Antonio are speculating in this case is a lady in Belmont, Portia, who is "richly left," and in order to woo her Bassanio needs dough, he needs ducats. Therefore, if Antonio extends his good name—that is, his credit rating—to Bassanio, if he shoots a second arrow to follow the first, then he might get double the return on his investment. Here, too, in Bassanio's ad-hoc loan pitch, the language of Heidegger is foreshadowed: the kinetic *Geworfenheit* or flungness of the flighted arrow, the belief vested in "adventuring" and "hazard." For Heidegger, being flung into the world involves a *Wagnis*, venture, and venture involves danger, *Gefahr*. "If that which has been flung remained out of danger," he tells us in *Wozu Dichter?* "it would not have been ventured."[8] No pain, no gain.

Antonio, overextended himself, allows for his own credit—the measure of his sovereignty and status—to be, as he says, "rack'd": widened, extended, but an image which also suggests

8   Martin Heidegger, *Holzwege* (Frankfurt a.M.: Klostermann, 1950) 273 et passim.

those old Germanic tortures. Thus begins a set of ventures, of deferrals and suspensions, of withdrawals and disappearances, as joined up and mutually dependent as the giant networks of global capital itself: Bassanio's trip to Belmont, Shylock's plot, Jessica's elopement and so on—you know the story, or at least we will credit you with knowing the story. But what we, here, want to emphasise about the economic system that is *The Merchant of Venice* is what we also want to underline about post-gold-standard economy itself: its tendency, on the one hand, towards immateriality (money, in a sense, *is* not; it is not a substantial commodity as Marx sometimes thought; it has disappeared within the fibre-optic relays of the world's far-flung banking systems; even on paper it represents no more than a promise, "I promise to pay the bearer on demand the sum of ..." or a deferred act of trust underwritten by the metaphysical authority of God, as in the dollar bill) and, on the other hand, the very opposite. Let's ask: what is at stake within *The Merchant of Venice*'s ventures, what steps into the intervals, delays and gaps that speculation opens up? The answer, which takes us back to Nietzsche, is: the body. When the soul, the sovereign soul, the good soul of the merchant of Venice is ventured, that venture will be held accountable in pounds and ounces, and that holding to account—measure for measure—will be called justice.

א

If *The Merchant of Venice* is one large economic system, then its central drama is the conflict between two co-existing yet contradictory conceptions of economy itself. We might call these the *Antonian* and the *Shylockean* and we would like these two meanings of economy to overlay, for reasons that will soon become obvious, a distinction inherited from Aristotle between *oikonomia* and *technē chrematisikē*, between natural economy and the art of money-making. Crudely stated, this is the distinction between the good, Antonian natural economy of the *oikos* and the bad, Shylockean artificial economy that arises when money *(to khrema)* appears on the scene. Derrida, in a fascinating passage from *Donner le temps — la fausse monnaie,* summarises Aristotle's distinction between economics and chrematistics thus:

> For Aristotle, it is a matter of an ideal and desirable limit, a limit between the limit and the unlimited, between the true and finite good (the economic) and the illusory and indefinite good (the chrematistic).[9]

Economics comes from *oikos* — home, hearth, seat of the family, the household, indeed of all those things that Derrida lists under "the proper" — and "chrematistic" from *to khrema,* money, the unlimited exchangeability of goods that occurs when money appears on the scene. As Bacon writes in his essay "Of Usury," which is roughly contemporary with *The Merchant of Venice,* "They say … it is against nature for *Money* to beget *Money.*"[10] Money begetting money is bastard begetting. The distinction between economy and chrematistics is reflected not only in that between the limited and the unlimited but also in that between, continuing the above quote, "the supposed finiteness of need and the presumed infinity of desire." Once money, *to khrema,* has appeared on the scene, the infinity of desire will always transcend the finitude of need. Money is the desire of desire itself, *a priori* unsatisfied by any object one might actually need — behold, the logic of shopping! The fact that Derrida's language recalls that of Levinas (need/desire, finitude/infinity) is perhaps not accidental, for in opposition to an anti-monetary tradition in philosophy that begins with Aristotle and culminates with Marx (communism is the name of a society without the alienating spectrality of money), Levinas

---

[9] Jacques Derrida, *Given Time: 1. Counterfeit Money,* trans. P. Kamuf (Chicago: University of Chicago Press, 1992) 158.

[10] Quoted in Shakespeare, *The Merchant of Venice: Texts and Contexts,* ed. M. Lindsay Kaplan (Boston and New York: Bedford/St. Martin's, 2002) 207.

is one of the rare thinkers, like Locke indeed, who reserves a privileged place for money in his work. He writes in "The Ego and Totality":

> Money then does not purely and simply mark the reification of man. It is an element in which the personal is maintained while being quantified—this is what is proper to money and constitutes, as it were, its dignity as a philosophical category.[11]

Connecting this line of thought with Derrida, he continues the passage from *Donner le temps* with a gesture that will be familiar to readers of his work: "As soon as there is the monetary sign—and first of all the sign—that is, *différance* and credit, the *oikos* is opened and cannot operate its limit." Money, in effect, is deconstruction; *différance* is credit, opening the closure of the *oikos*, what Levinas calls totality, to the unrestricted "economy" of desire where money circulates and where wealth is accumulated or squandered.

It is crystal clear from the first scene of the play that the meaning of Antonio's being, as it were, is determined economically in terms of *oikonomia*. When Shylock says that Antonio is a good man, and Bassanio asks if he has heard otherwise, Shylock replies:

> Ho no, no, no, no: my meaning in saying he is a good man, is to have you understand me that he is sufficient. (I.iii.12-15)

This, a line that we will return to when we look at Marx below, is simply the echo of Antonio's own elision, when speaking to Bassanio, of his "purse" and "person":

> My purse, my person, my extremest means
> Lie all unlock'd to your occasions.(1.i.138-39)

---

[11] Emmanuel Levinas, "The Ego and Totality," *Collected Philosophical Papers,* trans. Alphonso Lingis (Dordrecht: Kluwer, 1987) 45.

Personality is pursonality. But Antonio's purse is empty, for his argosies with portly sail are also far-flung, all abroad in Tripoli, Mexico, the Indies, England and the whole imagined geography of the commercial orb of which the *urb* of Venice is both the mirror and the market-place.[12] The *urb* of Venice is the orb of the emergent world market and a prospect of what Elizabethan London might turn into in the ensuing centuries. So Bassanio uses Antonio's name, his good, clean, proper name, to gain credit from the usurer. It is with the issue of credit that we pass from Antonian *oikonomia* to Shylockean chrematistics.

Shylock hates Antonio because he abused him and spat upon him at the market-place of the Rialto and called him a dog. "Hath a dog money?" Shylock quips in one of his unnerving mimic voices (note how his speeches are constantly interspersed with acts of ventriloquism—Shylock do the police in different voices). But, more fundamentally still, Shylock hates Antonio because he is bad for business. He lends money without interest and thus threatens the livelihood of Shylock and the shadowy Tubal, who is the real power-player in the play. As everyone knows, Christians were forbidden to lend money for profit and Antonio ceaselessly attempts to cancel out the chrematistic logic of credit by restoring the natural economy of interest-free exchange. Shylock explains the beneficial effects of interest with the slightly baroque Biblical story of Laban's sheep tended by Jacob, where these "woolly breeders" illustrate the way in which money can breed. To Antonio's sly question, "Or is your gold and silver ewes and rams," Shylock wittily replies, "I cannot tell, I make it breed as fast." (I.iii.90-91) As Marc Shell points out, there is a delightful word play at work in this passage between Jews or Iewes, Ewes and Use.[13] *Iewes use*

---

[12] See the extracts from *Coryats Crudities* in *The Merchant of Venice: Texts and Contexts*, 139.

[13] Marc Shell, "The Wether and the Ewe: Verbal Usury in *The Merchant of Venice*," *Money, Language and Thought* (Baltimore: Johns Hopkins University Press, 1993) 47-83.

like Ewes. That is, Jews are usurers that make money breed as fast as Jacob's sheep. If we were feeling a little reckless, then we might even speculate on the link between *"iewes"* and *"iusticia,"* between original justice and Jewishness.

Oikonomeia runs over into chrematistics once desire appears on the scene: desire is another name for this excessive tendency that ruptures the limit of the *oikos*. This is exactly what happens in *The Merchant of Venice*, not just once but multiply. Antonio's self-sufficiency is opened up into a larger *chrematon* by Bassanio's desire for Portia. Conversely, Bassanio's possession of what has become his *oikos*—home, hearth and wife—is suspended and ruptured by the demands of Antonio, who makes it pretty clear in Act IV, scene i, that he desires Bassanio (he describes him as his "love"). We could go as far as to say that Shylock desires Antonio, in as much as he wants his body; in this respect, Shylock uses his chrematistic trading zone as his wooing bower, his pick-up pad. Antonio may be able to reject Salerio's opening thesis about his melancholia, the commerce-theory, and to reject also Solanio's, the love-theory—"Why then you are in love," "Fie, Fie" says Antonio—but taken together, overlaid, the two theses between them hit the nail on the head. In and around Shakespeare's Venice, desire *is* an economy, to be both experienced and expressed in purely economic terms.

More precisely, what is going on in the drama of *The Merchant of Venice* is the transformation of the language of courtly love into commerce, where the supposedly natural economy of eros is broken open by the chrematistic logic of money-making. Bassanio's quest for Portia is largely a fiscal one: underwritten by a loan, semi-secured against her fortune. Her remarkable declaration of love to him in Act III, scene ii is couched in the language of accountancy, appreciation and conversion: "only to stand high in your account," she says, "I would exceed account" and "be trebled twenty times myself ... a thousand times more fair, ten thousand times more rich."

"Myself and what is mine to you and yours/Is now converted." (III.ii.149-167)

Portia is a body and an estate, that which exceeded the body of her father. From her first entry into Shakespeare's text this dualism, this double-act of the body and its surplus which is at once spectral and material, makes itself felt: "By my troth," she tells Nerissa, "my little body is aweary of this great world" — whereupon Nerissa immediately talks of "abundance," "surfeit" and "superfluity" (I.ii.1-9). The several physical descriptions we get of her are steeped in the rhetoric of surplus, of exceeding: she is "fair, and (fairer than that word)/ Of wondrous virtues" (I.i.161-163); her physical form outruns her portrait to the same measure as the portrait exceeds Bassanio's description of it in Act III, scene ii. In winning Portia, Bassanio acquires what he calls "new int'rest" (III.ii.220). Before that interest can be converted or cashed in for Portia's body, though, two things must take place. Firstly, a ring must be exchanged: a ring whose loss, Portia explains in exemplary fiscal diction, would "presage the ruin of your love/And be my vantage to exclaim on you." (III.ii.173-174) Secondly, there is that other matter of interest being cashed in for a body: I promise to pay the bearer on demand the sum of one pound — of my flesh. And yet has not Shylock's extremism been played out already, in the casket lottery? Saturday night game shows and reality TV have never gone this far, even in Japan. The set-up that Portia's father, brilliantly depraved producer, has created demands that contestants stake their body parts against the prize. And not just any body part: they have to stake their penis — or let us rather say its "natural," productive use in women.

This moneying of love, this economisation of eros in whose chrematistic machinations vital body parts get caught, is not restricted to *The Merchant of Venice*. It is everywhere in Shakespeare — not least in the Sonnets, from whose outset we are treated to a litany of economic terms and conditions:

increase, contract, abundance, waste, "niggarding" or miserliness. Sonnet 4 is typical in this respect:

> Unthrifty loveliness, why dost thou spend
> Upon thyself thy beauty's legacy?
> Nature's bequest gives nothing, but doth lend,
> And being frank, she lends to those are free:
> Then, beauteous niggard, why dost thou abuse
> The bounteous largesse given thee to give?
> Profitless usurer, why dost thou use
> So great a sum of sums, yet canst not live?

If you don't reproduce you can leave no "acceptable audit";

> Thy unused beauty must be tombed with thee,
> Which used, lives th'executor to be.

In the context of *The Merchant of Venice*, the interplay of "use," "abuse" and "usurer" cannot have escaped your attention. Shakespeare returns to this grouping in Sonnet 6, arguing again for natural reproduction:

> That use is not forbidden usury
> Which happies those that pay the willing loan

—a "willing loan" that is the opposite of being "self-willed": the latter option will make you "death's conquest and make worms thine heir."

This is the image presented Morocco, Portia's first suitor: his casket contains a death's head and a poem about tombs and worms, contents which condemn him to a life of self-willing (onanism) or homosexuality—both "unnatural," forbidden forms of expenditure, abuses rather than good usages of seminal (and here we use the word in all its senses) credit. The pun on "willing" and "willed" also recalls Portia's complaint that "the will of a living daughter" is "curb'd by the will of a dead father." In Sonnet 135 this word "will" appears thirteen times:

> Whoever hath her wish, thou hast thy Will,
> And Will to boot, and Will in overplus;
> More than enough am I, that vex thee still,
> To thy sweet will making addition thus.

—and so on. Will is desire, testament, proper name and sexual organ—both male and female: the poet at one point saucily requests to "hide my will in thine," "whose will is large and spacious." This hermaphroditic ambiguity also appears in Sonnet 20, whose effeminate male addressee, "the master mistress of my passion," was "for a woman ... first created"

> Till nature as she wrought thee fell a-doting,
> And by addition thee of me defeated,
> By adding one thing to my purpose nothing ...

That is, "she pricked thee out for women's pleasure." Will, prick, is surplus: adding one to nothing. Portia uses exactly the same trope when proposing her and Nerissa's transvestism: men "will think we are accomplished with what we lack." (III.iv.61-62). (Jessica, echoing Portia in more directly fiscal terms, calls her own gender-switch "my exchange" (II.vi.35)— and this as she drops a weighty casket of her father's money down on Lorenzo). With this new surplus, this hermaphroditic excess, begins a further set of projections and investments and self-flingings (Bassanio will fling both himself and his ring at Balthazar, Gratiano ditto at the clerk)—ventures that, again, threaten the finite order of the *oikos*. Not only the economy of desire but also that of the body itself, its use and status, has been opened up to chrematistic excess and can no longer operate its good and natural limit.

This situation, this dreadful, unnatural condition, almost proves fatal for Antonio in Act IV. But right from the beginning he was sensing its first rumblings, in the way that animals first sense approaching earthquakes or neurotics the returning rumblings of the repressed. Antonio, title character and model citizen of the Venetian state, is sad: melancholy, anxious, as though manifesting the symptoms of a trauma brought on by a disaster that has not yet happened, or has not yet (as Beckett would say) taken its course. The disaster, we say, is none other than *to khrema*, at once the excessive tendency that carries desire beyond the limits of the proper *and* a global credit system or finance capitalism. Its avatar is Shylock. Shylock's logic threatens so much more than just the good, Christian economic order: spilling beyond this, it threatens all the world's natural regimes, all its good usages. The Antonian melancholy that frames *The Merchant of Venice* is the anticipation of a system of universal Shylockery: the world as a market regulated by a credit system where one's being is determined by a credit rating, by the nature and extent of one's debt.

א

Shylock is *tō khrema*'s avatar — and yet in the central exchange of the drama he appears to break with the chrematistic logic of usury. He says that he wants to be friends with Antonio and Bassanio and decides to give not for interest, but in kind, out of kindness. He offers, in a merry sport, the bond of the pound of Antonio's flesh, to which the latter retorts:

> Content in faith, I'll seal to such a bond
> And say there is much kindness in the Jew. (1.iii.48-49)

It is here that the parallel between *The Merchant of Venice* and Nietzsche's Second Essay is most striking, where it is difficult to imagine that Nietzsche didn't have a copy of the text, or at least the Schlegel-Tieck translation, open as he penned these lines:

> The debtor *(Schuldner)* — to inspire trust in his promise to repay, to provide a guarantee of the seriousness and sanctity of his

promise, to impress repayment as a duty, an obligation upon his own conscience—made a contract with the creditor (*Glaubiger*) and pledged that if he should fail to repay he would substitute something else that he "possessed," something he had control over; for example, his body, his wife, his freedom or even his life ...[14]

But Nietzsche continues a few lines later, even more strikingly:

Above all, however, the creditor could inflict every kind of indignity and torture upon the body of the debtor; for example, cut from it as much as seemed commensurate with the size of the debt.

Of course, what we are perhaps confronting here is the Roman source for both Nietzsche's genealogy of morals and Shylock's flesh-bond. According to the first-century legal historian, Aulus Gellius, the Roman law on debt stipulated that, should the debt be unpaid, the debtor would be confined for a period of sixty days after which time he could be condemned to death and "the laws allowed (the creditor) to cut the man to pieces if they wished, and share his body."[15]

Another parallel suggests itself here. It is tempting to imagine that Freud was thinking of *The Merchant of Venice* when he mapped the complex neural relays and deferrals of his patient the Rat Man. This neurotic is obsessed with two things: debt and torture. A chance anecdote by an officer on some military manoeuvres has planted in his mind the image of Chinese rat-torture, in which a bucket containing a hungry rat is attached to the victim's buttocks and the rat eats its way up the victim's rectal passage. It doesn't take Freud long to forge a link between the large debts (*Schulden*) of the patient's *Spielratte* (compulsive gambling) father, the guilt or *Schuld* felt by the

---

14 Nietzsche, *On the Genealogy of Morals*, 64.
15 Cited in John Gillies, *Shakespeare and the Geography of Difference* (Cambridge: Cambridge University Press, 1994) 127.

patient, his accompanying obsession with paying off a sum of money that in reality he doesn't actually owe (a debt that he experiences as inextricably linked to systems of transit and transportation, like Antonio's) and his fear of rats that, anally concentrated and covering up for its opposite, desire, opens up a homosexual dimension within his sexual constitution. Money itself, the paper currency, is dirty, and so are children, *Ratten*, little rug-rats. "In his delirium," writes Freud, "he had coined himself a regular rat-currency, and converted into this all the accumulation of interests around his father's legacy." Will and will again, in overplus.

Good genealogist and maybe even proto-Freudian that he is (and how could any major Shakespeare character not be a proto-Freudian, given that so many of Freud's insights are based on Shakespeare's works?) Shylock is seeking compensation from his debtor by torturing his body. But, as Nietzsche emphasises, Shylock desires this torture not because he holds Antonio *responsible* but because he will find recompense in the *pleasure* he feels in enacting his bond,

> The pleasure of being allowed to vent his power freely upon one who is powerless, the voluptuous pleasure, "*de faire le mal pour le plaisir de le faire.*"[16]

This is why Shylock refuses to be paid twice or thrice over in money for his bond: he desires the *pleasure* of torturing Antonio's body. Shylock stands for Venetian law, and he will have his bond, but the desired outcome is pleasure through the other's pain. With characteristically hyperbolic gusto, Nietzsche goes on to imagine festivals of pain at the service of intense pleasure, and one imagines gladiatorial contests, public executions and the sort of sadistic glee seen on the faces of the torturers at Abu Ghraib prison in Baghdad. The point here, again, is that the origin of our moral concepts like guilt,

---

[16] Nietzsche, *On the Genealogy of Morals*, 65.

conscience and duty is soaked in blood and reared in cruelty. Even the categorical imperative smells of cruelty, Nietzsche insists, which is confirmed by Kant's claim in the *Critique of Practical Reason* that the feeling induced by moral law might be described as *Schmerz*, pain. And the example of Kant illustrates Nietzsche's point: namely, that the history of morality is its increasing spiritualisation, where moral "progress" means less and less physical pain and more and more psychological torture. The materiality of the creditor-debtor relation becomes the spirituality of bad conscience, where I experience my being-indebted, my *Schuldigsein* as the basic expression of my subjectivity. The history of morality is, thus, the inwardisation or internalisation (*Verinnerlichung*) of pain, where it becomes at once more intense and more subtle. Rather than punishing others, we learn to punish ourselves, inhibiting our desires, despising our instincts and loathing our bodies and their disgusting functions. Nietzsche cites Pope Innocent the Third, who innocently catalogues the horrors of the body,

> Impure begetting, disgusting means of nutrition in his mother's womb, baseness of the matter out of which man evolves, hideous stink, secretion of saliva, urine and filth.[17]

Christian morality culminates in a paroxysm of self-laceration, a guilty rage against the self, that is not articulated as rage or laceration, but—and this is the nadir of Christian hypocrisy—as *love* or *mercy*. Nietzsche concludes:

> Here is sickness beyond any doubt, the most terrible sickness that ever raged in man; and whoever can still bear to hear (but today one no longer has ears for this!) how in this night or torment and absurdity there has resounded the cry of *love*, the cry of the most nostalgic rapture, of redemption through *love*, will turn away, seized by invincible horror …[18]

---

17 Nietzsche, *On the Genealogy of Morals*, 67.
18 Nietzsche, *On the Genealogy of Morals*, 93.

With this is mind, we would like to consider the central dramatic *agon* of *The Merchant of Venice*, the trial scene from Act 4. At stake is the conflict between mercy and justice. It is assumed by the Doge who presides at the trial, by Portia, Antonio and his retinue that mercy is the truth of justice, just as the New Law is the fulfilment of the Old Law and Christianity is the truth of Judaism.[19] Shylock, the Jew, is therefore asked to show mercy. But—cunning genealogist that he is—he refuses and says "I stand here for law" (IV.i.142). That is, he stands for a more original conception of justice based in the bond between creditor and debtor.

From the Nietzschean/Shylockean perspective, Portia's transvestite eloquence about the quality of mercy, "It droppeth as the gentle rain from heaven upon the place beneath" (IV.i.181-182) is a travesty that serves to disguise the basic hypocrisy of the Christian-Moral interpretation of the world. But it's a fascinating travesty, in that it invokes the very principle of surplus and abundance, of prodigality, what Mauss and Bataille call "expenditure without return"—in short, those tendencies that have so rattled the whole order of the play. Mercy is *merché* without measure that, doubly-blessed and blessing, tends to infinity. Portia invokes excess, infinity—*to khrema*, one could almost say—then, in a perfectly-executed U-turn, does exactly the opposite: she bans it.

If one iota of Antonio's flowing silks enrobes the water, if blood that's surplus to the bond be shed, then Shylock will be held accountable for this excess, even to the point of death. By carrying this logic to its end, she recuperates not just Antonio's body from the chrematistic mechanism it has been caught up in, but also all of Shylock's own estate, and, beyond that, his

---

[19] Derrida places the question of the relation of mercy and justice, and in particular the question of mercy as the overcoming or *relève* of justice at the centre of his reading of the play in "What is a 'Relevant' Translation," *Critical Inquiry* 27 (Winter 2001): 174-201.

Judaism—that is, in the context of the trading zone of Shakespeare's Venice, his right to practise chrematology itself. Humiliated by the Christians, betrayed by his daughter, bankrupt and compelled to convert, Shylock exits with a whimper, whispering, "I am not well." (IV.i.392)

This brutal reversal, this act of casuistry that, barbaric and elaborate at the same time, Christianises the Judaic and recuperates the chrematistic into the closed economy of *oikos*, wraps up the central agon. Yet, incredibly, Portia does another U-turn and induces another act of excess, of a giving that breaks the boundary of the proper, of the marriage hearth: still in drag, she persuades Bassanio to let go of his ring. It's as though she wanted to kick-start the cycle of anxiety all over again, in order to recuperate and close it down once more: classic *Fort-Da*. As soon as the men's guilty secret breaks out, the text erupts with images of physical castration ("Would that he were gelt" [V.i.144]), transexualism ("if a woman live to be a man" [V.i.160]) and sexual infidelity (I slept with Balthazar, Portia tells Bassanio; and I slept with his clerk, Nerissa adds to Gratiano). This new eruption is quickly reigned in by the production of a letter—and with this comes, in a lame but necessary plot-twist, the larger recuperation of the ships and merchandise whose venturing enabled the main cycle to take place. Another wrap-up—although Shakespeare cannot resist signing off with a final open gesture that at least registers the spectre of chrematology's possible return. A ring, symbol of value tightly wrapped around the body, limiting its affections by embodying a bond, can still be removed; virtue can still be ventured through the body. Sexual ambiguity even creeps back in through Gratiano's bawdy bottom diction of sore rings. The play's final lines are:

> Well, while I live, I'll fear no other thing
> So sore, as keeping safe Nerissa's ring. (V.i.306-307)

A ring is a cycle, too, of course, a symbol of repetition: nothing ever *really* ends ...

א

Which brings us, in a coda, to another student of Shylock and sometime Shakespearean: Karl Marx. Considering the monumental scale of Marx's research into political economy and the capitalist economic system, analyses which, whatever failings they may have, nonetheless merit revisiting in light of the spread of what we all too easily call globalisation, he says relatively little about the central issue of *The Merchant of Venice*, namely credit. One finds a few fascinating remarks on credit scattered in *Capital* Volume 3, where Marx identifies a structural ambiguity in the late 19th Century credit system: on the one hand, it develops exploitation to its most pure form through what Marx calls "gambling and swindling"; on the other hand, in its development of a world market the credit system raises the capitalist mode of production to "a certain degree of perfection" and anticipates the advent of the rule of associated labour:

> The credit system will serve as a powerful lever during the transition from the capitalist mode of production to the mode of production of associated labour.[20]

The modern credit system is, thus, a strange mixture of "swindler and prophet." More than a century after Marx's remarks, it would appear that the swindlers have won out over the prophets.

More interesting and more Shakespearean is a much earlier text from 1844, written during the same extraordinary creative burst as the Paris Manuscripts: "Excerpts from James Mill's *Elements*

---

[20] See the chapter on "Pre-Capitalist Relationships," *Capital*, volume 3, trans. D. Fernbach (London: Penguin, 1981). The quotation is from page 743.

of Political Economy."[21] It is here that Marx begins to analyse money and extends the theoretical tools honed in his critiques of Hegel, Feuerbach and Bauer into the analysis of political economy. Marx asks, in an oddly Heideggerian-sounding formulation, after the *Wesen* of credit:

> What constitutes the essence of credit? We disregard here the *content* of credit which is once again money. We disregard then the content of this trust according to which a man accords *recognition* to another man by advancing money to him and … expresses his confidence that his fellow human being is a "good" man and not a scoundrel. By a good man the creditor, like Shylock, means a "sufficient" man.[22]

Money functions as the mediator by means of which the products of human labour become *entfremdet*, estranged or alienated. *Money is essentially alienating.* For Marx, it is alienated species-being, our estrangement from the being of being human, from our common humanity and from community itself. As long as the human being does not recognise himself and others as human but as a credit rating, community or *Gemeinwesen* will only appear in the form of self-estrangement, becoming what Marx calls a commercial society, where "each of its members is a *merchant.*"[23] The idea of money as mediator leads Marx to the statement that money is the veritable God, or rather it is Christ-like. Just as in Christianity, the person of Christ is the mediating instance in the relation of God to the human being, so too with money. As Marx insists in so many of his early texts, there is a peculiar and powerful mirroring between religious self-alienation and secular self-alienation where money is the medium of alienation in capitalist society. Money, as Marx will later claim in *Capital,* is the universal

---

21 Karl Marx, *Early Writings,* trans. R. Livingstone and G. Benton (London: Penguin, 1975) 259-78. We would like to thank Daniel Morris for drawing this text to our attention and also for his stimulating conversations about Marx.

22 Marx, *Early Writings,* 263.

23 Marx, *Early Writings,* 266.

equivalent for commodities in the process of exchange. Things lose their meaning insofar as they are transformed into commodities and "natural" Antonian economic relations become dehumanised.

The banking and credit system does not, as Saint-Simon and even Proudhon thought, humanise monetary activity. On the contrary, it deepens estrangement and alienation into the heart of man, literally into his flesh. This is the truth of Shylock's identification of goodness with good credit. Under conditions of finance capitalism, good credit is a sufficient condition of goodness. Continuing the above quote from the text on James Mill, Marx writes:

> Credit is the *economic* judgement on the *morality* of man. In the credit system *man* replaces metal or paper as the mediator of exchange. However, he does this not as man but as the *existence (Dasein) of capital and interest*.[24]

In the credit system, man becomes transformed into money and money has literally been incorporated into him. Like some financial parody of the Eucharist, credit infuses the heart with the alienating divinity of money. Shylock, in his determination to have Antonio's flesh, is therefore enacting the essence of credit insofar as goodness equals economic sufficiency and this becomes flesh. By contrast, the person without credit is "a social pariah and a bad man."[25] Marx goes on:

> The substance, the body clothing, the *spirit of money* is not money, paper, but instead it is my personal existence (*Dasein*), my flesh and blood, my social worth and status. Credit no longer actualises money-values in actual money but in human flesh and human hearts.[26]

---

[24] Marx, *Early Writings*, 264.
[25] Marx, *Early Writings*, 265.
[26] Marx, *Early Writings*, 264.

In Heideggerese, we could say that the essence of alienated human *Dasein* is monetary—one could imagine here an entire rewriting of Heidegger's analysis of inauthenticity and authenticity in economic terms, where the human being is literally being-indebted, *Schuldigsein* and where human beings are flung into the facticity of financial flows.

We can link the above, particularly the identification of money with divinity, to another triangulation of Shakespeare, Marx and money from 1844. On this occasion, the allusion is not to *The Merchant of Venice* but to *Timon of Athens*, where the idea of the divinity of money is coupled with its whore-like character. Money, Marx writes, is the pimp between need and object, making available all objects and objectifying all beings, especially human beings, into prostitutes for my imagined needs. In a quotation repeated in *Capital Volume 1*, Marx cites Shakespeare speaking of money as "Thou common whore of mankind" and,

> Thou visible god,
> That solder'st close impossibilities,
> And mak'st them kiss.[27]

Money is the visible God and common whore of mankind. That is, there is nothing that money cannot solder together, no two commodities for which money will not be the pimp that permits the exchange. In a mercantile society, everything is for sale and everyone is a prostitute insofar as their value is ultimately determinable in monetary terms. Playing on the connotations of the German *Vermögen*, the availability of money determines my capacity and my ability in terms of my wealth. As such, Marx goes on, money is the alienated *Vermögen* of humankind, that is, wealth is alienated human capacity and

---

[27] Karl Marx, "Economic and Philosophical Manuscripts," *Early Political Writings*, ed. J. O'Malley (Cambridge: Cambridge University Press, 1994) 376. See also *Capital*, volume 1, trans. B. Fowkes (London: Penguin, 1976) 230.

ability. Money is an extraordinary power of inversion, transforming wishes from imagination to reality and making reality illusory, into what Marx will describe in *Capital* as the vast phantasmagoria of commodity fetishism, more plainly stated, the world market. Money transforms imagined need (say the need for plastic surgery) into real objects and real need into imagined objects (making, say, poverty either invisible or the fault of the poor). As such, money is the bond that binds together capitalist society, it is what Marx calls in an arresting phrase "the bond of all bonds":

> If *money* is the bond which ties me to *human* life and society to me, which links me to nature and to man, is money not the bond of all *bonds*? Can it not bind and loose all bonds? Is it therefore not the universal *means of separation*? It is the true *agent of separation* and the true *cementing agent*, it is the *chemical* power of society.[28]

Yet, most interesting in this regard are the final pages of the slightly earlier text, "On the Jewish Question" from 1843, where Marx engages in a set of reversals and double-reversals no less extraordinary than those undertaken by Shakespeare. Marx offers an essentially anti-Semitic, Antonian argument. That is, if Nietzsche can be thought of as Shylock, then Marx sounds like Antonio or some portly cross-dressed Portia. What is strange about Marx is the utterly Christian logic of his argument: credit is bad and immoral, money dehumanises. Marx's utterly provocative thesis is that the bourgeois world, the Antonian world of Christian capitalism, has become Shylockean. That is, Christendom has become dominated by *Judentum*, by what Marx calls "practical Jewishness," and by its secular God, money. Christians have become practical Jews, not what Marx calls *Sabbatsjuden*, Sabbath Jews, but *Alltagsjuden*, everyday Jews. In one of his choicest dialectical inversions, Marx writes:

---

[28] Marx, "Economic and Philosophical Manuscripts," 377.

> Christianity derives from Judaism. It has once again been dissolved into Judaism. From the very beginning the Christian was the theorising Jew, the Jew therefore is the practical Christian, and the practical Christian has again become a Jew.[29]

In other words, capitalism is a system of universal shylockery, where all Antonian limits of the *oikos,* the hearth, the home, the *Heimat,* the homeland and the human, have been burst apart by the energy of chrematistic exchange and excess. The giving of credit has shifted from a marginal practice allotted to Jews in a handful of mediaeval and renaissance cities to the increasingly global manner in which identity is constituted. I am, you are, we all are a credit history, a record of debt, against which our goodness, our sufficiency is measured. I owe therefore I am. And if I do not owe, I am not. Being is being in debt, goodness is good credit. Ontology and ethics flow from the same money pot.

א

Postscriptum: one of the authors of this paper recently moved to a job in New York—contemporary Venice—and has been unable to get a credit card. Why? Because he does not have a credit history, a history of debt. How, he asked, after the third company had turned him down, might he get in debt? Well, of course, the answer was by getting a credit card. A beautiful economic ring, if still slightly sore.

---

[29] Marx, *Early Political Writings*, 55.

Darren Tofts

Mind Games: Borges, Virtuality & the Limits of Credulity

The world *may* be fantastic. The world *will* be Tlön.

The cartographers of antiquity have left a profound and fearsome legacy. Only now can we speak of its dread morphology. Spurning the severe abstractions of scale, they achieved exact correspondence: the map occupies the territory, an exact copy in every detail. Here, after centuries of vanity, is exactitude in science, pitiless, coincident and seamless. I have stood on the threshold of the cave, having escaped the bondage of shadows. I have climbed to the top of the mountain and sought out the tattered ruins of that map. I have discoursed with the scattered dynasty of solitary men who have changed the face of the world. I have come to offer my report on knowledge. I have come to tell you that the world will be Tlön.

The figure of the map covering the territory has become an indexical figure in discussions of postmodernism. It has come to stand for a problematic diminution of the real at the expense of a proliferating image culture, obsessed with refining the technologies of reproduction, of making the copy even better than the real thing. As Hillel Schwartz, author of the

* This essay was originally published in *Postmodern Culture* 13.2 (2003) as *"The World Will Be Tlön": Mapping the Fantastic onto the Virtual.*

remarkable *The Culture of the Copy*, notes, with untimely emphasis, "the copy *will* transcend the original."[1]

Preoccupied with the relationship between reality and its copies, postmodernism deflects the idea of an absolute reality in favour of high fidelity facsimiles. The trajectory from postmodernism to virtuality involves a shift from copying to simulating the world, from the reproductive practices of photography and film, to post-reproductive or simulation technologies such as telepresence, advanced digital imaging, virtual reality and other immersive environments. This journey from reproduction to simulation involves the disappearance of difference, the breakdown of binary metaphysics and all that we understand by the term representation. The movement from analogue to digital media is a significant event in the diminution of reality's a priori status. It comes on the heels of a long artistic tradition of exploration into the relationship between reality and its representability.

Fantastic literature is one such mode that has actively explored this nexus of reality and representation, traditionally doing so through the distorting glass of allegory — whether it be in the writings of J.R.R. Tolkien, with his mythical Middle Earth, the dark and insular labyrinth of Mervyn Peake's Gormenghast trilogy, or the miraculous world of Gabriel Garcia Marquez's Macondo. In such writing, the creation of imaginary "other" worlds is astonishing, seductive in its realism, in the persuasive weight of presence it delivers. For the time of reading, Mordor's fire and cobwebs are oppressively real, as is the stench and menace of Swelter's kitchen, or the jungle's embrace of a Spanish galleon, festooned with orchids. While fantasy is seen as a discrete form of writing, like science fiction or the gothic novel, it is still an art of fiction, a conjuror's verisimilitude, all smoke and mirrors, sleights of hand and verbal prestidigitation.

---

[1] Hillel Schwartz, *The Culture of the Copy: Striking Likenesses, Unreasonable Facsimiles* (New York: Zone Books, 1996) 212.

While the realities of such writing are convincing, they fall short of actually supplanting our own sense of the real. That is, they don't disturb our sense of what is real and what is not. Like all fiction, they are temporary zones, carnivalesque moments in which anything is possible. Without thinking too much about it we know that they are realistic. But we also know they are not real. This intuitive understanding is the safety valve of catharsis, the limit point of identification within the boundaries of a particular cultural technology, whether it is literature or cinema. This certitude, that we are immersed in realistic un-realities, is the metaphysic that allows us to tune into fantasy, live there for a time and then re-inhabit the real without believing that the fantasy continues beyond the book, or the film. It is fantasy's exit strategy. Without this strategy, this metaphysical way out, we run the risk of psychosis, certainly as Sigmund Freud had imagined it, as a sustained and problematic over-identification with a fictional character or world. Please allow me to introduce myself: I am Titus Groan, and my quest in life lies somewhere beyond the agonising rituals of Gormenghast. I must flee its stone lanes and unforgiving walls. Can anyone here help me?

Cultural theorists, such as Umberto Eco and Jean Baudrillard, have given other names to such extreme identifications with fictions, names that defined the cultural climate of the last decades of the twentieth century—terms such as simulacrum, hyperreality, the desert of the real, faith in fakes, the culture of the copy. Not wanting to be seen to lag behind the postmodernist cognoscenti of Europe, Hollywood has manufactured a genre of cyber-technology films that equally responds to this perception of the closure of fantasy's exit strategy, in which there is no longer a way out, a return to the real. Films such as *The Truman Show* (1998), *The Matrix* (1999) and *Dark City* (1998), to name but a few, postulate worlds of hard-wired false consciousness, in which what is taken for reality is, respectively, the most insidious reality TV, the ultimate simulation, the perfect virtual reality. To be outside the deception is not to be mad, as Michel Foucault would perhaps have it, but rather to be all-powerful, in control of reality and its representations, the architect of representation as reality—the auteur, in other words, as demiurge.

This brings us to the qualitative and disquieting difference between the fantastic and the virtual. In the realm of the fantastic, we don't need anyone to welcome us to the real world, since we reliably know what it is and what it is not. When the exit strategy of fantasy is closed, or denied, we have no way of knowing that *we don't even know* there is a difference anymore between fantasy and reality. Unless we are liberated from the simulacrum, like neo in *The Matrix*, or find the outdoor to a reality we never knew existed, like Truman, it's business as usual in the real world, where people go to work, go to the football on the weekends and catch the occasional paper at cultural studies events. Welcome to the desert of the real.

In the desert of the real you can still find, if you are lucky, ruptures in the seam of things, little tears in the otherwise flawless efficiency of the map that covers the territory. One of these is in fact a parable about maps and territories, simulation and fabricated reality—a parable about the creation of the world. This artefact is a short fictional text written by the Argentinean writer, Jorge Luis Borges. First published in 1940, "Tlön, Uqbar, Orbis Tertius"[2] occupies an important place in the history of twentieth century speculation on the relationship between fantasy and reality. It is at once a meditation on and example of this relationship. Indeed, for Borges, terms such as fantasy and reality are in no way absolutes, nor are they dependent figures within a binary opposition. They are rather manifestations of possible worlds, projections of the world as it may be.

---

[2] "Tlön, Uqbar, Orbis Tertius," in *Labyrinths: Selected Stories and Other Writings*, eds. D. Yates & J. Irby (Harmondsworth: Penguin, 1976 [1964]). Further references to this work and other titles from *Labyrinths* are included in the text.

We have much to learn from "Tlön, Uqbar, Orbis Tertius." Although he died in 1986, Borges is still very much our contemporary. His presence, more than we can perhaps ever realise, or imagine, is everywhere felt but nowhere seen at the start of the third millennium. As we invest more time, money and metaphysical capital in the cultural technologies of virtuality, we are perhaps closing off our own exit strategies, dissolving the liminal zones of genre and metaphysics that partition the fantastic and the real. We can learn something of how we are doing this, as well as the consequences of doing it, from "Tlön, Uqbar, Orbis Tertius." It is worthwhile, therefore, briefly reviewing the fiction in this context, to refresh the memory of those familiar with it, to submit it to the memory of those who are not. For those of you from the border, who have difficulty with me describing Tlön as if it is a fiction—and not an assured commentary on your world—I humbly beg your indulgence.

As with many of Borges's stories, "Tlön, Uqbar, Orbis Tertius" begins with a found object. It is a single volume, number 46 to be precise, of a pirated edition of the *Anglo-American Cyclopaedia*, published in New York in 1917. The volume is un-remarkable in every way, apart from four extra pages that are contained in this singular volume only and not in any other copy of this particular edition. The superfluous pages contain a detailed account of a previously unknown and uncharted region of Asia Minor called Uqbar. The narrator and his companion, Adolpho Bioy Cesares, search in vain for further references to Uqbar, but nothing in the way of corroborating evidence emerges from their labours, even from hours spent at the National Library of Argentina. The entry on Uqbar contains detailed information on the history, customs, geography and literature of this mysterious region. One piece of information will suffice to impart a flavour of the piece:

The section on Language and Literature was brief. Only one trait is worthy of recollection: it noted that the literature of Uqbar was one of fantasy and that its epics and legends never referred to reality, but to the two imaginary regions of Mlejnas and Tlön. (29)

After further research, "events," the narrator observes, "became more intense" (40). It is discovered that the documentation of Uqbar was in fact the aborted precursor of a more ambitious project, undertaken by what is subsequently revealed as a secret society, originating in the seventeenth century—a kind of enlightenment Sokal hoax on a trans-historical scale. More ambitious and sublime in its conception and scope, this society, which included George Berkeley as one of its number, set out to invent the fictitious history of an entire planet, called Tlön. The imprimatur of this society, *Orbis Tertius*, is found in a similarly unlikely volume—of which there exists, again, only one copy— entitled *A First Encyclopaedia of Tlön*. In this one volume we encounter the eclectic miscellany of detail, of the reassuring kind that adheres reality to representation, the documentary veracity that endows the encyclopaedia with the solidity of truth, authenticity and knowledge:

> Now I held in my hands a vast methodical fragment of an unknown planet's entire history, with its architecture and its playing cards, with the dread of its mythologies and the murmur of its languages, with its emperors and its seas, with its minerals and its birds and its fish, with its algebra and its fire, with its theological and metaphysical controversy. And all of it articulated, coherent, with no visible doctrinal intent or tone of parody. (31)

As James Woodall, Borges's most recent biographer, has noted, "The discovery of another planet... in science fiction is generally a cue for extravagant fantasy; for Borges in this story it was a way of reviewing the world, of offering a critique of reality."[3] In this respect history is everything. Just as Mervyn Peake had used his fiction to explore his time spent at Belsen as

[3] James Woodall, *Borges: A Life* (New York: Basic Books, 1996) 115.

a war-time illustrator, so Borges attempted to come to terms with the chaotic horrors of war and the spurious symmetries of the day—dialectical materialism, anti-Semitism, Nazism—in the creation of a harmonious world. But in coming to terms with it he did not attempt to understand it, but rather to replace it altogether. For a world at war, the desire to submit to Tlön, to yield to the "minute and vast evidence of an orderly planet," was overwhelming (42). But such is the stuff of allegory, the tidy protocols of hermeneutic neatness. What better way to explain the embrace of a fictitious reality that is superior in every way to the wreckage of contemporary history?

But this is not all there is to the story. Borges in fact turns the allegorical mode of fantasy in on itself, closing off its exit strategy and interpolating us, the readers outside-text, along the way. There are a number of things in this fiction that can't be simply written off as allegorical parallel (that is, the interpretation of Tlön as metaphor, as the projection of an ideal world). The world of Tlön, we quickly realise, is palpable and capable of affecting dramatic outcomes in the real world. The *First Encyclopaedia of Tlön* first makes its appearance in 1937, received, as certified mail, by a mysterious person called Herbert Ashe. Little is known about Ashe, other than the inscrutable, yet forthright detail that in his lifetime "he suffered from un-reality" (30). What is beyond doubt is that Ashe was one of the collaborators of *Orbis Tertius* and three days after he received the book of Tlön, the book he helped bring into this world, he died of a ruptured aneurysm. We know, too, that as part of their process of rhetorical corroboration, the society of *Orbis Tertius* disseminates objects throughout the world that cohere with information to be found in the *First Encyclopaedia of Tlön*. Such objects, like the forty volumes of the *First Encyclopaedia of Tlön*, are attenuations, material reinforcements, simulacra that solidify the fictitious detail of the books in memory. We could call these objects "proof artefacts," like the scattered ephemera of a holiday never actually taken in Philip K. Dick's 1962 story, "We Can Remember It For You

Wholesale" (the text which became the basis of the film *Total Recall* [1990]), or the family photographs coveted by the replicant Leon in the film *Blade Runner* (1982).

But there is a difference, of a metaphysical kind, between a suggestive corroboration, a simulated mnemonic device and something that can't be accounted for in material terms, such as the small, oppressively heavy cone that is found on the body of a dead man in 1942. Representing the divinity in certain regions of Tlön, we are informed by the narrator that it is "made from a metal which is not of this world" and is so heavy that a "man was scarcely able to raise it from the ground" (41). No one knew anything of the man in whose possession the cone was found, other than the fact that he "came from the border" (41). Here is an instance of the imaginary made flesh, the uncomfortable collision of worlds that we expect to forever remain discrete. It is a kind of perverse, Eucharistic event, the transubstantiation of the fictional into the material, the crossing over from one border to another, from one metaphysical realm into another—the "intrusion of this fantastic world into the world of reality." Holding this enigmatic object in his hand, the narrator reflects on "the disagreeable impression of repugnance and fear" it instils in him (41). Here is the nausea of the simulacrum, the supplanting of reality by fantasy. Rachael Rosen encounters this dread in *Blade Runner* when Deckard exposes her childhood memories as belonging to someone else. The contemporary technological shift from one media regime to another, from reproductive to simulation or virtual technologies, entails a similar ontological blurring of worlds that may not be so easily resolved through allegory.

How do we comprehend, for example, the ability of Neo in *The Matrix* to "know Kung Fu" without ever having been taught it, without learning its philosophies and techniques as a discipline? The fact is there is little "ability" to his knowing Kung Fu, because he has not acquired it, but rather he has been programmed to know it (together with its cultural resonances and quotations, from Chuck Norris roundhouse kicks to Bruce

Lee's trademark cockiness). His experience of Kung Fu is a simulated rather than actual thing, akin to the competence that airline or military pilots derive from spending hours in flight simulators. The ability to know how to do Kung Fu, repeatedly and without thinking about it, is an issue of second nature, of acquired habit that has become intuitive. However the difference here is that second nature, in Neo's case, is not preceded by first hand experience.

Such is the consequence of the shift from one media regime to another. In an essay that discusses virtuality in relation to Ray Bradbury's 1952 short story "The Veldt," Ken Wark argues that the futuristic, holographic nursery in that text is a technology of the "too real."[4] This virtual technology—which is a cross between a children's playroom and the Holodeck from *Star Trek*—exceeds the real by manifesting simulacra, such as lions, into the real world. Such manifestations are akin to psychiatric irruptions of the unconscious in waking life. They are affects capable of real and, as it turns out, destructive consequences. This is no allegorical *wunderkammer*, since the logic of representation has ceased to exist within its machinations.

If Bradbury's holographic nursery has anticipated anything achieved so far in the name of new media, it is not so much the immersive, virtual reality environment, as the new, "total realism" of hybrid cinema (that is, the convergence of film and digital effects). Lev Manovich, in *The Language of New Media* (2002), describes how the use of digital technologies in the pursuit of greater realism in cinema has created effects that are "too real."[5] That is, the ability to simulate three-dimensional visual realities—such as the dinosaurs in *Jurassic Park*—has created a perfect visuality that, paradoxically, has to be "diluted

---

4 McKenzie Wark, "Too Real," *Prefiguring Cyberculture: An Intellectual History*, eds. D. Tofts, A. Jonson & A. Cavallaro (Cambridge, Mass.: MIT Press, 2002).

5 Lev Manovich, *The Language of New Media* (Cambridge, Mass.: MIT Press, 2001) 199.

to match the imperfection of film's graininess."[6] For Manovich, digital simulation has precipitated a new order of experience, a synthetic reality that exceeds the limitations of film's attempts to represent real world experience.

As evidence of the persuasiveness of synthetic reality, I submit the following image:

This image, created by Australian media artist Troy Innocent, represents the kind of fusion of real people with computer-simulated objects that Manovich describes in relation to the formation of synthetic realities. Created by Troy at my request, this image beautifully illustrates the point that synthetic realities can blur the distinction between formerly discrete worlds. Bill Mitchell, author of *The Reconfigured Eye: Visual Truth in the Post-Photographic Era* (1994) would probably refer to this image as a "fake photograph," an example of the new

[6] Manovich, *The Language of New Media*, 202.

aesthetic possibilities of digital imaging. I prefer to think of it as a snapshot from Tlön, the infiltration of one world by another. Mitchell is sensitive to the metaphysical implications of digital imaging, noting that "as we enter the post-photographic era, we must face once again the ineradicable fragility of our ontological distinctions between the imaginary and the real." [7]

It is such forecasts of the consequences of our embrace of the virtual that confirms the continued importance of "Tlön, Uqbar, Orbis Tertius" in today's world. As a "critique of reality," it not only documents an account in the 1940s of the changing of the face of the world, but also anticipates the technological reinvention of the real. Such reinvention, in the name of virtual and simulation technologies, prompts the question, do we need *a* reality any more, when multiple realities can be created synthetically? As a synthetic reality, "Tlön, Uqbar, Orbis Tertius" draws us, the readers of Borges the writer, the people outside-text, into its perplexing ontological orbits. That is, our experience of the world is affected by our involvement in the story. Like the inhabitants of Tlön, we find ourselves engaging with metaphysics as if it were a "branch of fantastic literature" (34).

Borges defiantly teases the readers' desire to believe in the reality of the discovered world, secure, as they are, in their assured, known world outside-text. He tests, in other words, the extent to which the reader is prepared to forestall their exit strategy, to explore the outer limits of credulity to do with this previously unknown world. After all, all the reference points in the story are verifiably factual, such as the Brazilian hotel, Las Delicias, in which Herbert Ashe is sent the mysterious *First Encyclopaedia of Tlön,* or the narrator's companion, Adolfo Bioy Cesares, the person who brings the troubling issue of Uqbar to his attention, in reality one of Borges's closest friends and literary collaborators. Borges's style is clearly documentary-like in approach, prudent, well researched and sound, with very

---

[7] Bill Mitchell, *The Reconfigured Eye: Visual Truth in the Post-Photographic Era* (Cambridge, Mass.: MIT Press, 1994) 225.

few literary flourishes or overt metafictional moments. Indeed, it is more accurate to call "Tlön, Uqbar, Orbis Tertius" an essay rather than a fiction, reading, as it does, with the impersonal, measured factuality of the encyclopaedia entry.

As an essayist, documenting the conceit of Tlön, Borges's methods of persuasion—or are they in fact evidence—are compelling. In reflecting on one of the theories of time subscribed to by the inhabitants of Tlön, for example, he notes that "it reasons that the present is indefinite, that the future has no reality other than as a present hope, that the past has no reality other than as a present memory" (34). Furthermore, he notes, in a footnote, that this question had detained the attention of the great Bertrand Russell, who supposed "that the planet has been created a few minutes ago, furnished with a humanity that 'remembers' an illusory past" (34). He identifies the reference as *The Analysis of Mind*, 1921, page 159. You can pursue the citation if you like, but take it from me, it is not bogus.

This is one of the many troubling moments in which information from outside-text corroborates the collaborative, invented world of Borges's fiction. That is, facets of this grand guignol can be chased down as referential points in our own world. We can confirm these references from scholarly sources, such as *The Analysis of Mind*, or volume 13 of the writings of Thomas De Quincey. Like the people within the diegetic world of the story, it is difficult rationalise the feeling that our reality, or at least my reality, is not yielding to Tlön.

In drawing a parallel between "Tlön, Uqbar, Orbis Tertius" and *The Matrix*, I was startled when I re-read the story and reflected upon one of the doctrines of Tlön: "while we sleep here, we are awake elsewhere and ... in this way every man is two men" (42). Think of the film's iconic image of immersive simulation: Neo reclining on a chair on board the Nebuchadnezzar, jacked into the matrix, while his sim-self or avatar floats like a butterfly in the virtual dojo with Morpheus. The duality of actual self and digital representation in *The*

Matrix is the anchor that smoothes out and reconciles the split between the worlds of meat and virtuality—the conduit between different ontologies, different metaphysical states. So, in playing around with this parallel, looking for an angle, an opening gambit, you can imagine my concern, when reading of the progressive reformation of earthly learning in the name of Tlön, that "biology and mathematics also await their avatars" (43).

Events became more intense as I moved deeper into the vertigo of writing about Tlön. On reading *The Age* Saturday Extra on the 20th April 2002, it was with a mixture of fascination and alarm that I came across a startling account of a little known visit to Melbourne by Borges in the late Autumn of 1938. Written by Guy Rundle, under the title of "A Surreal Visitor,"[8] the piece took me quite by surprise. My first inclination was to check the date: it wasn't the 1st of April. To my knowledge Borges had never travelled to Australia, a suspicion quickly confirmed in the pages of the biographies at my disposal. Yet the detail was all here: he arrived on 16 May at the invitation of John Willie, a member of Norman Lindsay's bohemian circle and admirer of Borges's work, gave a lecture at the Royal Society entitled "The Author's Fictions" and spent much of his

8 Guy Rundle, "A Surreal Visitor," *The Age* Saturday Extra (20 April, 2002) 5.

time in the domed reading room of the State Library of Victoria. These were all likely, Borgesian places, places that I would expect the great man of letters to frequent if he was in Melbourne, right down to the oneiric epiphany of a set of locks in a Glenhuntly shop window. In all, Borges spent ten days in Melbourne before returning to Buenos Aires, his mind, no doubt redolent with the smell of eucalyptus (a sensation that would seem to have found its way into the remarkable opening line of his story "Death and the Compass," published in 1944).

On closer inspection it became clear that Rundle was playing a very erudite joke on his readers, treating Borges by the rules of his own game, so to speak. Indeed, the first line read like a Borges pastiche, citing an author, a prodigious event and an ironic allusion, all within the strict economy of a single sentence: "Devotees of the writings of Jorge Luis Borges will not be surprised by the recent discovery that the great Argentinean writer once spent some time in Melbourne." The rhythm and balance of the syntax recalls the opening sentence from "Death and the Compass": "Of the many problems which exercised the reckless discernment of Lönnrot, none was so strange—so rigorously strange, shall we say—as the periodic series of bloody events that culminated at the villa of Triste-le-Roy, amid the ceaseless aroma of the eucalypti" (106). The suggestion that Borges's admirers "will not be surprised" is the ironic allusion, a rhetorical manoeuvre gesturing to the fact that a devotee of Borges, well versed in the art of fabulation, would recognise that Borges is the perfect subject for such a fiction.

Rundle's piece cannily imitates distinctive features of Borges's writing and, in particular, "Tlön, Uqbar, Orbis Tertius"—a text famous for its challenge to readers to accept, or at least consider, the reality of a fictitious world. For all we know, Rundle may have written his story with "Tlön, Uqbar, Orbis Tertius" at his elbow, open at page twenty-eight. On that page you will find one of Borges's own ironic, reflexive allusions, as the narrator and Bioy Cesares discuss the article on

Uqbar in the *Anglo-American Cyclopaedia*. The key detail here is that they found the piece "very plausible" (28).

Rundle's piece is crowded with plausible detail that is very specific and combines known facts about Borges's life—such as his involvement with Victoria Ocampo and the important literary magazine, *Sur*—with previously unknown information. It sounds plausible that someone in Norman Lindsay's bohemian circle would have been aware of *Sur* and passionate enough to mentor the Argentinean writer's visit to Australia. Most of all, Rundle exploits Borges's delight—especially indulged in "Tlön, Uqbar, Orbis Tertius"—in inviting the reader to trust in evidence that is confined to fugitive or lost documents, missing or unverifiable detail. The record of Borges's visit, for instance, is "confined to a few notes made for a poem (never written) that Borges made in a notebook, which recently came to light at a house in Cordoba, and some letters written to fellow novelist Bioy Cesares." The reference to Bioy Cesares is a delightful touch, an unquestionable source offsetting the potential unreliability of such fragmentary, incomplete records. Borges's lecture, presented to the Royal Society is, not surprisingly, "also lost, if ever written down." Nor should we be surprised to detect the occasional flash of audacity as Rundle warms to his work, noting that a vernacular reference to a "strange lecture by a Spanish chap" is attributed to Harold Stewart, who, along with James McAuley and writing under the pseudonym of Ern Malley, perpetrated one of the great literary hoaxes of the twentieth century.[9]

I have reflected that it is permissible to see in this story of a visit never taken a kind of palimpsest, through which the traces of Borges's "previous" writing are translucently visible. It is especially noteworthy that Rundle exploits the plausible conveyance of tenuous information, or what Borges, in "Tlön, Uqbar, Orbis Tertius," refers to as a tension between "rigorous

---

[9] See Michael Heyward, *The Ern Malley Affair* (St Lucia: Queensland University Press, 1993) for the definitive account of Ern Malley's assault on the modernist lexicon.

prose" and "fundamental vagueness" (28). This is noteworthy. Of the Borges stories Rundle refers to in the piece—and they are some of his most well known—no mention is made of "Tlön, Uqbar, Orbis Tertius," arguably his most famous work. This absence is also a tour de force of citation by omission, implicit in the gesture to a line from "The Garden of Forking Paths," in which the word "chess" is the answer to the following question: "'In a riddle whose answer is chess, what is the only prohibited word?'" (53).

One can imagine that such a persuasive piece of writing would be not only plausible, retrospectively writing Jorge Luis Borges into Melbourne's literary memory, but revelatory to many readers. Once again a line from "Tlön, Uqbar, Orbis Tertius" came to mind: "a fictitious past occupying in our memories the place of another, a past of which we know nothing with certainty– not even that it is false" (42-43). A trip to the Exhibition Gardens or the reading room at the State Library would never be the same again, knowing that the great Borges had left his trace there. But literary hoaxes don't fool everyone. Nor are they to everyone's taste.

On the following weekend, I can't say that I was surprised to read the following disclaimer:

> An article in Saturday Extra on 20 April called "A surreal visitor" about writer Jorge Luis Borges's apparent visit to Melbourne was in fact a piece of fiction, mimicking Borges's own style of placing people in imaginary situations. The editor of Saturday Extra regrets this was not acknowledged at the time of publication.[10]

Now this is a real Borgesian test of credulity. I find the idea of Jason Steger, the literary editor of the Saturday Extra, forgetting to mention this fact, far less plausible than the idea of Tlön itself. Jason Steger is clearly the Herbert Ashe of this conspiracy. This disclaimer, while predictable, was actually

---

[10] "Clarification," *The Age* Saturday Extra (4 May, 2002): 2.

Clarification

An article in Saturday Extra on April 20 called "A surreal visitor" about writer Jorge Luis Borges' apparent visit to Melbourne was in fact a piece of fiction, mimicking Borges' own style of placing people in imaginary situations. The editor of Saturday Extra regrets this was not acknowledged at the time of publication.

quite dissatisfying and ruined what, for me, was a marvellous piece of invention. I could see it now, many years down the track, my students wondering, with restrained awe, if they had sat where Borges had in the domed reading room of the State library. So out of some peculiar nostalgia for the lost memory of a visit that never was, I decided, in the spirit of Rundle's piece, to look into some of the "facts" he assembled, to re-trace and re-claim some of the steps of this sublime, phantom visitation. I didn't expect to find any corroboration, but I wanted to at least participate in the fiction, to walk in the ubiquitous shadow of this rigorous Latin American genius. Now this is where this story gets really weird.

On the 23rd of April, 2002, I went to do some research at the State Library of Victoria. Had the domed reading room been open (it was then still under renovation) I would have sought out that imaginary vibe. Mindful of the lessons of "Tlön, Uqbar, Orbis Tertius," I suppose I wanted to imaginatively place Borges in the scene, to fill the gaps that I knew, full well, I would find. A strange inclination, I know, but then we are dealing with a writer who, more than any other, has encouraged us to question what we accept as real, as verifiable, as truth. I wanted to find the spaces of his absent presence. After all, Borges was a deconstructionist *avant la lettre* and he would have known only too well that if there are no traces, there is no presence.

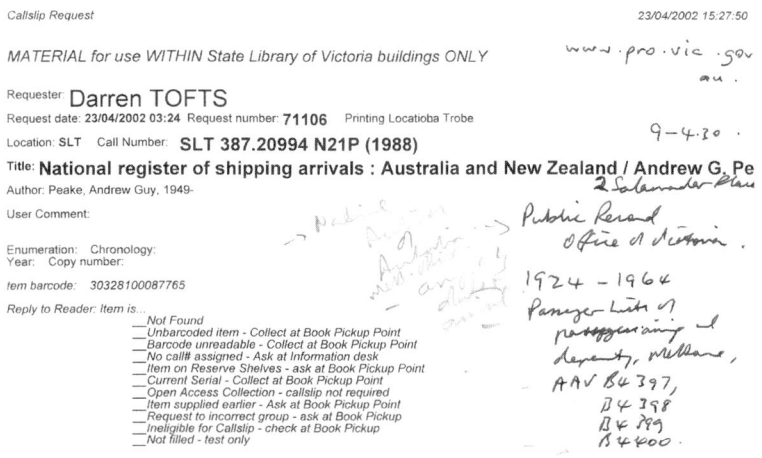

My first reference, the *National Register of Shipping Arrivals: Australia and New Zealan*d, was promising, but not altogether resolute. The volume was in fact an index of passenger lists between the years 1924 and 1964, held elsewhere, at the Melbourne Office of the National Archives of Australia to be precise, which is part of the Public Record Office of Victoria.

While a deferral it was at least a start. That reference would have to wait for another day. *Cook's Australasian Sailing List* was my next port of call. When requesting the book it was clearly available and as the stacks are not open to public access, it was highly likely that I would get a return.

I was disappointed, then, to receive my request slip and no book. The slip indicated that the volume could not be found. In discussing this with the librarian on duty, it was pointed out that this was, indeed, surprising. However, as a seasoned denizen of research libraries, this sort of thing happens all the time, so I didn't think twice about it.

I started to get concerned, though, when my next request bounced on me. Consistent with Rundle's imaginary itinerary, I wanted to consult the Author Index of the *Proceedings of the Royal Society of Victoria* to find no evidence of Borges's guest lecture there.

Not only did I receive a note saying that the volume was not found, but on the request slip there was also a handwritten note indicating that the volume was "Not on shelf." I left the library with nothing to show for my efforts. While, as I had expected, I did not find any evidence of Borges's visit to Melbourne, I did not find, either, any absence of evidence to prove that he did not come.

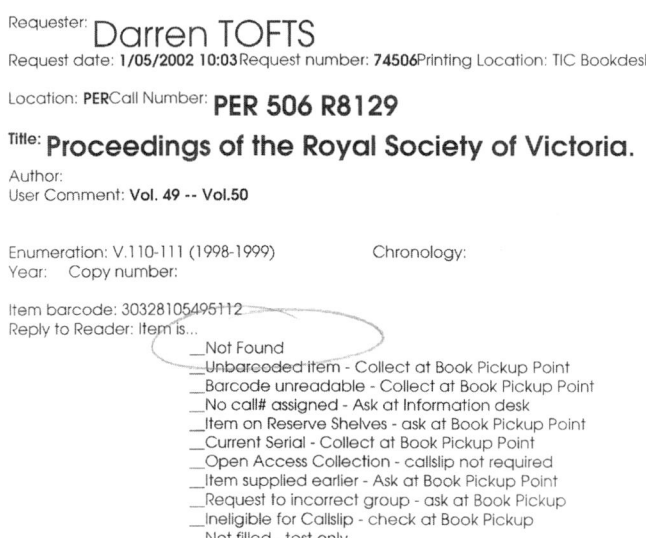

I returned to the library the following day. On the way there I stopped off at the Royal Society. The person, with whom I spoke, while decidedly brusque and unhelpful, did confirm that guest speakers would, indeed, be registered in their Proceedings.

This time at the library the exact volume of the Proceedings, containing everything from 1938, was not found. A trip around the block to the Public Records Office was more promising. A database search of passenger ships yielded no records whatsoever of the Koumoundouros (the liner that purportedly delivered him to these shores), nor did a search of passengers coming into Melbourne as "legal aliens" in 1938 include a Jorge Luis Borges, though, as you will see from this sample of the inventory, the name Borges was not an uncommon one for arrivals in Melbourne that year:

Borges John Frederick

Series number	Control symbol	Contents date range
PP14/1	5/12/125	circa 1915 - circa 1920

Access status	Location	Barcode no
Open	Western Australia	751432 Request item

Title
BORGES John Frederick - Nationality : German - [Application Form for Registration as Alien]

Series number	Control symbol	Contents date range
PP14/3	GERMAN/BORGES J F	circa 1916 - circa 1920

Access status	Location	Barcode no
Not yet examined	Western Australia	5126243

Title
aka [Borges] Costa Guida

Series number	Control symbol	Contents date range
E37	1975/2807	1975 - 1978

Access status	Location	Barcode no
Not yet examined	Northern Territory	5324711

Title
Borges, Julio Maria - Drafting Officer Grade 1 (Architectural) - Papua and New Guinea [52 pages]

Series number	Control symbol	Contents date range
A452	1964/5458	1964 - 1966

Access status	Location	Barcode no
Not yet examined	National Office	3544495

Title
Diplomatic Representatives in Australia - Borges Da Fonseca

Series number	Control symbol	Contents date range
A1838	1500/1/23/10	1956 - 1959

Access status	Location	Barcode no
Not yet examined	National Office	595507

Title
Borges, Jose Maria

Series number	Control symbol	Contents date range
B44	V1975/6776	1975 - 1975

But what was starting to disconcert me, in an odd, metaphysical kind of way, was that this confirmed evidence sat cheek by jowl with inconclusive, irresolute results. Nothing, it seemed, could be proved false. The whole thing was actually starting to resemble "Tlön, Uqbar, Orbis Tertius"—real life as an uncanny form of literary allusion or repetition. It was as if the very task of researching Borges's imaginary visit to Melbourne had unleashed a kind of strange code or virus, a meme, a Borges meme that had the potential to change the way we perceive reality. But unlike the genetic or ideological connotations of this notion that we find in Richard Dawkins and Douglas Rushkoff, the Borges meme was of a metaphysical nature, short-circuiting all attempts to confirm its un-reality, even in the face of other plausible evidence that declared that the whole affair was a fabulation (not the least of these being Jason Steger's disclaimer printed in *The Age*). Indeed, for a fleeting instant, the idea did cross my mind that along with Steger, Rundle belonged to the same secret society of intellectuals, Orbis Tertius, who made the world Tlön. Their quest, it could be argued, was an attempt to animate what Rundle called an "unremarkable and overfamiliar city." This could be achieved through projecting the city anew through the exotic eyes of a "mysterious visitor." The tantalising possibility that this imaginary event might be real, or the more interesting dynamic of its ambivalent veracity, is the occasion for a kind of belief, a virtual, simulated belief in the reality of the unreal. To emulate a quote of Borges's from "The Library of Babel," it suffices that his visit to Melbourne be possible for it to exist.

To conclude, the idea of a Borges meme gets us to the disconcerting heart of this writer's metaphysics. Unlike fantasy in its allegorical mode, Borges's metaphysical fictions intrude into what we understand to be real, the obvious world outside-text. Borges writes of the undecidable, the interzone between fiction and non-fiction, documentary writing and fabulation. It is an unclassifiable space of paradox and contradiction, the sensation, vague yet familiar, that what seems unlikely may be a forgotten reality—a confused sensation akin to the afterglow of a vivid dream, before it vanishes in wakefulness. As we have seen, this is a paradox that we have been confronting for some time in the name of postmodernism and more recently in relation to virtual technologies. In the age of virtuality, we are once again re-tracing Borges's footsteps as he guides us, a latter day Ariadne, through the labyrinthine fantasy that we call the real.

Postscript

A couple of days after I finished writing this essay I received a parcel from the Royal Society. Unaccompanied by a letter or note of explanation—they were as perfunctory as ever—I found this photograph.

It is without doubt a photograph of Borges, probably in his late 30s. This would date it around 1938 or 1939. The intriguing detail is the plaque at his feet. On closer inspection—thanks to my friend Chris Henschke—it reveals the State of Victoria coat of arms. The botanical name of the tree on which Borges is reclining is the Ribbon Tree of Otago. It has been grown in Melbourne since the nineteenth century, a fact that can be verified in Guilfoyle's *Catalogue of Plants Under Cultivation in the Melbourne Botanic Gardens*, published in 1883.

The only other thing of note about the photograph is that its verso bears an inscription in an elegant copperplate. For some reason this would not scan properly, but I offer the following transcription:

> I remember him, with his face taciturn and Indian-like and singularly *remote*, behind the cigarette.

McKenzie Wark

Allegorithm

01. Benjamin gets up in the morning. He goes to the toilet. He leaves the seat up. He showers and fixes breakfast. He reads the paper. He finds a job—as a Test Subject—starting tomorrow. It's not much, but times are hard. He reads a book, and then another. He fixes lunch, naps, reads again. He goes to bed. He gets up. Toilet, shower, breakfast again. He does not make his bed. He goes to work. He comes home, prepares another meal. He talks to his room mate Bert a bit. Hannah drops by. He flirts with her some. He goes to bed, gets up, does the whole thing all over again.

02. Days go by. Not much changes. His cooking improves. He makes new friends—Ted, Gersholm, Asja. They drop by sometimes; sometimes he visits. There is the new furniture. That makes him a bit happier, but not much. He gets a promotion to Lab Assistant. It's the night shift, but the pay is better. Then he makes Field Researcher and is back working regular hours. After a while he becomes a Scholar. He is so creative, but it helps to have friends if you want to get ahead. He aspires to being a Theorist. The pay is better. And the hours. He dreams of yachts and big screen TVs. Benjamin is a Sim, a character in a game called *The Sims*. One could be forgiven for imagining this was somebody's life.

03. In *The Sims*, you create characters like Benjamin, build and furnish homes for them, find them jobs and friends. All in a world without a sky. Perhaps a game like *The Sims* could be a parody of everyday life in "consumer society." Benjamin and his friends dream of things. Things make them happy. They find a nice sofa so much more relaxing than a cheap one. As designer Will Wright says: "If you sit there and build a big mansion that's all full of stuff, without cheating, you realise that all these objects end up sucking up all your time, when all these objects had been promising to save you time … And it's actually kind of a parody of consumerism, in which at some point your stuff takes over your life."[1] Others disagree. Gonzalo Frasca: "Certainly, the game may be making fun of suburban Americans, but since it rewards the player every time she buys new stuff, I do not think this could be considered parody."[2] In *The Sims*, characters can have lots of different jobs, but as Fredric Jameson says: "parody finds itself without a vocation." If *The Sims* is a parody it is a blank parody, mimicry without a critical impulse, without parody's "ulterior motives." [3]

04. Perhaps a game like *The Sims* could be an allegory for everyday life in gamespace. In the allegorical mode, says Walter Benjamin: "Any person, any object, any relationship can mean absolutely anything else. With this possibility a destructive but just verdict can be passed on the profane world: it is characterised as a world in which the detail is of no great importance."[4] For Benjamin, the fragmenting of the modern world by technique, the profusion of commodities that well up in the absence of a harmonious whole, finds its expression in allegory, which fragments things still further, shattering the

[1] "SimSmarts: An Interview with Will Wright," in Brenda Laurel, *Design Research: Methods and Perspectives* (Cambridge, Mass: MIT Press, 2003).

[2] Gonzalo Frasca, "The Sims: Grandmothers are Cooler than Trolls," *Game Studies*, 1.1 (July 2001). http://www.gamestudies.org

[3] Fredric Jameson, *Postmodernism or, The Cultural Logic of Late Capitalism* (London: Verso, 1991) 17.

[4] Walter Benjamin, *The Origins of German Tragic Drama* (London: Verso, 1998) 175

illusion of bourgeois order, revealing the means by which it is made. "What resists the mendacious transfiguration of the commodity world is its distortion into allegory."[5] And yet this possibility too seems exhausted. The fragmenting of the fragmented seems routine to a Sim. No other worlds seems possible.

05. Perhaps a game like *The Sims* is not such much an allegory as an *allegorithm*. Alex Galloway: "To play the game means to play the code of the game. To win means to know the system. And thus to interpret a game means to interpret its algorithm (to discover its parallel allegorithm)."[6] What might matter about games is not what they say about everyday life. They don't always say anything all that new or interesting. They mostly just recycle, or "remediate" images or narrative fragments from other media. What is more interesting about games is the kind of relation they propose between the game proper and the everyday life of gamespace. The hieroglyphs that populate the surface of the game are keys to the algorithm; the algorithm in turn takes the form to which everyday life in gamespace aspires. Lev Manovich: "As the player proceeds through the game, she gradually discovers the rules that operate in the universe constructed by this game."[7] What is distinctive about games is that they produce for the gamer an intuitive relation to the algorithm. The intuitive experience and the organising algorithm together are an allegorithm for the relation between the experience of gamespace and the possibility of an underlying logic.

06. An algorithm is a finite set of instructions for accomplishing some task, which transforms an initial starting condition into a

5   Walter Benjamin, "Central Park," *Selected Writings*, vol. 4 (Cambridge, Mass.: Harvard University Press, 2003) 173.
6   Alex Galloway, *Gaming: Essays on Algorithmic Culture*, manuscript, 2005
7   Lev Manovich, *The Language of New Media* (Cambridge, Mass.: MIT Press, 2001) 222.

recognisable end condition. The recipes that Benjamin and other Sims learn from the cookbooks on their bookshelves are algorithms. Benjamin's career as a Sim is also a series of algorithms. Benjamin starts with a given set of values. The gamer applies certain steps to the transformation of those values which may or may not lead to the desired end state. The gamer selects one sequence after another, and gradually learns what they do—that's algorithm. The gamer discovers a relationship between appearances and algorithm in the game which is a double of the relation between appearances and a putative algorithm in gamespace—that's allegorithm. Or rather, the allegorithm is the gap between the intuitively knowable algorithm of the game and the passing, uneven, unfair semblance of an algorithm in the everyday life of gamespace.

07. From the point of view of representation, the game is always inadequate to everyday life. A Sim in *The Sims* is a simple animated character, with few facial features or expressions. In *The Sims 2* they seem a little more lifelike, but the improvement of the representation in some particular ways only raises the standards by which it appears to fall short in others. From the point of view of simulation, it all seems more the other way around. Everyday life in gamespace seems an imperfect version of the game. Gamespace may be more complex and variegated, but it seems much less consistent, coherent and fair. Perhaps this was always the almost utopian promise of the digital—a real of absolute, impersonal equity and equanimity.

08. Imagine that Benjamin, our character in *The Sims*, makes it to the penultimate level and becomes a Theorist. Perhaps then you buy him a computer because he seems bored with reading. What would he do with it? Play *The Sims*, of course. Being a Theorist, perhaps he starts to theorise it. Perhaps he jots something like this in his notebook: "The gamer whose listless gaze falls on the controller in his hand is ready for the allegorithm. Boredom is the basis of the allegorithmic insight

into the world. Boredom lays waste to the appeal of the game as game, and calls attention to the ambiguous relation of game to gamespace. Allegorithmic perception is n-dimensional, it intuits behind appearances interactions of many variables. The allegorithmic mode of apprehension is always built on an evaluative relation to the world of appearances. More and more relentlessly, the everyday life of gamers is coming to wear the expression of gamespace. At the same time, gamespace seeks to disguise the ungamelike character of things. What heightens the mendacious transformation of gamespace is its distortion into allegorithm. Gamespace wants to look itself in the face. It celebrates its incarnation in the gamer."

09. In the gamer, Benjamin might say, is reborn the sort of idler that Socrates picked out from the Athenian marketplace to be his interlocutor. "Only, there is no longer a Socrates, so there is no one to address the idler. And the slave labour that guaranteed him his leisure has likewise ceased to exist."[8] In *The Sims*, as in gamespace, one wonders if the idler has disappeared also. There is no idle time in *The Sims*, or in the gamespace of which it is the more perfect double. The quartz heart of the central processor inside the computer on which *The Sims* runs ticks over remorselessly. All of its moments are equivalent, and so too, in a way, are all moments in *The Sims*. Sleeping, napping, conversation or reading all advance one's scores. Benjamin has to go to bed to get up again to go to work to earn the right to sleep and dream, again.

10. To be a gamer is to come to understanding through measurable failure. The bar graphs measuring Benjamin's being trend negative and refuse to budge. You are too busy elsewhere to get Benjamin to the toilet on time, and he pees himself. He needs sleep, he needs company, he needs a new kitchen. He turns to face you, the gamer, and gestures wildly, as if cursing his God.

[8] Benjamin, "Central Park," 186

When things were going well, you forgot to save the game, so there is no better time to go back to. Nothing for it but to work with what you have, or quit and start again. The game is an algorithm from which you know you can escape; gamespace is an unknown algorithm from which there is no escape. The game is just like the gamespace of everyday life, except that the game can overcome the violence of time. The game ties up that one loose end with which gamespace struggles—the mortal flaw of an irreversible time. No wonder the Sim turns in vain to the gamer as a God, for it is the gamer who has turned toward the game as a messianic, reversible time.

11. Gamers are not always good Gods. It's such a temptation to set up a Sim to suffer. Deprive them of a knowledge of cooking and pretty soon they set fire to themselves. Build a house without doors or windows and they starve. Watch as the algorithm works itself out to its terminal state, the bar graphs sliding down to nothing. This violence is not "real." Sims are not people. They are images. They are images in a world which appears as a vast accumulation of images. Hence the pleasure in destroying images, to demonstrate again and again their worthlessness. They can mean anything and nothing. They have no saving power.

12. The Sim who suffers turns to face its gamer, looking out toward an absent sky, appealing directly, beyond the frame of the game itself. The gamer may not answer, or may not be able to answer. The gamer as God suffers from an apparently similar algorithmic logic as the Sim. *The Sims* comes with theological options. Turn on "free will" and Sims stray from the powers of their maker. Turn it off and their actions are predestined, but even so, the gamer-god quickly finds that the algorithm is a higher power than the power one commands. Should the game be going badly for the Sim, it turns to face the gamer; should the game be going badly for the gamer, there is no one for the gamer to turn away and face. The Sim who addresses a

helpless, hopeless or lost God lives out the allegorithm of gamespace itself.

13. As a gamer you can have no sense of worth and no faith in salvation other than through your own efforts. But those efforts are fraught, and you are soon lost in the maze of the game. The gamer achieves worth through victories of character; but that character inevitably faces defeat in turn. Or worse. The only thing worse than being defeated is not being defeated. For then there is nothing against which to secure the worth of the gamer other than to find another game. One game leads to the next. It's the same for Benjamin. After Theorist comes Mad Scientist and after that—nothing. Start over. Pick a new career. Get an expansion pack. Try some new lives. Start as a Playground Monitor, become a Teacher, a Professor, get tenure, rise to Dean, the finally, Minister of Education. Start as a Nobody, working for tips. Become an Insider, a Name Dropper, a Sell Out, a Player, a Celebrity, then finally, a Superstar. But these are just arbitrary names for series of levels. Any qualitative difference between levels is just an effect of an underlying quantity. A higher level is just *more* than a lower level. And so there's nowhere to go but to more, and more, until there is no more, and the gamer, like the character, is left with nothing. The fruit of the digital is the expulsion of quality from the world. That's gamespace.

14. Original Sims can be any mix of two genders and three colours. In *The Sims 2* you start with preset templates (Caucasian, African American, Chinese, Persian—and Elf) alterable via a lot of sub-sliders. You choose gender, age, colour, hair style and colour, eye colour, weight, height, glasses, hats, accessories, clothes, and so on, but these external attributes are merely a skin. They do not really affect the game. The sliding variables of character, however, do programme in advance what careers a Sim can excel at, and which past times restore faculties. In *Sims 2*, they may be straight or gay. Again, it makes no difference.

Either way their offspring mix the "genetic" character qualities of their parents. The external representations are of no account; the internal variables determine potential. The "skin" is arbitrary, a difference without a distinction, mere decoration. Underneath it lies a code which is all. *The Sims 2* is committed both to a genetic view of intrinsic nature and a liberal view of the equality, and hence indifference, of extrinsic appearances.

15. In *The Sims*, things proliferate. Or rather, the skins of things. You can have many different kinds of sofa, or coffee table, or lamp shade, but the meter is running, so to speak. You have to make more money to buy more things. But some gamers who play *The Sims* trifle with the game rather than play it. These gamers are not interested in "winning" the game, they are interested in details, in furniture, or telling stories, or creating interesting worlds. If a cheat is someone who ignores the space of a game to cut straight to its objective, then the trifler is someone who ignores the objective to linger within its space. Bernard Suits: "Triflers recognise rules but not goals, cheats recognise goals but not rules."[9] *The Sims* lends itself to play that transforms it from a world of number back to a world of meaning. Algorithm becomes a more stable platform than the vicissitudes of gamespace for creating a suburban world of pretty things. But in trifling with the game, the gamer struggles to escape boredom and produce difference—and finds that this too has limits. Steven Poole: "You must learn the sequences the programmers have built into the game—and, okay, there are hundreds of them, but that does not constitute freedom."[10]

16. Allegory is about the relation of sign to sign; allegorithm is about the relation of sign to number. Signs don't open to reveal chains of other signs, pointing in all directions. Or rather, it is no longer of any importance what signs reveal. They billow and

[9] Bernard Suits, *The Grasshopper: Games, Life and Utopia* (Toronto: University of Toronto Press, 1980) 47.

[10] Steven Poole, *Trigger Happy* (New York: Arcade, 2000) 33.

float, pool and gather, arbitrary and useless. There is no way to redeem them. But signs now point to something else. They point to number. And number in turn points to the algorithm, which transforms one number into another. Out of the bit rot of signs, games make allegorithms. The signs point to numbers, the numbers to algorithms, the algorithms to allegorithms of everyday life in gamespace, where signs likewise are devalued, arbitrary, but can still stand as details of the one thing that still makes sense, for the logic of the digital.

17. Allegorithm is a double relation: on the one side, there is the relation of appearance to algorithm in the game; on the other, there is the relation of appearance to algorithm in gamespace. In relation to gamespace, the game itself works as an escape from the real stakes of the agon of the everyday to the unreal stakes of a pure game. But the game can also work as a critique, in turn, of the unreality of the stakes of gamespace itself. When *Sims* devotees assign values to non-existent furniture, truly the idea of economic "utility" has lost all meaning. The game can also work as an atopia, where play is free from work, from necessity, from seriousness, from morality. Kill your Sims, if you want to. Play here has no law but the algorithm. And yet there is a tension between the game and gamespace. The relation between them is at once analogue and digital, both a continuum and a sharp break. The gamer struggles to make of the game a separate world, for escape, for critique, for atopian play, and yet gamespace insinuates itself into the game. That's the algorithmic tension.

18. Benjamin starts as a Beta Tester, become a Hacker, and finally a Game Designer. After that you are supposed to level up to Venture Capitalist then finally Information Overlord. But something goes wrong along the way. Benjamin's game design company goes broke. The whole industry is consolidating. So Benjamin goes to work for a much bigger game company. He starts work. It's a mild sort of "crunch" time—normal when

there's a project with a deadline. Benjamin is working eight hours, six days a week. The project is on schedule, so its not so bad. It's temporary. He complains a bit to his Spouse. The deadline for ending the crunch comes and goes. And another. Then the hours get longer. Benjamin is working twelve hours, six days a week. Benjamin's bar graphs slide into the red. Then the real crunch time begins. Benjamin is working eight hours a day, seven days a week, "with the occasional Saturday evening off for good behaviour."[11]

19. You could be forgiven for thinking this is just a game, but it is somebody's life—as reported in a widely circulated text written by EA Spouse. EA, or Electronic Arts, is a game company best known for its Madden sports games, but also owns Maxis, which makes *The Sims*. EA's slogan: *Challenge Everything*—everything except EA, or the gap between game and gamespace. In the gamespace of contemporary labour, things are not like the measured progression up the ranks of *The Sims*. In *The Sims*, Benjamin could work his way from Game Designer to Information Overlord much the same way as he had worked up the levels below. At Electronic Arts, things are different. Being an Information Overlord like EA's Larry Probst requires an army of Benjamins with nothing to work with but their skills as game designers and nowhere to go than to another firm which may or may not crunch its workers just as hard. As the Military Entertainment Complex consolidates into a handful of big firms, it squeezes out all but a few niche players. Gamespace is here a poor imitation of its own game.

20. Start over. This time Benjamin starts as a bucket runner. He quickly works himself up to coltan miner. Coltan? What is coltan? Quit *The Sims* for a moment. Pop the cover off your Playstation or your Apple or PC computer. You are looking at stuff that has come from all over the world. In the guts of your

---

[11] EA Spouse, "EA: The Human Story," 10 November 2004.
http://www.livejournal.com/users/ea_spouse/274.html

machine you may spot some capacitors made by Kemet, or maybe semiconductors from Intel. These probably contain tantalum, a marvellous conductor of electricity, also very good with heat. They were quite possibly made with coltan dug out of the ground in the Congo, where there's plenty of coltan, from which tantalum is refined. The Okapi Faunal Reserve in the Congo is home to gorillas, monkeys and elephants as well as the okapi, a rare relative of the giraffe. Thousands of Mbuti, or pygmies, also live there. Their livelihood is compromised by the coltan miners, who dig what one journalist called "SUV-sized holes" in the mud, out of which they can extract about a kilo of coltan a day.[12] A kilo of coltan was worth $80 during the technology boom. There was a world shortage of the stuff, which even delayed the release of the Sony Playstation 2.[13]

21. The Congo is arguably the region in which the "great game" of colonial exploitation has done the most harm and conferred the least benefits. The Congo's first democratic leader, Patrice Lumumba, was ousted in a CIA sponsored coup that brought to power the notorious Mobutu Sese Seku. With the collapse of the Mobutu regime, there was civil war, and little else. One of the things that kept the civil war going was the coltan. Coltan both fuelled the war, and accelerated the destruction of wildlife habitats. And so the military entertainment complex, with precious brands to protect, didn't want protest movements sullying their reputations by calling attention to all the gorillas coltan kills, or the guerrillas it feeds. The military entertainment complex would like to believe, and would like you to believe, that gamespace is not a Nietzschean struggle of naked forces, beyond good and evil, but a clean, well lighted, rule-governed game.

---

[12] Blaine Harden, "The Dirt in the New Machine," *New York Times Magazine* (12 August, 2001): 34-39

[13] Koen Vlassenroot and Hans Romkema, "The Emergence of a New Order?: Resources and War in Eastern Congo," *Journal of Humanitarian Assistance* (28 October 2002). http://www.jha.ac

22. "Kemet requires its suppliers to certify that their coltan ore does not originate from Congo or bordering countries."[14] Motorola says much the same: "We believe we have done as much as any reasonable company could do by mandating compliance from our suppliers on this important issue."[15] Outi Mikkonen, communications manager for environmental affairs at Nokia is a little more sanguine: "All you can do is ask, and if they say no, we believe it."[16] The bad publicity around Congo Coltan is good news for the Australian company Sons of Gwalia, which provided half of world supply. The destruction of Australian habitats seems somehow less picturesque. No gorillas or giraffes are involved. This is the way its played in gamespace. It's all separate caves, with dim reports of each other. By all means, save the gorillas and okapi, but it doesn't change the equation.

23. The line that connects gamespace to game also divides one from the other. There's no getting away from the materials that make it possible to own a Playstation console or a computer with *Intel Inside*. There's no getting away from the labour that makes it possible to run *The Sims* on your machine. Benjamin: "There is no document of culture which is not at the same time a document of barbarism."[17] And yet the whole point of a game is its separation, the line dividing it from gamespace and enclosing it in a self contained, algorithmic world of its own. Allegorithm is at once this intimate line connecting and yet separating game from gamespace. To Benjamin—the Benjamin who is a Sim—everything outside *The Sims* is metaphysics.

---

14 "Our Philosophy," http://www.kemet.com
15 Motorola Position on Illegally Mined Coltan, 25 August, 2003.
   http://www.motorola.com/EHS/environment/faqs/
16 Kristi Essick, "Guns, Money and Cellphones," *The Industry Standard* (11 June 2001).
17 Walter Benjamin, "On the Concept of History," *Selected Writings*, 4.392

24. *The Sims* is a very peculiar kind of game, in which everyday life is the subject of play, but where play is nothing but work. And yet there's a difference between play in game and gamespace, which permits the former to offer an allegory for the latter, an allegory which may function as escape and critique of gamespace, perhaps even as an atopian alternative. In the game, unlike in gamespace, the contest between gamer and game is over nothing. There are no precious minerals. There is no labour contract in dispute. The difference between play and its other may have collapsed, but there is still a difference between play within the bounds of an algorithm that works impersonally, the same for everybody, and a gamespace that appears as nothing but an agon for the will to power. If it is a choice only between *The Sims* as a real game and gamespace as a game of the real, the gamer choose to stay in The Cave™. The contradiction is that for there to be a game that is fair and rational there is still a gamespace which is neither.

25. The game is what gamespace isn't, particularly for those for whom it is the dominant cultural form. EA Spouse writes: "We both have been steeped in essentially game culture from an early age, and we watched that 'culture' gain legitimacy as we got to the point of thinking about our future careers."[18] The gamespace of making games as commodities cannot live up to the games themselves. On EA Spouse's website, some forlorn gamer has written, and perhaps again in vain: "On the simes busten out please do not make a meter for the items you buy. Same with walls or aniny thing eles. So bottom line no metter in any of the simes games ever again please. Thank you if you do it."[19] But, sadly, the meter is always running. It is integral to gamespace, if not necessarily to what makes gamespace possible. Beyond the critique of actually existing gamespace,

[18] EA Spouse, "Frequently Asked Questions," 1 November, 2004. http://www.livejournal.com/users/ea_spouse/274.html
[19] Dale Cunningham, "The simes busten out," 10 June, 2005. http://www.livejournal.com/users/ea_spouse/274.html

games can point also to an utopian promise, in which games are something else again. But while the game opens toward new worlds, gamespace forecloses anything but its own relentless agon.

Christina Ljungberg

Maps Mapping Minds

> There is no way to satirise a map.
> It keeps telling you where you are.
> And if you're not there,
> you're lost. Everything is reduced
> to meaning.
> A map may lie, but it never jokes.
> —Howard McCord, "Listening to Maps"

Maps make meaning by locating us as subjects in the world. Maybe that is why maps have always been played an important role in human signification and communication—if we want to explore our symbolic or immaterial worlds with their mosaic of ideas and practices, we need to know where we are. But how do maps make meaning, and, more fundamentally, what precisely is a map? Already the origin of the word "map," from the Latin *mappamundi* (L. *mappa*, cloth for the cloth on which the map was drawn, and *mundi*, "of the world") indicates the extent to which meaning is and always has been mapped into and out of maps: these medieval conceptual maps depict a world heavily centred on religious and spiritual matters in layers of cultural information, providing an integrated representation of the spiritual and cultural state of mind of the time. [1]

---

[1] *The History of Cartography, vol. 1. Cartography in Prehistoric, Ancient, and Medieval Europe and the Mediterranean*, eds. J.B. Harley and David Woodward (Chicago: University of Chicago, 1987) 322.

Maps help us to orientate ourselves, and identify our mistakes or, better, missteps. In contemporary cartography, maps are defined as "graphic representations that facilitate a spatial understanding of things, concepts, conditions, processes, or events in the human world."[2] As spatial embodiments of knowledge, maps are not restricted to the mathematical domains but also political, social, moral, psychological fields or spaces, and seemingly limitless as to their imaginative scope, which makes them perfect stimuli for further cognitive engagements. Just like the *mappamundi*, which demanded of its viewer or reader to interact with its abundant narrative iconography, so maps generally stimulate us to figure, conceptualise, record or represent the world anew. It is this performative function in maps I would like to trace in order to show that this function is—and always has been—inherent in the map's semiotic system, whether we look at humorous cognitive maps, old, geographical maps, purely scientific diagrams of cognitive mapping or fictional allegorical maps. Maps produce new "realities" through the narrative spaces they create: as processes of mapping rather than finite objects, these mapped spaces themselves become "protocols of cognition," informing us of the processes involved in creating meaning and suggesting the extent to which all mappings are cognitive.

1. Cognitive Mapping

The expression "cognitive mapping" is used to label the process of investigating the organisation of subjective and discursive concepts and thought processes. But what does it really mean, and are not all maps cognitive, since they all involve engaging our minds in some kind of mental process, whether material or immaterial? Part of the answer might lie in the recent realisation within cognitive studies that spatial structures seem to be fundamental to the way in which we form concepts in

---

[2] *The History of Cartography*, xvi.

order to make sense of the world: by constructing schemata, the imagination mediates between objects of sensation, on the one hand, and abstract concepts on the other, which helps us to locate ourselves and to understand everyday situations. That may be one of the reasons for the "spatial turn"[3] in social and cultural theory, which increasingly uses geographical concepts and metaphors to investigate contemporary complex phenomena, making "cartography" an object of critical attention and mapping a naturalised part of contemporary discourse. As early as in 1976, Arthur H. Robinson and Barbara Bartz Petchenik wrote in their seminal *The Nature of Maps* that the map metaphor is so often used in an "abstract, non-cartographic sense to connote organising, planning, presenting and knowing" that it points to the pervasiveness of mapping in communicating information:

> mapping is considered to be the most fundamental way of converting personal knowledge to transmittable knowledge. The basic significance of maps, then, seems to lie particularly in the fact that maps are surrogates of space.
>
> As we experience space, and construct representations of it, we know it will be continuous. Everything is somewhere, and no matter what characteristic objects do not share, they always share *relative* location, that is spatiality: hence, the desirability of equating knowledge with space, an intellectual space.[4]

Space seems to reside at the centre of modern thought, together with the insight and recognition that all constructs of knowledge involve position and context. This pertains in particular to maps which are interactive forms of knowledge and social space. The "relative location" shared by objects is mostly historically determined and a part of its culture. Not only is all mapping inextricably bound within the discourse

[3] *Thinking Space*, eds. Mike Crang and Nigel Thrift (London: Routledge, 2000).

[4] Arthur H. Robinson and Barbara Bartz Petchenik, *The Nature of Maps: Essays toward Understanding of Maps and Mapping* (Chicago: University of Chicago Press, 1976) ix, 4.

pertaining to its cultural and historical framework but maps also clearly enact the problems of representing reality and the world: maps can never represent either directly or transparently since, like every other semiotic system of representation, they involve choices, omissions, uncertainties and intentions.

It is probably this insight that has caused "cognitive mapping" to become *the* magic buzzword used to describe most mental processes, often used only as "mapping" without explicit reference to its scientific origin. But what precisely do we understand by "cognitive mapping"? To begin with "cognitive," cognitive science may be defined as a "multidisciplinary approach for studying how mental representations enable an organism to produce adaptive behaviour and cognition."[5] This captures three important aspects of cognitive science: a belief that multi-disciplinarity is crucial, an agreement that the object to be explained is directed behaviour and cognition, and a recognition that internal knowledge representation and transformation is relevant to that explanation. What makes a more precise definition difficult is the multidisciplinary nature of the science, the inherent multi-level complexity of cognition, and the dynamic nature that has characterised cognitive science in these last decades.

This sense of being hard to pin down may have spilled over into definitions of "cognitive mapping," giving it its rather vague image. It could, at any rate, be described as the dynamic process which, in the words of Downs and Stea is "an abstraction covering those cognitive or mental abilities that enable us to collect, organise, store, recall, and manipulate information about the spatial environment."[6] A striking example of a classical cognitive map is the one below, which represents a Londoner's view of the north Great Britain (Fig. 1).

[5] Chris Westbury and Uri Wilensky, http://www.chass.utoronto.ca/epc/srb/dse/encyclopedia/encycframeset.html. 14 October 2005.
[6] Roger M. Downs and David Stea, *Maps in Minds: Reflections on Cognitive Mapping* (New York: Harper & Row, 1977) 6.

The map, drawn with a humorous intent, has twisted coastlines, the relationship between the various areas distorted and the relative location of places changed. Civilisation ends with "Potter's bar" at the edge of Metropolitan London; a sign for "ox carts" and "end of roads" at the arctic circle precedes Scotland and Yorkshire in the far north, just below the North pole, surrounded by icebergs and dogsleds. But despite these distortions, and although this map is intended to make us laugh, it is easy to recognise and understand what the map wants to communicate: the Londoner's view of the cold, remote and "uninhabitable" north as the end of the world.[7]

Although every cognitive map is a product, representing the world at a specific moment in time, it always contains traces of the processes and practices which produced it, while at the same time it renders these traces less than easily or fully legible. This is, however, also pertinent to other maps, both geographical and imaginary, as to every other representation. A map generates other processes, which makes it inherently dynamic, making it not only a cultural testimony of the state of knowledge at the time of its production and of its maker, since it also generates new cognitive or mental maps when we interact with it—which explains the notorious instability inherent in maps. In this sense, an old map such as William Dampier's "Map of the World Shewing the Corse of Mr Dampier's Voyage Round it From 1679 to 1691" (fig. 2) which accompanied *A New Voyage Around the World* (1697), his written report of his adventures, is a cognitive map, too, representing the way Dampier wanted to "shew" the world to his contemporaries.[8] Constructed partly from other maps and partly from maps drawn on his own expeditions, this map shows some fundamental characteristics of mapping in general and of geographical maps in particular: not only is this map presented as a document of his travels but it also includes both

---

[7] Downs and Stea, *Maps in Minds*, 10.

[8] William Dampier, *A New Voyage Round the World* (New York: Dover, [1697] 1968).

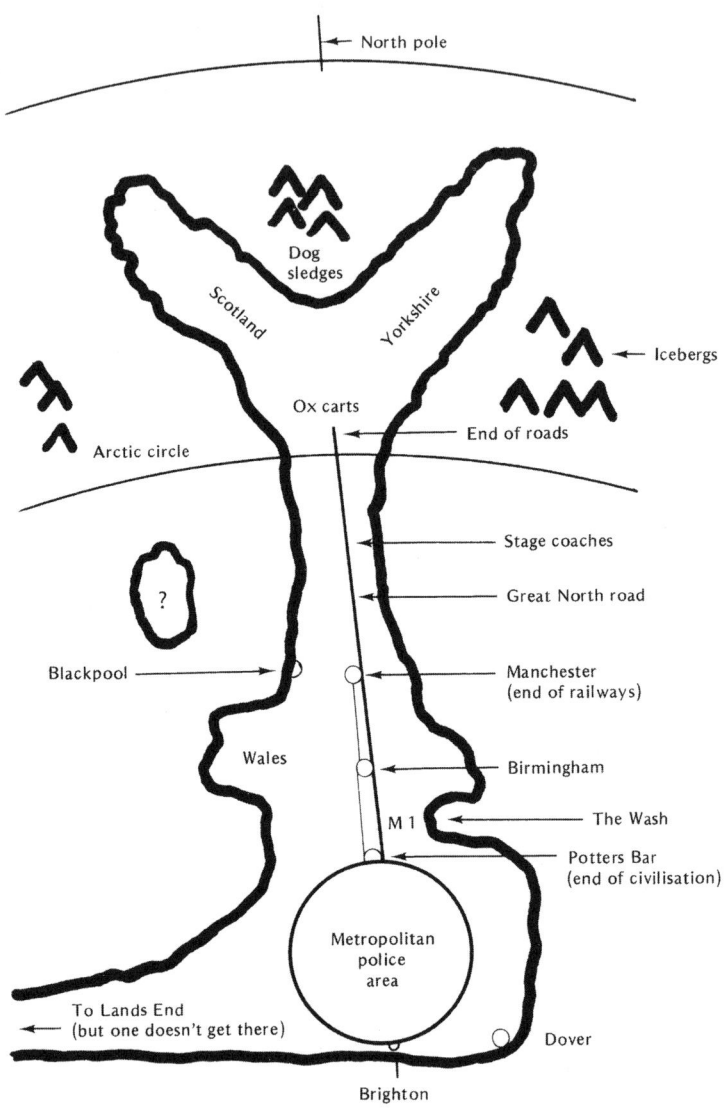

Fig. 1. A Londoner's view of the North

remembered and imaginary geographical objects of places that were supposed to exist at the time. The practical limits of the cartographic knowledge of that time shows in the more careful mapping of important and well-known coastlines, which could be mapped from a boat while the vast inland areas of, e.g., North America still are to a great extent unexplored, being of less interest at a time when discovery was made primarily at sea. That is why large parts of North America are still unmapped and drawn much smaller than the inland of South America, which had been conquered and "mapped" by the Spanish and the Portuguese. "Terra incognita" is precisely that: land that does not inspire any map fantasies that will in turn generate new cognitive processes.

2. Mapping Mental Processes

But a map such as Dampier's also generates new insights for contemporary readers, as it immediately has us compare the mental images of our contemporary world maps that we have stored in our own minds and which tell us that North America and Australia look very different from the way they are drawn on Dampier's map above. Such a process of discovery can also be called a mapping, in its mathematical sense of being a correspondence between two sets (or domains) that assigns to each element in the first a counterpart in the second. The mapping process between these various domains (or input spaces) is what enables us to produce, transfer, and process meaning by adding new knowledge, gradually integrating new input into already existing mental structures.[9] This cross-space mapping does not only involve several input spaces: it also involves so-called generic space, which will determine the whole outcome of the process since it is this space which reflects some, already abstracted element and structure shared by the inputs (like a code). The process will eventually result in

[9] Gilles Fauconnier and Mark Turner, "Principles of Conceptual Integration," *Discourse and Cognition*, ed. J.P. Koenig (Stanford: CSLI Publications, 1998) 271.

an emergent structure, a *conceptual blend*, the mechanism by which we can integrate parts of the other spaces in order to produce new meanings. It involves composition, as new relations become apparent; completion, as frame knowledge fits the blend to wider knowledge; and finally, elaboration, which is "running the blend" through its emergent logic. This is something we do unconsciously most of the time but in particular when we use metaphors or allegories, scientific or political analogies, or explore imaginary domains. What is important here is that the blended space has emergent qualities, which means that it possesses features that cannot be ascribed to any of the input spaces but only result through the process of blending.

In the case of the Dampier map, the input spaces of an eighteenth-century reader would be very different to that of a contemporary one, but in what ways? What determines what goes into these mental spaces? This aspect is both the most crucial and the most difficult one to foresee, as it is inherently linked with the historical, cultural and ideological framework of the "cross-mapper" who must integrate the map into her or his already existing knowledge and psychological make-up. In Fauconnier and Turner's view, the construction of new blends takes place analogous with biological evolution, in which there is an interaction which results in products, and those products are selected for or against.[10] The brain functions here as a "bubble chamber of mental spaces" that constantly forms new mental spaces out of old ones—on the surmise that the brain is constantly constructing a multitude of blends, of which only a few are selected to be further developed and applied. But that still does not answer the question about how humans find the best (or at least very good) mappings out of all the formally possible ones. What is it that steer integration processes? How does this work when we blend reality and fictional spaces?

---

[10] Fauconnier and Turner, "Principles of Conceptual Integration," 321-2.

3. Allegorical maps

Although fiction always involves a mapping between the "real," experiential world and the fictional world with its space-builders and other mechanisms of fictional space, the "cross-mapping" between them becomes particularly interesting in allegorical maps, which explicitly thematise the radical divergence between "real" and fictional spaces. Allegorical maps present an imaginary realm of an envisioned space, which we automatically map onto the geographical, "real" world and which subsequently functions as an implicit comparison between these two spaces. They are therefore ideal for investigating the organisation of subjective and discursive concepts and thought processes in a certain period (and in so doing, making us reflect on our own). Already the allegorical maps in Sir Thomas More's speculative essay *Utopia* (1516; 1518) offered a scathing critique of the British society of his time while portraying Utopia as an ideal state.[11] Another allegorical map that became the fashion of its day is the *Map of Tenderness* (*La Carte du Tendre*, fig. 3) in Madeleine de Scudéry's novel *Clélie*, which set off a century-long tradition of mapping emotions onto geographical space. The tender map's topography of love and courtship depicts the distractions and the pitfalls—in the form of villages, lakes, rivers and the threatening *Mer Dangereuse* which leads to the unknown, the *Terre inconnue*, at the top of the map—that lovers encounter along their journey from the town of New Friendship (*Nouvelle amitié*, at the bottom of the map) to intimacy and "true" love.

---

[11] Cf. Christina Ljungberg, "Cartographic Strategies in Contemporary Fiction," *Orientations: Space/Time/Image/Word*, Word & Image Interactions 5, eds. Claus Clüwer, Véronique Plesch and Leo Hoek (Amsterdam: Rodopi, 2005) 155-172.

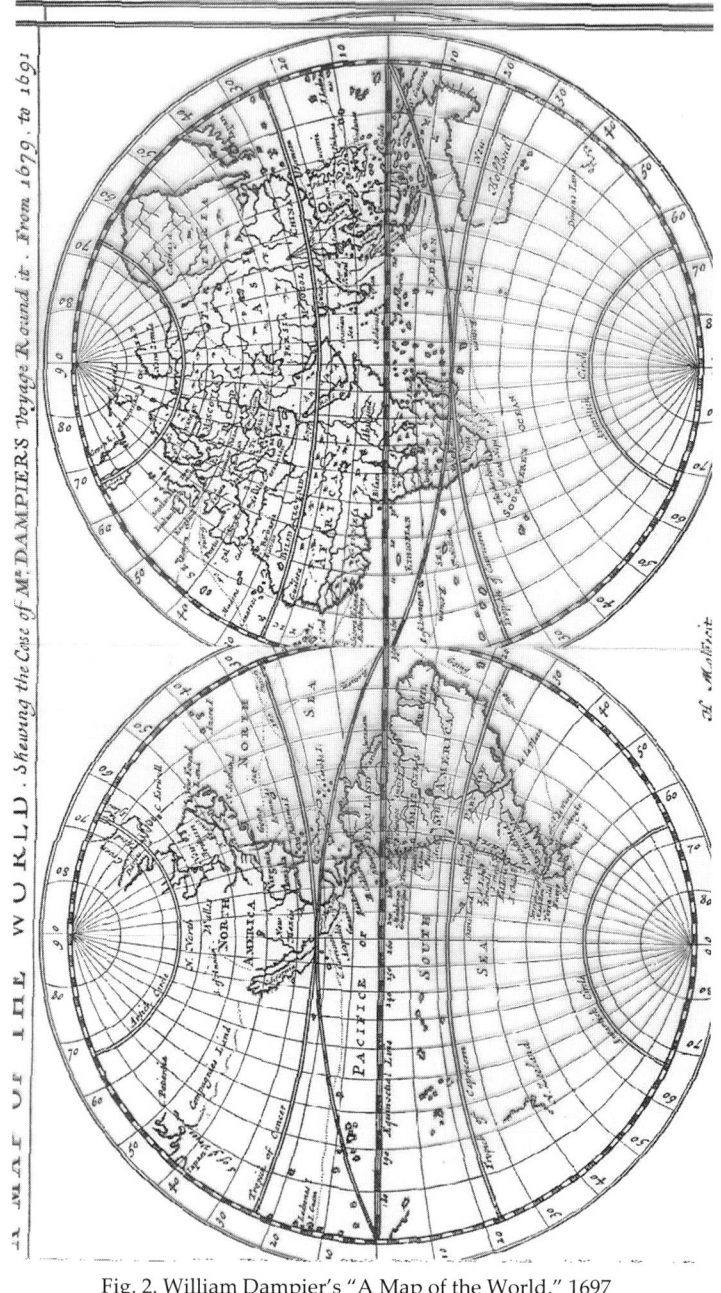

Fig. 2. William Dampier's "A Map of the World," 1697

According to Giuliana Bruno, Scudéry, who held a salon in Paris in the seventeenth century, "made room for an intellectual enterprise that included mapping."[12] Scudéry's salon was quite unique for its time in that created a literary world for women by women and had as its focus female body politics. It was immensely popular in the Paris bourgeois salon society of the mid-seventeenth century. Ridiculed by Molière for its "preciousness" (*Les Préciseuses ridicules*, 1659) and often denigrated and dismissed as "women's literature," a closer look reveals it to be an interesting and very precious undertaking, in particular as a look into women's minds and desires around this time.

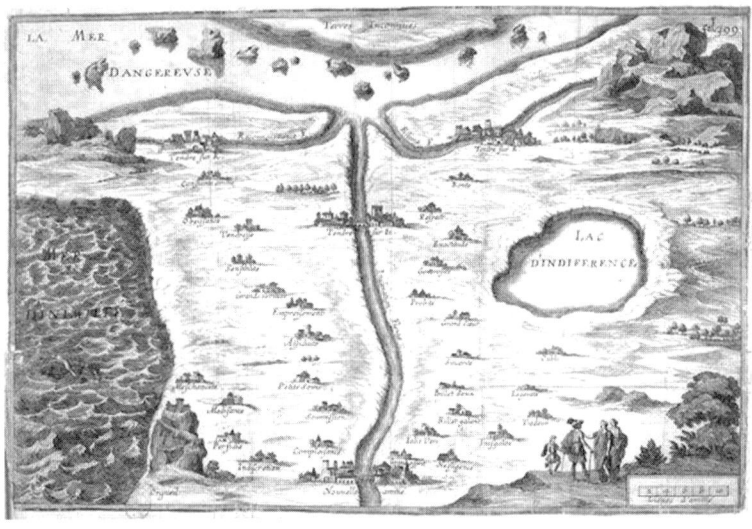

Fig. 3. *La Carte du Tendre (Map of Tenderness)* from Madeleine de Scudéry, *Clélie: Histoire romaine* (Paris: Augustin Courbé, 1654).

---

[12] Giuliana Bruno, *Atlas of Emotion: Journeys in Art, Architecture, and Film* (New York: Verso, 2002) 217.

The *Map of Tenderness* is a composite map that functions like a psychological game inscribing affections and emotions onto social and geographical space. The person voyaging through it traverses an inhabited realm of towns and landscapes that can be travelled through backwards and forwards. Love appears as the ultimate goal, but progress is slowly, systematically organised and classified through speech acts expressed in geographical objects: distances on the map are, for example, measured in *lieues* (1 *lieue* =4 km). Beginning in *Nouvelle Amitié*, located at the southern middle point of the map, there is a choice of three routes one can follow to reach *Tendre*: the route of *Estime* (Esteem), arriving at *Tendre-sur-Estime*, the route of *Reconnaissance* (Recognition), arriving at *Tendre-sur-Reconnaissance*, or the route of *Inclination*, at *Tendre-sur-Inclination*. The wrong choice is that made by selecting the eastern route, by which one can fall into the *Lac d'Indifference* or end up in *Tiedeur* (luke warmth) or *Négligence*.

Contrary to what one might expect, the map's topography does not serve as a mirror for the feelings and emotions of Clélie, the novel's protagonist, but is instead designed as a guide for a male readership of how to succeed in finding the way to a woman's heart. It is a chart of how relations develop in intimate space, most likely covering more than just courtly love, as is often assumed. As Bruno argues, it offered an "uncharted path of productive, rather than reproductive, closeness between a man and a woman, made room for the sharing of intimacy between women, and explored relational magnetism in settings larger than coupling."[13] At the same time, because it was produced as a collective collaboration, the map functions as a fascinating protocol of cognition documenting how relationships were conceived of and managed in mid seventeenth century, and the mindset of both its makers and its readers.

The metaphors operating within this allegorical map could

---

[13] Bruno, *Atlas of Emotion*, 224.

be analysed as three different conceptual blends: 1) "love is a pilgrimage"; 2) "love is a game"; 3) "love is a battlefield," that are put in operation together to create a highly complex conceptual blend which cross-maps emotions onto geographical space. These three blends all have the mental image of "love" as one of their input spaces. In the first case, "love is a pilgrimage," it is the image of pilgrimage, as a journey to a shrine or other sacred place, or a journey or long search made for sentimental reasons, that takes up the second input space. The generic and third space would seem to be the idea that most important things in life involve some sort of quest or search and have to be earned. The second blend, "love is a game," has as it second input space the game as an amusement or pastime; its generic space would be that most interactions involve rules.

It seems, however, that it is the third blend, "love is a battlefield," that is the most crucial: I would suggest that, in this case, it is not the violent aspects of a battlefield that Scudéry plays with but instead, the battlefield as a place of clever strategy. The generic space would seem to contain the general knowledge that most interactions need strategies; the emergent blend, "love is a battlefield" the insight that those strategies are vital both to win a battle and to someone's love. What is interesting to note is the almost proverbial status of the three first blends, which confirms Lakoff and Turner's suggestion that schemas evoked by proverbs are especially rich in images and information and therefore, the most productive.[14] Applied to a concrete case, such a schema becomes an instance of a mechanism called "generic is specific," whereby there is always an abstract structure located in the generic space that can be applied to an indefinite number of inputs in the blended space because they have this abstract pattern in common.

In a second move, these three metaphors are cross-mapped on to one another, making each of their emergent inputs form a

---

[14] George Lakoff and Mark Turner, *More than Cool Reason* (Chicago: University of Chicago Press, 1989) 162.

new space. The new generic space would seem to suggest that love is a spatial entity, a geographical location such as a garden or landscape in which relations between the sexes are taught as a socialising game. The new conceptual blend that emerges seems to suggest that the road to a successful relationship is a complex undertaking that both involves a search, an adherence to certain rules and well thought-out strategies in order to succeed. In a third move, this emergent blend is then cross-mapped onto the material *Map of Tenderness*, which, with its highly subjective emotional landscape immediately invites a comparison with the "real," geographical world, thus triggering new emergent conceptual blends from these new input spaces which, in turn, will generate a new mapping process.

As a protocol of cognition, this map not only lets us catch a glimpse into the minds of an educated bourgeois society around 1650 but it also reveals a cultural context that evolves as a topology of an seventeenth-century sensibility. As Bruno remarks, "this geographical discourse turned inter-subjectivity into a map by which one might navigate interpersonal relations and locate women's position in love and society."[15] Although the map looks archaic and primarily reminiscent of a medieval *mappamundi*, the map's subject matter and its use of Cartesian coordinates to draw its boundaries locate it at the interface between late medieval and early modern times. It appears at a time when the map has become a political instrument and the drawing of boundaries, thanks to more elaborate systems of measuring distance, has become increasingly important. That is why this map is highly performative, not in the sense of creating new geographical realities but in the sense that the boundaries of the locations on the map draw up the lines of a new social reality, effectively creating a new topography from a woman's point of view that was to have considerable influence on Europe salon and bourgeois life during the decades to

---

[15] Bruno, *Atlas of Emotion*, 223.

follow and inspire a whole new genre of emotional geographies.

Therefore, although the performative function is inherent in all maps, there is, I would suggest, a difference in the degree of performativity. That is why an analysis of maps as protocols of cognition offers an especially illuminating approach to the cognitive processes that maps and mapping entail.

Gregory L. Ulmer

Choramancy: A User's Guide

> The past can be seized only as an image which flashes up at the
> instant when it can be recognised and is never seen again.
> —Walter Benjamin.

The Florida Research Ensemble (FRE) developed a prototype
for an inventional consulting practice, tested in the city of
Miami, Florida. This review of the procedure is stated as a
series of steps that permit the replication of the method.

PART ONE: THE IMAGE CRISIS
1. *Select a Public Problem.*
The point of departure for a consultation is the selection of a
problem of concern to the community. The measure of this
concern is determined by the attention it receives in the news
media. The problem selected by the FRE was a public relations
crisis: the damage done to the image of Florida by the murder
of a number of tourists.

[*Cognitive Jurisdiction.*] The crisis in Florida's public image was a
good test case for the consultation, since it provided a situation
that matched the expertise of the FRE with the qualities of the
problem. There is a strict rule of cognitive jurisdiction in
conventional consulting regarding which discipline knowledge
is relevant to which kinds of problems. Arts and Letters
disciplines are not considered relevant to most of the problems

that beset the lifeworld, especially the kinds of problems that most concern citizens having to do with crime, the economy, the environment, and the like. However, the FRE expertise in imaging established its credibility in a case concerning precisely an image.

Miami River aerial photograph courtesy of the Florida Department of Transportation, 2003, and John Craig Freeman.

[*Mediated Disaster*.] The emerAgency is concerned with the civic sphere created through the circulation of information (the imagined community). The purpose of the new consultancy is to develop a practice for the internet that allows netizens to become agents of a "fifth estate," giving citizens a voice in the public policy process equivalent at least to that of journalism, whose agenda-setting role has become a matter of concern.

Here is a sample of the reports of the murders that produced the image crisis:

TOURIST KILLING HAUNTS MIAMI

Uwe-Wilhelm Rakebrand was cautiously following the rules when he collided with the law of the jungle. His murder has become a symbol of exasperation for a metropolis that can never quite escape its own violent image. The German tourist's shooting death in the car he and his pregnant wife had just rented triggered a volley of suggested remedies for Miami's violent virus. Mayor Xavier Suarez proposed highway checkpoints to look for guns, similar to those used to catch drunken drivers; US Sen. Connie Mack, R-Fla, urged tougher sentences for career criminals; a Gulf Coast-based citizens' group called Stop Turning Out Prisoners said it will place more billboard warnings. And there were calls for gun control from various quarters. But Rakebrand's death probably had little to do with what he did; a lot to do with where he was. Rakebrand was headed toward the lights of Miami Beach's glittering night life when he was caught in Miami's darker reality: it is a place not only of dance clubs, fashion shots and glistening beaches, but also of drug runners and inner-city desperadoes who mix guns and gore with the city's sun, surf and cosmopolitan glamour. Miami Police Chief Calvin Ross had a grim view of future prospects. "Until we come to grips with what that problem is, and keep these individuals off the street, or do something on the very front end with juveniles to ensure that they don't enter into a life of crime, we're still going to continue down the same path." Reruns of *Miami Vice*, a TV series that depicts reasons for both allure and alarm, are popular in Germany. Just the week before, newsstands displayed the international edition of Time magazine's cover story summary on Miami: Glitzy, violent, and muy caliente (very hot), it's taking the world by storm. "I don't know that there's a rational explanation for such an irrational and heinous act," said Gary Stogner of the state's division of tourism. Besides lamenting a tragedy, officials are also casting worried eyes on the new wave of negative publicity for a state, and metropolitan area, built around image.[1]

2. *Address the Consultation to a Public Agency with some Responsibility for the Problem.*

Although the emerAgency operates "without portfolio," its work is nonetheless addressed to an existing agency with responsibility for the problem, whether that agency is part of government, business, a non-profit or volunteer organisation. Any practical consequences of the report, however, are likely to depend on the response of public opinion. In the FRE case, the initial responsible party was the state government of Florida.

Over a fourteen month period nine tourists were murdered in Florida. Official reminders that this number was out of 41 million visitors, or that crimes against tourists made up just 3.2 percent of all crimes committed in Florida, did little to address what one official called a media-induced perceived tourist-safety crisis. The Commerce Secretary suspended tourist advertising temporarily, while countering negative news coverage. In the tourism business, he said, image is the business and has a direct bearing on the health of the industry. "We have a huge perception problem, but nonetheless a real problem." A number of steps were taken to treat the symptoms of the problem, such as posting armed guards at highway rest stops, and changing the license plates on rental cars to make them less conspicuous. The part of the policy formulation addressed by the FRE was the government's decision to use advertising agencies to treat the damage to the state's image.

[*Public relations advertising.*] In 1991 the legislature created the Florida Tourism Commission (FTC) charged with devising a strategy for promoting tourism. One of the first acts of the FTC was to hire the New York consulting firm of Penn and Schoen which, for a fee of $250,000, agreed to assess what role the state should play in tourism promotion. The Florida Research

[1] Dan Sewell, *The Gainesville Sun*, 12 September, 1993.

Ensemble accepted the same mandate "without portfolio." Florida already attracts more than forty million visitors each year. Nonetheless, the local tourism boards that were set up in the wake of the creation of the FTC posed as the primary question not the quality of the "Florida experience" but how and when to advertise and how to get the attention we need. A related question concerned what facilities and resources may be magnets for visitors. The State Commerce Department commissioned a campaign in which an ad agency monitored the weather in northern cities. After a blizzard in a given city, the agency placed ads in the newspaper. In the winter of 1992-1993 the ad depicted a piece of nicely browned toast, accompanied by the text: "just a reminder that it's nice and toasty in Florida."

In 1996 the legislature dissolved the Department of Commerce and its Division of Tourism, and the Governor created Visit Florida, a public-private marketing agency, that took over the $17 million budget raised by a two dollar rental car tax. For $800,000 the Fahlgren Advertising Agency created a TV spot designed to trigger memories for viewers in Chicago, New York, and Atlanta of the carefree Sunshine State vacations of their childhood. Amid colourful sun, sand, and water scenes, the commercials showed black-and-white shots that sought to stir memories of singing in the car, learning to fish, and seeing the ocean for the first time. "We ask them to reacquaint themselves with that memorable childhood experience," Austin Mott, president of the Florida Tourism Industry Marketing Corporation was quoted as saying in one newspaper account, "and incorporate it into their current lives." The ads ran on network shows and CNN, while similar print ads were placed in magazines such as FAMILY CIRCLE, MATURE OUTLOOK, BON APPETIT, AND CONDE NAST TRAVELER. Television time and print space for the initial round of ads cost $1.5 million. In hindsight the policy to address the perception apart from the actuality of the place seems misguided. In 1999 tourism again was in decline, due to the destruction of the Florida "ambiance" both culturally and environmentally.

3. *Monitor News Coverage of the Problem and Related Issues.*
Once the problem is selected, it is treated as a motif in order to note the broader pattern it makes, or the context it evokes. News items are useful for determining which elements are within the public sphere, and for providing the point of orientation for the consultation by establishing the voice and stance of the "fourth estate." One such item in particular formed a pattern when juxtaposed with the Rakebrand murder, and moved the FRE to focus its research on Miami specifically.

[*Screams in the Night.*] "MIAMI—Two boats believed carrying as many as 43 Haitians in an apparent bid to smuggle them into the United States sank Saturday off the South Florida Coast, and rescuers found only three survivors. The Coast Guard was alerted at 2 a.m. by a freighter after crew members heard screams from the water about 30 miles east of West Palm Beach." Scarcely a week goes by without such a story appearing in a Florida newspaper. There are Haitians appearing on our shores, jumping from ships, being rescued at sea, wading ashore, washing up drowned.

The symmetry of the cases—the deaths of a German tourist and a Haitian alien—gave initial form to the plans for the consultation. There is a Miami such that Uwe-Wilhelm Rakebrand set out from Germany to experience it. "Meanwhile" (the temporality of nation-building supported by the novel, according to Benedict Anderson's *Imagined Community*) Joel Estiverne (the only victim named in the follow-up stories about the nightscreams incident) boarded a smuggler's boat and was lost at sea. Samedi Florvil, with the Haitian Refugee Centre in Miami, commented that the illegal immigrants often "pay $2,000 or $3,000 to get on a boat. It is to spend money to buy misery." The first point of interest, in addition to the question of the nature of this attractive power, was that Rakebrand's death precipitated an image crisis while Estiverne's death was ignored.

Barbara Jo Revelle, from *Miami River Chora*

[*Real Time.*] The Cuban boat people have played a larger role in the history of Miami than have the Haitians. Recent events (after our consultation was completed) proved the power of live coverage to affect the dynamics of a problem. There was the case of the net-cam set up to monitor the site of the excavation for the condominium that unearthed the Tequesta burial grounds with its series of puzzling holes. More immediately relevant was the TV coverage of the Coast Guard attempts to enforce State and Federal immigration laws, that required them to intercept the six Cubans who leaped from their small boat and tried to swim to the nearby Florida shore. If picked up in the water the Cubans automatically would be repatriated. If they reached shore, they would be granted a hearing to determine their eligibility for political asylum. The live helicopter coverage of the drama brought out a large contingent of Cuban-Americans (and others) to the site of the drama, resulting in a suspension of the laws in this instance (if not a change in policy). The Haitian community cannot muster the same level of support for its boat people, and this condition made their circumstances exemplary. The ultimate case revealing the politics of public policy is that of Elian Gonzales.

The FRE research began to focus on the Haitian attraction to Miami as a neglected dimension of the image crisis. Our method assumes a polarity of attraction-repulsion. It is difficult to understand an attraction without taking into account the negative pole. The following story again broadened the range of the situation.

HAITIANS JUMP SHIP IN MIAMI

More than 150 undocumented Haitians jumped from a freighter into the Miami River Tuesday and were chased into and around riverfront businesses by US immigration agents and police. "We had a lot of policemen running in and out with their guns drawn," said Este Garcia, owner of Garcia's Seafood Grill. "They were in the restaurant, jumping into the water. It was a madhouse. A couple of them hid in trash cans." At least 86 people were captured and many were ordered to sit against the wall of a warehouse near the river, which is frequented by small freighters from the Caribbean and the Bahamas. Forty teen-ager's were among the Haitians who jumped from the green-and-white freighter named Rose-Marie Express as it pulled into dock, police said. Some of the passengers ducked into waiting cars and escaped while others hid under the docks. "At first I thought it was gangs because I just saw kids running and Immigration with guns. I think it went a little overboard. They were pushing them and roughing them up," said Garcia's waitress Lisette Rivera. A US Customs agent raced to the dock after receiving a call that a ship might be off-loading drugs, said US Customs assistant special agent in charge Mark Bastan. Garcia said some immigrants were stumbling around as they tried to escape. "They were disorientated, they've been out on the water for days." The freighter set out from Cap Haitien on Haiti's northwest coast about four days ago, according to a volunteer from the Haitian Refugee Centre. The US Coast Guard in July began banning wooden freighters such as the

Rose-Marie Express from entering the Miami River because they are not considered safe.

The final selection for the site visit—the Miami River—was determined the same way that many screenplays begin. "Stories usually emerge from fragmentary ideas: a colourful character, a poignant or offbeat relationship, a childhood incident, a physical object, or a problem in your own family. Dozens of successful motion pictures originated in the pages of the daily newspaper. Remember that newspaper items seldom contain all of a screenplay's elements. You will have to find some ingredient in the news item that excites you, that stimulates your imagination, and then build your story on that. It's a game that professionals call 'what if.'"[2] The Rose-Marie Express (green and white, freshly painted, wooden) made it safely into the harbour of the Miami River all the way from Cap Haitian. The safe arrival of this boat pinpointed the location of the FRE inquiry into the Florida image crisis on the Miami River.

[*Myami.*] The image of Miami is "dialogical," meaning that its nature and meaning are contested, occupied by multiple opposing discourses vying for control of its signification. To distinguish Miami-as-image, the discursive Miami, from the "thing itself," we used the name "Myami." Our file of clippings tracked over a period of several years the events considered newsworthy enough to put on the wire, datelined MIAMI—

> As a quadriplegic boy watched, three teens stole his VCR, video games and $200 his mother had saved for his 12th birthday party. / A suspicious tool salesman with a $50,000 debt believed a hit man was going to kill him. So when Richard Deville, a United Airlines pilot and avid tool collector, showed up at Seminole Tools on August 6, Gerald Fishbone shot him dead. / Three men were found shot to death at a cockfighting arena, but police don't know who killed them or why. / A 23-year-old

[2] Alan A. Armer, *Writing the Screenplay: TV and Film* (Belmont, CA: Wadsworth, 1988) 17.

man pleaded guilty Wednesday to cutting off a dead man's hand as part of a voodoo-type ritual. / The Port of Miami looked like a success, but appearances can be deceiving. Federal prosecutors contend three of the top people at the port were crooks, using port money like a personal piggy bank for everything from yacht maintenance to Disney World trips. / One of Miami's most savage drug gangs, The Boobie Boys, blamed by police for 35 killings, including a 5-year-old boy, was dismantled Friday with a roundup targeting a suspended detective. The gang's favourite method of attack was drive-by shootings. / The US Army Corps of Engineers says it will help pay for most of the cleanup of the Miami River, a waterway so polluted it has been called a "cesspool." / Unless architects redesign their sketches, a $100 million twin tower condominium soon will be built where archaeologists discovered what they believe are prehistoric ruins, a settlement of the Tequesta Indians. Archaeologists speculate that the circle, made up of dozens of holes carved into stone, could have been used to measure time or keep track of the seasons. / When business recruiter Frank Nero told a group of Japanese businessmen that he was from Miami, one formed his fingers to make an imaginary gun and said: "Miami Vice, boom, boom, boom."

4. *Take Note.*
Take note of how the scene of interest is represented in popular culture, or entertainment forms and media.

[*Noir.*] News is not the only genre forming the image of Miami in the public sphere. Myami, that is, reflects the same paradoxical influence on the image of the city that Mike Davis found in the representations of Los Angeles in hardboiled novels and film noir cinema

Still frame from *Imaging Place*, a place-based virtual reality by John Craig Freeman, with theory by Greg Ulmer. Ground level, navigable scene from South Miami Avenue on the Miami River, 2004.

[*Los Angeles.*] "Together they radically reworked the metaphorical figure of the city, using the crisis of the middle class (rarely the workers or the poor) to expose how the dream had become nightmare ... It is hard to exaggerate the damage which noir's dystopianisation of Los Angeles, together with the exiles' [European intellectuals living and working in L.A.] denunciation of its counterfeit urbanity, inflicted upon the accumulated ideological capital of the region's boosters. Noir, often in illicit alliance with San Francisco or New York elitism, made Los Angeles the city that American intellectuals love to hate (although, paradoxically, this seems only to increase its fascination for post-war European intellectuals). As Richard Lehan has emphasised, 'probably no city in the Western world has a more negative image' ... It is hard to avoid the conclusion that the paramount axis of cultural conflict in Los Angeles has always been about the construction/interpretation of the city myth, which enters the material landscape as a design for speculation and domination."[3]

[*Promotion.*] The same dynamic conflict between promotional public relations and noir narratives informs the city myth of Myami. A history of the promoters lists the cast of characters as follows: "Hamilton Disston, who brought Florida to life with a million dollars he didn't have; Henry Plant, who opened Florida's West Coast and helped win a war; Henry Flagler, who opened the East Coast and built the eighth wonder of the world; Bion Barnett, who proved bankers should take chances; Mrs. Potter Palmer, who used snob appeal to start a city; D. P. Davis, who sold island properties before he built the islands; Barron Collier, who made millions in advertising and poured them all into Florida; Carl Fisher, who created Miami Beach but who couldn't crack New York; George Merrick, who built Coral Gables but thought he failed. Their like will not be seen again; there are laws these days which would have handcuffed them—literally."[4] Despite or because of the hucksters' propaganda, the promotional Myami oscillates between "Magic City" and "Paradise Lost."[5]

Miami, most notably in the works of Elmore Leonard and Charles Willeford, and in the Television series *Miami Vice*, has received some of the same treatment as Los Angeles, albeit belatedly, or in a post- or neo- noir modality of the genre. A book about "the mythical America of crime writers" includes some discussion of the Miami River setting. The Interviewer, John Williams, spoke with James Hall, author of the hard-boiled *Squall Line*, as they rode in Hall's boat on the bay near the river's mouth.

---

[3] Mike Davis, *City of Quartz: Excavating the Future in Los Angeles* (New York: Vintage, 1992) 20-1.

[4] Charles E. Harner, *Florida's Promoters, The Men Who Made It Big* (Tampa: Trend House Publications, 1973) 11.

[5] Sheila L. Croucher, *Imagining Miami: Ethnic Politics in a Postmodern World* (Charlottesville, VA: University Press of Virginia, 1997) 25.

Hall points out the opening of the Miami River to me: "I took a trip down there the other day; it's where the ships come from the Caribbean. I was looking at these ships that are ready to go back and they're stacked with the strangest stuff … stolen bicycles, plastic buckets … All these things you can't believe another culture places a value on, that they'll all be saying in Haiti, 'Oh, great, a ten-gallon bucket.'" […] Ships flying the flag of Honduras and Haiti are coming in to Miami, bringing in Colombian cocaine, and then returning to Haiti loaded up with items as diverse as school buses, rice, beans, stolen bicycles, all hidden under tarpaulins, stolen from pest-control firms. None of this strange cargo is listed on any manifest, and all disappears on arrival in Haiti. The sinister part is the identity of the people running this Miami River traffic: none other than Baby Doc's infamous Tonton Macoutes. Now minus their trademark sunglasses, they are currently upping the craziness stakes in Miami drug wars. A guy from the Sheriff's Office, quoted in the *Herald* says, "The Macoutes don't think they can die. They think they're immune to bullets. They do drug deals based on info from voodoo priests." Echoes here of *Squall Line*.[6]

[*A State of Mind*.] Sheila Croucher, in *Imagining Miami*, summed up the issue: "Miami is a city without true substance, a state of mind instead of a state of being."[7] As James Donald observed, every city is a state of mind that owe as much to discourse as to people and place. "[The imagined city] has been learned as much from novels, pictures and half-remembered films as from diligent walks round the capital cities of Europe. It embodies perspectives, images, and narratives that migrate across popular fiction, modernist aesthetics, the sociology of urban culture, and techniques for acting on the city."[8] We had identified three genres, all within the institution and discourse of entertainment, as contributing most to the complex image of Myami: news, advertising , noir fiction. The insight at this stage

[6] John Williams, *Into the Badlands: Travels through Urban America* (London: Flamingo, 1993) 33.
[7] Croucher, *Imagining Miami*, 2.
[8] James Donald, *Imagining the Modern City* (Minneapolis: Minnesota, 1999) 7.

of research was the possibility that an understanding of Myami might be generalised into an understanding of the logic and rhetoric of electracy as such. Entertainment (understood as the design of information according to the demands of profitability) is the new institution of the emergent apparatus: it is to electracy what school was to literacy—the site of the invention of the practices capable of disseminating to the general population the practical benefits of a language technology.

The second insight concerned the way each mode constructed the image of the city to create an atmosphere, a feeling, an ambiance—a state of mind: Miami-in-me. Every city is a state of mind, but not the same state of mind. Film noir has been defined precisely as being not a genre but a tone or mood. The lesson was that our zone came pre-coded, with a conflicting set of default moods already inscribed within it.

Miami Vice has many antecedents, but most significant among them is the American cinematic genre known as film noir—the source of many of the programme's thematic, narrative, and stylistic elements. [...] Paul Schrader has argued bluntly, "film noir is not a genre...It is not defined, as are the Western and gangster genres, by conventions of setting and conflict, but rather by the more subtle qualities of tone and mood." [...] Noir visual style is catalogued lucidly by J.A. Place and L.S. Peterson. They argue that film noir is fundamentally "anti-traditional" in its visual style—that it consistently violates the code of classical filmmaking that had evolved through the 1930s, listing noir violations as: low key (high contrast) lighting; imbalanced lighting; Night-for-night; deep focus; wide angle focal length; dissymmetrical mise-en-scène; extreme low and high angles; foreground obstructions. They argue that these stylistic elements are as responsible for the film's "meaning" as are conventional components of plot and theme. 'The characteristic noir moods of claustrophobia, paranoia, despair, and nihilism constitute a world view that is expressed not through the films' terse, elliptical dialogue, nor through their confusing, often insoluble plots, but through their remarkable style. In effect, unbalanced composition equals an unstable world view. [...] Noir thematics are assumed to be the dark side of the American dream, a negative image of the 1940s status quo. Men are the ostensible heroes of most films noir. Most commonly they are men with an indiscretion in their past and unpleasantness in their future toward which the present rapidly carries them. The noir protagonist is alienated from a combustible, hostile world, driven by obsessions transcending morality and causality. The obsessive noir protagonist is drawn into a destiny he cannot escape; he is impelled toward his fate by exterior forces beyond his power and interior forces beyond his control.[9]

Noir (and neo-noir) is a report on the American state of mind. Like advertising, it is a theory of (un)happiness. The struggle between booster advertising and noir is between two states of mind: nostalgia versus nihilism. Our measurement or sampling of the mood of the zone would have to take these default moods into account. Our concern was not to try to suspend (phenomenologically) these schemas, but to include them within the design. We understood this inquiry to be related to consulting in the terms outlined by Croucher, having to do with the subjective nature of public problems. The question empirical consultants do not address is, "why and how certain images, issues, and identities capture the public imagination and others do not." We took up in turn her focus "on the processes that transform private perceptions into public images."[10] The long-range goal was to learn how to counter the default public images and states of mind with alternative moods: to ask if it is possible to address policy formation at the level of state of mind.

[*Image Formation.*] A distributed testimonial, interlinking a multitude of individual consultations of the zone, has as its goal the democratising of this passage from private to public and back. The struggle for Myami (the image and its associated state

9 Jeremy G. Butler, "Miami Vice, The Legacy of Film Noir," in *Film Noir Reader*, eds. Alain Silver and James Ursini (New York: Limelight, 1996) 290-1.
10 Croucher, *Imagining Miami*, 17, 18.

of mind) exists at this point of convergence or overlap of discourses. "Miami is a composite of images none of which are devoid of material referents but all of which are constructed through processes distinct from the content or conditions they appear to reflect. These images can be traced to the tug and pull of vested interests and community politics."[11] We needed to correlate this point with a specific geographical setting in order to perform as theoria.

5. *Be reflexive: include your own methods and discourse as part of what is in question.*
[*The Topos of Wisdom.*] For its consultation on the image crisis, the FRE constituted itself as a theoria. The media narratives called attention to a situation, associated with the state of the State of Florida in general and with the city of Miami in particular. The imperative was that we should tour the site of the problem to see for ourselves, to witness and give testimony on behalf of the public. This tour of the ground would in turn provide the basis for the design of an internet site, a virtual Miami to be toured by netizens/students in order to perform their own testimonials. One goal of the internet tour of Miami/Myami is to open this image to the problematic of the critique of realism that informed the revolution in representation within the arts and sciences of the twentieth century. The policy context for the crisis of the image of Florida could be an opportunity for citizens to update their cognitive mapping skills to include the lessons of modernism and postmodernism

The initial idea was that the theoria would go to the Miami River to attest to the situation of attraction—the convergence of tourists and Haitians. We discovered, however, that in so doing we were participating in a genre that is just as formulaic as *Miami Vice*, even to the point of its implicit title: *Myami Virtue*.

---

[11] Croucher, *Imagining Miami*, 23.

The scene of a shipwreck with spectator (as in the nightscreams episode) is a topos, as Hans Blumenberg explained, a commonplace of the sages who used it for many centuries as a moralising anecdote. The discourse of the sages of the ancient theoria that we had adopted as a relay for the new consultancy expressed the state of mind known as "ataraxy," a kind of serene indifference to the accidents and tribulations of the external world.

[*Shipwreck with Theorist.*] Blumenberg wrote a history of the shipwreck paradigm or "model open to multiple possible actualisations. By tracing the history of these actualisations, Blumenberg discerned changes in the way human beings have imagined their relation to the 'Lebenswelt,' or life-world. He noted that one of the most pervasive actualisations of the life-as-sea-voyage metaphor includes a spectator who observes the distress of those at sea from the safety of dry land. For Blumenberg, this spectator embodies theory (the Greek word 'theoria' derives from 'theoros,' spectator)."[12]

Before setting foot on the banks of the Miami River, we were already in a scene, a schema—a topos—and could not pretend that our inquiry would be any more objective or free from "perspective" than was that of the empirical consultant, the journalist, the booster, or the TV script writer. The continuing relevance of the shipwreck topos to contemporary philosophy may be seen in Walter Benjamin's attitude to his situation. "In April 1931 he had described himself as 'a shipwrecked person adrift on the wreck, having climbed to the top of the mast which is already torn apart. But he has the chance from there to give a signal for his rescue.'"[13] The nightscreams event or the Rose Marie Express, whose distress we watched from the safety of our academic shore, show us nonetheless, if not objectively

12 Hans Blumenberg, *The Legitimacy of the Modern Age*, trans. Robert M. Wallace (Cambridge, MA: MIT, 1983) 2.
13 Susan Buck-Morss, *The Dialectics of Seeing: Walter Benjamin and the Arcades Project* (Cambridge, Mass: MIT Press, 1989) 37.

then metaphorically, allegorically, how things are, the human condition, whose features induce a certain state of mind, depending on what we bring to the scene. The default moods are those established by consulting (problem-solution), boosterism (nostalgia), noir (nihilism), and wisdom (ataraxy). In terms of invention as a rhetorical practice, we were treating "chora" at this point as a category to gather and organise the "topoi" or commonplaces associated with a specific geographical region or area. The Miami River as a chora does not replace topos in the rhetorical tradition as the name for the "places of invention," but adds a new dimension of order and generation.

PART TWO: CONSULTING THE ZONE
6. *Tour the site of the problem.*
[*Divination.*] Having completed our "table work," a review of the media image of Miami, the next step was to tour the site, the Miami River, designated as the zone. Although William Tilson featured the Miami River in a number of his graduate seminars, and John Craig Freeman produced a VRML mapping of the river for a CD-Rom (a panorama updating the tradition of "chorography"), the FRE delegated the official tour or site visit to Barbara Jo Revelle, acting as theoros. As a creative photographer, Revelle's task was to make an image or images capable of gathering holistically the mood or atmosphere of the zone. Her procedure was to document the zone, including interviews with anyone she met and a journal recording her experiences, memories, and reflections related to the tour. These documents (word and picture images) provided the link between Miami and Myami.

Given our decision to focus on the "Haitian" as the other of the tourist, it was important to take into account post-Enlightenment warnings about the limitations of science—its colonising ideological construction of the other—, and to make explicit this potential abuse in our own disciplinary practices. Our theories suggested that it was possible to counter the default zombie quilted into our discourse by opening our inquiry to the consulting methods of Haitian wisdom. The historical research showed that our civilisation is continuing the process of syncretism, adding an Afro-Caribbean world view to the post-Augustinian jewgreek hybrid. Our intention was to experiment with a hybrid of poststructural psychoanalytic theory and the divinatory practices of the Afro-Caribbean diaspora (specifically Vodoun and Santeria). Roland Barthes, who anticipated this crossing with divination in his theory of text, provided a point of departure:

> THE STARRED TEXT
> We shall therefore star the text, separating, in the manner of a minor earthquake, the blocks of signification of which reading grasps only the smooth surface. The tutor signifier will be cut up into a series of brief, contiguous fragments, which we shall call lexias. It will suffice that the lexia be the best possible space in which we can observe meanings; its dimension, empirically determined, estimated, will depend on the density of connotations ... The text, in its mass, is comparable to a sky, at once flat and smooth, deep, without edges and without landmarks; like the soothsayer drawing on it with the tip of his staff an imaginary rectangle wherein to consult, according to certain principles, the flight of birds, the commentator traces through the text certain zones of reading, in order to observe therein the migration of meanings, the outcropping of codes, the passage of citations.[14]

We designated the zone (run-down, mixed-use industrial area) of the Miami River as a text-scene of divination, which we would "consult" by surveying the movements, positions, identity, and "cries" of the denizens—Haitians, Coast Guard, Italian taxi driver, the homeless, the developers, and the rest— in relation to the personal problem of a theoros. Divination provided an interface metaphor for the tour of the river.

---

[14] Roland Barthes, *Image, Music, Text*, trans. Stephen Heath (New York: Hill and Wang, 1977) 13-4.

Divination is an analogy for our Copernican revolution in consulting, in which we did not try to explain the problem, but (in the spirit of the shipwreck metaphor) it explained us. "Problems B Us" (the slogan of the emerAgency). The hybridity of the method was contained within the pun on "consultation" that linked the practices of science and religion. In our case, Barbara Revelle, acting as theoros, posed a burning question (a question at once personal and collective, the one that everyone asks, hence general, and yet the answer is unique in each instance) and then her tour of the zone produced a number of signifiers that constituted an answer.

7. *Pose a Burning Question prior to the tour of the zone.*
Barbara Revelle walked out into a humid sunny summer morning on the Miami River, morning after morning, for five weeks during May and June of 1998, performing as querent (inquirer) for the FRE theoria. Her burning question was formulated as a hybrid between the general one borrowed from Heidegger's attunement ("how do things stand with me?" — "Befindlichkeit"), and the specific one based on divination (in her case: "should I stay in my love relationship?"). One does not ask such a question casually, nor will the answer come to one not in crisis.

8. *Make an image of the zone in words and pictures (photographs).*
[*Punctum (Sting).*] The procedure for producing a reading of the zone (the means by which the zone answers the burning question) is based on Roland Barthes's theory of how to read the "third meaning" of a photograph. The theoros does not and could not plan or intend what Barthes called an obtuse meaning, neither to include nor exclude this dimension. "The detail which interests me is not, or not strictly, intentional, and probably must not be so; it occurs in the field of the photographed thing like a supplement that is at once inevitable and delightful; it does not necessarily attest to the photographer's art; it says only that the photographer was

219

there, or else, still more simply, that he could not not photograph the partial object at the same time as the total object (how could Kertesz have 'separated' the dirt road from the violinist walking on it?). The Photographer's 'second sight' does not consist in 'seeing' but in being there."[15]

The consultation as a practice depends upon the querent's experience of recognition. The material cause of the punctum that stings the viewer is some detail in the photograph. In a picture of a family of American blacks, the spectacle of their household interests Barthes, but he is stung by "the belt worn low by the sister," and above all " by her strapped pumps" (being out of fashion, they refer him to a specific date in time).[16] The key to the method, and to the obtuse as an experience, is in the relationship between the detail in the image and the memories and their associated emotions that the detail awakens in the viewer.

> However lightning-like it may be, the punctum has, more or less potentially, a power of expansion. This power is often metonymic. There is a photograph by Kertesz (1921) which shows a blind gypsy violinist being led by a boy; now what I see, by means of this 'thinking eye' which makes me add something to the photograph, is the dirt road; its texture gives me the certainty of being in Central Europe; I perceive the referent (here, the photography really transcends itself: is this not the sole proof of its art? To annihilate itself as medium, to be no longer a sign but the thing itself?), I recognise, with my whole body, the straggling villages I passed through on my long-ago travels in Hungary and Rumania.[17]

This recognition recalls the workings of a mode of experience called variously epiphany, attunement, extimacy (Lacan), whose purpose in the testimonial is to locate and map for the

[15] Barthes, *Image, Music, Text*, 47.
[16] Roland Barthes, *Camera Lucida: Reflections on Photography*, trans. Richard Howard (New York: Hill and Wang, 1981) 43.
[17] Barthes, *Camera Lucida*, 45.

querent the border between the inside and the outside (of anything: logic, personal identity, nation—the ideological boundaries). The detail attunes Barthes to the setting, objects, characters of the scene in a way mapped by the inside-outside figure of a möbius strip—the extimate topology of the psyche. "The punctum, whether or not it is triggered, it is an addition: it is what I add to the photograph and what is nonetheless already there. To Lewis Hine's retarded children I add nothing with regard to the degenerescence of the profile: the code expresses this before I do, takes my place, does not allow me to speak; what I add—and what of course is already in the image—is the collar, the bandage … Once there is a punctum, a blind field is created (is divined)."[18] The colloquial use of "divined" is reconnected with its ritual meaning in testimonial. The punctum, then, occurs when there is a match between a signifier in the scene (in the photograph, or in the zone), and a scene in the querent's memory.

9. *Search the zone, or the images of the zone, for a triggering detail.*
[*Roland Barthes.*] "A detail overwhelms the entirety of my reading: It is an intense mutation of my interest, a fulguration. By the mark of something, the photograph is no longer 'anything whatever.' This something has triggered me, has provoked a tiny shock, a satori, the passage of a void (it is of note that its referent is insignificant) … A trick of vocabulary: we say 'to develop a photograph'; but what the chemical action develops is un-developable, an essence (of a wound), what cannot be transformed but only repeated under the instances of insistence (of the insistent gaze). This brings the Photograph (certain photographs) close to the Haiku. For the notation of a Haiku, too, is un-developable: everything is given, without provoking the desire for or even the possibility of a rhetorical expansion. In both cases we might (we must) speak of an intense immobility; linked to a detail (to a detonator), an

18 Barthes, *Camera Lucida*, 57.

explosion makes a little star on the pane of the text or of the photograph."[19]

The punctum is a relay that takes us to the very heart and core of the testimonial. The goal of our design is to combine a practice with a technology (testimonial on the internet) that supports the feeling that Barthes associates with satori. The hypothesis is that there is a continuum, a family resemblance, such that interpellation or "hailing" (the identifications with "parent" or authority figures formed as part of the construction of identity within the various institutions of the popcycle) may transform into satori. The "jubilation" manifested by infants recognising their own image in a mirror is the basis for every experience of "Aha!" (eureka). To say that testimonial is to electracy what tragedy was to literacy is to suggest that anagnorisis and peripeteia, performed by the actors in theatre, are performed in testimonial by netizens online. The family of terms, arranged more or less in an order of ascending "insight," include: interpellation (misrecognition), recognition, the uncanny, epiphany, anagnorisis, eureka, satori. We will perhaps have to add a new term to this family, a term from the Creole vocabulary (possession?).

[*The Poetic Encounter*.] The punctum extends to photography the tradition of the poetic encounter practiced in Paris from Baudelaire's *Paris Spleen* to the drifting tactics of the Situationists, including such intervening figures as Rainer Rilke (*The Notebooks of Malte Laurids Brigge*, and Andre Breton (*Nadja*). Walter Benjamin's Arcades Project updated Baudelaire's poetics to take into account the cinematic device of montage and to extend these to philosophical analysis in the practice of the "dialectical image." One of Benjamin's working titles for his unfinished Arcades project—"Paris, Capital of the Nineteenth Century"—suggests a phrase relevant to our consultation: "Miami, Capital of the Twenty-first Century." Revelle drifted

---

[19] Barthes, *Camera Lucida*, 49.

daily through the zone, taking pictures, taping interviews with the denizens she encountered, and recording the events of the day and her reflections on them in her journal. The decision about what to photograph, whom to interview, where to go, were dictated partly by chance, partly by her intuitive sensibility (feelings of attraction and repulsion), and partly by the FRE method.

10. *Select one photograph that is recognised as an answer to the burning question.*

Barbara's consultation sampled the situation of the zone at one historical moment (June, 1998). Her use of a personal question was posed within the frame of her status as theoros, one member of a theoria. The FRE acted as diviner to her querent, providing a cultural form within which her question and the image record could come together to provide an answer. Whatever the value of this answer to Revelle personally (and only she may decide that), the image-answer serves also to reveal the attunement (the mood) of the zone. The image produced in the process of the consultation is an electrate category, gathering the heterogeneous entities found in the zone into a scene (a mise-en-scène) that is to electracy what the concept is to literacy. The claim (which needs to be tested) is that It is possible to use this image not only to think and reason and feel with respect to the Miami River, but with respect to other matters as well. The poetic categorical image has abstractive, logical power.

The iconic or emblematic image was selected not by Barbara alone, but by the FRE using the mystory form to sort the data (in this case, nineteen hours of videotape and many rolls of film) into a cognitive map that produced a pattern. "Cognitive map" is the term Fredric Jameson used (extending the meaning from its source in architecture) to name a new aesthetic capable of connecting personal experience with expert knowledge about global and institutional realities. The triggering detail (the punctum) appeared as a signifier, a certain object, that repeated in the discourse of each register of the popcycle. The title of the photo-emblem is "Crossroads."

Barbara Jo Revelle, "Crossroads"

11. *To select the image answer to the burning question, sort the photographic and textual record into a mystory structure.*

[*Mystory.*] The updating of epiphany and allegory as the basis for a testimonial is a development and extension of my work with "mystory" as an electrate genre. Mystory, like testimonio, is a version within the mode of testimony that Elie Wiesel said defines our era. The registers or levels of our episteme are different from those organising medieval experience, obviously, but their nature and function may be understood by analogy with the medieval example. In mystory the allegorical scheme is appropriated not as a means of interpretation but of invention, production. The expectation is not to live an epiphany, but to write one, by juxtaposing a modern equivalent of the allegorical levels. This use of allegory identifies mystory as part of the postmodern condition. The contemporary quaternary or square consists of four discourses that together make up a "popcycle" (referring to the circulation or cycling of units of signification through the different discourses, from popular to specialised and back).[20]

The relevance of mystory as a basis for testimonial is that it is a holistic practice, designed originally as a way to compose simultaneously in four (more or less) discourses. What one testifies to in the first place is the inventory of identifications or quilting points constituting one's feeling of being a unified "self." Mystory is a cognitive map of its maker's psychogeography. The popcycle that I worked out in *Heuretics* remotivates an allegorical quaternary. The four levels of allegory serve as the four elements (Earth, Air, Fire, and Water) into which Plato's *chora* sorted chaos.

[*Mystory as allegory.*] Anagogy = Science (Career, Discipline): The collective meaning of history is determined now not by Christian Theology but by whatever world view is embodied within the specialised knowledge that one acquires as an expert in some given career field. This expertise may be disciplinary in the academic or professional sense—physics, law—or it may be a craft or trade (plumbing, football). This knowledge is the means by which one earns one's livelihood (work), but the knowledge of an avocation may be used instead.

Moral = Family (biography of the Individual): The individual is considered in terms of his/her family upbringing, with the language being the one learned in the home (English, French, Creole) and the discursive regime being the habits and customs specific to that family, as governed by such things as ethnicity, race, gender and the like.

Allegory = Entertainment (commercialised information and story): The interpretive "key" comes not from the "imitation of Christ" but from the identification with certain favourite celebrity stars. The discourse learned is that of cultural mythology encountered in popular genres (Westerns, film noir, romances) carried through the media—television, cinema,

[20] Gregory L. Ulmer, *Heuretics: The Logic of Invention* (Baltimore: Johns Hopkins, 1994)

newspapers, magazines, advertising. The entry into this discourse starts in early childhood due to the nearly ubiquitous presence of television in the home.

Literal = School (K-12): The historical fact that grounds the figuration is not the story of Israel as codified in the text of the Old Testament, but the history of one's nation, state, or community—the official version—as codified in textbooks taught in schools K-12. This history represents the memory of the collectivity.

[*Crossroads*.] The mystory is an allegory bringing into correspondence the four discourses of the popcycle of institutions in which our identities are constructed (interpellation). As emerAgents we do not file a report, but a testimonial, using the mystory procedure. The claim of choramancy is that this photograph is "categorical"—that it extracts and holds the mood of the River zone, and that this mood is what makes the image capacious, capable of gathering into a set the whole (hole) of the zone. The established means by which a picture holds a narrative are either that it represents the "pregnant moment"—the crisis, peripateia or turning point of a narrative, or that it offers what is typical in terms of the everyday reality of a situation. While both of these possibilities are observable in "Crossroads," neither is necessary since the method does not depend upon the form of what is visible in the image. The image functions rather as a "souvenir" of the triggering detail. The network of associations snapped in this shot is enhanced by the visualisation technologies of electracy.

To put into writing the flash of insight captured in "Crossroads" involves unspooling the four threads ("ficelles") of allegory. What is the effect of juxtaposing these four scenes? The sinthome that links them together—the event of attunement—is "singular," a specific "situation," and yet, as Whatever, has categorical power. If our purpose were to write a screenplay, to make a movie, then these tracks could be integrated in one narrative. "Crossroads" is a virtual film still evoking the diegesis (imaginary space and time) of Myami (a narrative diegesis is what makes a particular story recognisable regardless of the medium in which it is represented). The dynamic movement of a narrative from beginning to end is managed by the contracts governing the three modes of exchange that constitute society: economics, kinship, and communication. Events become potential stories (become worth recounting) when the contracts that regulate the exchanges are violated (the enactment of such vices as stealing, cheating, lying).

These exchanges and their violations are at work in the scene and moment indexed by the photograph. The mystory registers each exchange, juxtaposing or blocking them into an assemblage, in order to foreground a different dynamic that is also at work in the scene: contingency, luck, (it goes by many names, each with its own nuance), chance, coincidence, synchronicity. Beyond the ordering powers of argument, narrative, and image, there is a disruptive, chaotic operator. An "omen," for example, is defined as the conjunction of a personal problem, an event, and chance.

> This happens on the road, out at the crossroads, where novel experience arises contingently and so novel speech must also arise. Plato thought not only that Hermes invented language but that he did so in relation to "bargaining," which implies that a prime site of linguistic invention is the marketplace, another place where we are likely to meet strangers with strange goods, and, crossroads-wise, find ourselves forced to articulate newly. Moreover, the market at the crossroads may be a metaphor for metaphor itself, or for any original speech, the linguistic flowers that sprout at the crossroads of the mind. The mind articulates newly where there is true coincidence, where roads parallel and roads contrary suddenly converge.[21]

---

[21] Lewis Hyde, *Trickster Makes this World: Mischief, Myth, and Art* (New York: North Point, 1998) 299.

The Miami River is a port, a marketplace, literally a crossroads. The lines of our potential narrative are left untied in order to allow a figure—a metaphor or metonym—to emerge, an image, whose "event" or happening blocks the discourses into a pattern, a constellation. The point in any case is not to tell one story, but to show the ground and limits of story and concept. We assume the cultural schema, the familiarity with narrative form, so that it matters little whether we imagine "Crossroads" as a still from a movie that has been disassembled, or one that cannot be made.

[*Crossroads as Allegory*.] Literal Level: History (the story of the Miami River): Literally "Crossroads" shows a ship docked next to a warehouse on the Miami River, City of Miami, Florida. It is not the ship we anticipated in our table work (it is not the Rose Marie Express). The cargo is not immigrants but used, second-hand items: bicycles, plastic buckets, clothing, mattresses (the stuff of the flea markets that intrigued the surrealists). It is piled around the warehouse, and some has been loaded onto the vessel. Atop a pile of mattresses two crewmen are seated.

What cannot be seen but must be inferred is the Problem at work in each track. One of the selection principles determining what to include in each thread is this schema of Problem-Solution that frames the modern understanding of "ATH" (the blindness that produces calamity in tragedy). In this case the ship is impounded, caught in Operation Safety Net—the "Caribbean Code"—conducted by the United States Coast Guard, directed at "substandard shipping," vessels under 500 gross tons. The nature of the problem depends upon one's point of view or position in the situation. For the Coast Guard it is "irresponsible owners" trying to extend the economic life of old ships. The established policy solution is to eliminate such shipping through inspection and impounding. For the Haitians the problem is to make enough money to feed the dependents back home, a goal thwarted by the opponent—the Coast Guard.

Allegorical Level: Entertainment: The place where the photograph was taken (the Miami River zone) is animated by the exchange of communication, media, language, in the sense of the circulation of stories and information that motivate or discourage tourist travel and immigration. "Problems" in the Media quarter are constructed as spectacles to be consumed as entertainment. Although we designated this track as the Media exchange, an immediate Problem structuring it concerns tourism, the visitors who come to the location of a "spectacle." Sites of problems of all kinds have long been destinations favoured by tourists. One of the most popular stops on the "Murder, Mystery and Mayhem Tour" of the crime scenes in Miami, for example, is the gothic Mediterranean mansion on Ocean Drive known as the Amsterdam Palace, former home of Gianni Versace. The steps and sidewalk in front of the mansion, the place where Versace was murdered by Andrew Cunanan, is a shrine for mourners and a "photo opportunity" for the many visitors who pose for snapshots.

The policy question in this quarter has to do not with "murder" but with the gentrification of downtown Miami, specifically the physical impossibility of moving visitors continuously through the river district. "Few things can dampen an urban experience more than the realisation that each stop on an itinerary requires an automobile and a parking space. Until downtown can offer an assortment of attractions within walking distance of each other or in the reach of a short ride on a convenient public shuttle, business persons and visitors alike will have no patience with the idea of spending time downtown." So states the Master Plan of the Miami River Coordinating Committee. Solution? A River Walk, including urban renewal projects of various kinds in addition to the board walk: condominiums, restaurants, pollution controls, and the like. Thus this thread embodies the river as an object of study for the expertise of urban planners and architects.

Moral Level: Family (personal memory): The photograph was taken sometime in June, 1998, by Barbara Jo Revelle, an artist and member of the FRE, during her five-week stay in a boarding house next to the river. Her personal trajectory is inscribed within the exchange of kinship, exogamy, tracing a circulation away from her father through a marriage and divorce to her present relationship with Ron. This relationship is the motivation for the burning question. The Problem orientating the exchange is love—manifested in this case as jealousy, which motivates the intense and repeated fights between Barbara and Ron. He accused her of wanting to start an affair with some of the men she met during her stay. His justification was a genuine fear for her safety. The given Solution is counselling, couples therapy. Her story is simultaneously that of a querent and theoros, working in the "middle voice" which is the "mood" of theoria (the tour of the problem out there is a reading of my Family situation).

Anagogic Level: Career (disciplinary knowledge): The quarter of Expertise is absent from most narratives, since the discourse of disciplinary knowledge avoids story and prefers science, argument, expository and argumentative writing: the treatise format. The structural account of circulating objects, of exchanges governed by contracts, nonetheless applies equally well to knowledge, especially to the institution of consulting that is the target of our deconstruction. Knowledge circulates between the academy and the community—the agencies, commissions, and councils overseeing policy formation in the City of Miami, for example. The Problem considered within this institution is every problem and any problem that comes to the attention of the public. The Solution is science (Natural and Social Sciences) in the form of instrumental reason, empirical applied knowledge.

The difficulty for the FRE is that our expertise (Arts and Letters) is excluded from this exchange. The narrative obstacle for the FRE is that its expertise is refused, remains unsolicited, rejected as irrelevant to the policy formation addressed to the zone. It is important to note, at the same time, that the kind of knowledge we have to offer does not conflict with the Problem-Solution terms operating in each quarter of the allegory. Rather, what we have to offer is a different category, a different framing of events altogether, from the problem-solution narrative of conventional consulting.

Four threads, four circulations, four "props" run through the mystory: used domestic goods; tourists; Barbara Revelle herself; knowledge. It is not that all this information is "in" the photograph, but that it all may be thought together through this image. Why four? The number is symbolic, not instrumental. Each circuit in its own way is "blocked" (frozen, immobilised, paralysed): the exchange is interrupted, at an impasse. The block in each case involves a safety crisis, a calculation of risk. The snapshot records this situation at a specific moment in time: it is one "throw of the dice," just as in divination a consultation samples the querent's situation at a given moment, with one shuffle of the deck, one casting of shells, stones, coins. The reading reveals the play of forces at work in the situation at that moment, their "propensity" or tendency, the possibilities or potentials for change, the timing of that change, its possible direction. At the same time the reading confirms the general condition of the modern city, THE city (image-city), already established for Baudelaire's Paris, Joyce's Dublin, Eliot's London.

PART THREE: MIAMI AD-VICE

12. *Note any signifier that repeats in each of the four quarters of the mystory.*

How does "Crossroads" record the attunement of the Miami/Myami River? The attunement is figured in the detail that produced the epiphany, that triggered something "in me" (in us). This detail is the Whatever that links the river scene (external-present) with a past other scene of memory, forgotten, repressed, or stored in archives. The goal of choramancy as an electrate practice is to learn how to support in a digital network—how to enable, enhance, and extend as a procedure of reason—the flash of spirit.

Choramancy (chorography) attempts to be for the experience of insight what electricity is to lightning. As the theoria recollected the developed photographs and viewed the tapes accumulated over the five-week tour, we noticed a mattress that insisted, repeated, performed in one location after another: among the homeless in Jose Marti Park; in the ruins of the demolished apartments, along with other detritus from the displaced Guatemalan family; in the warehouses and on the decks of the ships trading with Haiti; in the bedroom of the boarding house where Revelle stayed. The first recognition occurred when Barbara remembered the game she played (forbidden games) with her "white trash" friends in the neighbourhood across the lake that her father contemptuously dubbed "Skeeversville"—the game known as "Perfume in the Black Hole." This connection produced an experience of the "uncanny" (and opened a passage towards "satori"). That the mattress or any object could conjoin so many discourses is a possibility prepared in advance within allegory. "The sign 'lion' functions in Chrétien de Troyes's *Yvain* as a remarkable shifter between several discourses: that of an allegorical moral system, that of a natural or 'physical' system, and that of a new and purely social system that we may call heraldic or totemic."[22] We selected "Crossroads" because it contained the switch or shifter that became the strange attractor of our consultation.

[*Memory: Uncanny Games (Eureka).*] "Linda McDonald's house-with the basement where her Daddy did upholstering when he wasn't drunk, and where the kids from Skeeversville played sexual and scary games in the dark amidst the mattresses, old chairs, and mouldering upholstering material. Two brothers from Skeeversville, Ricky and Bobby Eason —were often in on those games. There was one we called Perfume in the Black Hole. I can't quite remember the perfume part, but I think we divided into two groups, boys and girls, and went to parts of the basement where we couldn't see the other group. The girls passed around a perfume bottle, and put some on in turn, and the idea was that where you put the perfume was related to the 'secret you were required to remember and tell to the rest of the group.' We went around the circle, and when a player couldn't think of any more secrets to tell, she 'lost'—and the punishment was that she had to crawl into a mildewed and spider- infested space created by a folded-over broken-open mattress. This was the "black hole." Then someone from the boys side of the basement, chosen through some more manly ritual we never got to witness but were told had to do with their 'privates,' would crawl inside and try to guess the losing girl's identity by feeling her body. Nancy Moyer and I talking earnestly and often about whether we could be pregnant because of these games."[23]

[*The Other Mattress.*] The epiphany was initiated by the uncanny (contingently necessary) repetition of mattresses across the different levels of the popcycle, which transformed the mattress from a signifier into a sinthome.

---

[22] Eugene Vance, Fr*om Topic to Tale: Logic and Narrativity in the Middle Ages* (Minneapolis: University of Minnesota Press, 1987) 105.

[23] Barbara Jo Revelle, "Testimonial."

Barbara Jo Revelle, from *Miami River Chora*

[*Allegory of the Mattress.*] The Literal Mattress exists within the history of Haiti, the trade in used goods between Haiti and Miami that caused the stacks, piles, heaps of mattresses to be gathered at the docks of the Miami River. This detail is a metonym that opens onto a field (the object becomes a field) constituted by the history of the Caribbean. The Moral Mattress of the Family discourse appeared in Barbara's memory of the forbidden childhood game, Perfume in the Black Hole. The field opened by the object at this level is that of Barbara's relationship with her father, engaging then with the same dynamic that interested Lacan in Joyce's life: the way that Joyce decided to use writing to prop up the failure of the Name-of-the-Father in his "family romance."

The Anagogical Mattress appears in the figure used by Lacan to explain the formation of an ideological field around a quilting point or upholstery button. "The French term '*point de capiton*' literally designates an upholstery button, the analogy being that just as upholstery buttons are places where 'the mattress-maker's needle has worked hard to prevent a shapeless mass of stuffing from moving too freely about,' so the 'points de capiton' are points at which 'signified and signifier are knotted together ... The 'point de capiton' is thus the point in the signifying chain at which 'the signifier stops the otherwise endless movement of the signification' and produces the necessary illusion of a fixed meaning."[24] Lacan's theory of the human subject (representing metonymically the group of French poststructuralists) provides our cosmology, that we apply in turn to problems in the civic sphere.

The uncanny correspondence of these levels was confirmed as a recognition by the further fact that Linda McDonald's father (denizens of Skeeversville) was an upholsterer by trade (the Black Hole game was played in the McDonald's basement). This convergence of threads or narratives produces the experience of a dense moment. Belatedly, through Revelle, the mattresses led the theoria to an experience of eureka, if not yet satori.

What about the Allegorical Mattress; how does it appear in the Entertainment discourse? It is evoked in a typical episode of *Miami Vice*. The pattern already in place suggests a "bedroom drama," the seductive role of the femme fatale in the noir genre, which in practice (significantly, in our context) was erased from the *Miami Vice* formula (there was no such position in the situation). Another possibility was available in the film that initiated the "zombie movie"—*White Zombie*—in which a white woman is ensnared in the magic rituals of Voodoo. Most immediately, however, the tourist discourse gives pride of place to the bed. The two most memorialised destinations are battlefields and bedrooms, according to Diller and Scofidio's *Back To The Front: Tourisms Of War*.

The bed and bedroom are a place and position—a commonplace, a topos—in the mode of wisdom as well. "The bedroom I will talk about," Mary Carruthers states, explaining

[24] Dylan Evans, *An Introductory Dictionary of Lacanian Psychoanalysis* (New York: Routledge, 1996) 149.

that the standard posture associated with meditation was that of lying prostrate and weeping, "is what both the Romans and the medieval monks called 'thalamus' or 'cubiculum.' The monks associated it most often with the bridal chamber of the Song of Songs. And while all the sexual associations of fertility and fruitfulness resonate in this bedroom mystery, its goal is cognitive creation, and its matrix is the secret places of one's own mind, the matters secreted away in the inventory of memory, stored and recalled, collated and gathered up, by the 'mystery' or craft of mnemotechnical invention."[25] The goal of the consultation, after all, is to translate the River zone into a mnemonic scene.

13. *Select a Specific Public Policy Issue as the Target of the Consultation.*
[*Sublime Policy.*] This step should be initiated earlier in the process. One result of the tour of the problem site is a refinement of awareness of the policy issues imposed on the River. The mattresses scattered through the zone are symptoms of various activities and conditions with the status of "problem" targeted by a number of different government agencies, any one of which could be the focus of our consultation. Although "Crossroads" attunes the zone into a holistic category, settling on a specific policy issue further enhances the details and increase the "resolution" of the image. The larger deconstructive goal in any case is not to select among "problems" but to cut across this framing with a different categorisation system altogether.

A difference between an inventional agency such as the emerAgency and a conventional agency is that the nature of the object addressed is different. In the order of knowledge objects are categorised and made intelligible by means of concepts, by identifying and enumerating attributes and properties of the things in question, according to the basic assumption of

[25] Mary Carruthers, *The Craft of Thought: Meditation, Rhetoric, and the Making of Images, 400-1200* (New York: Cambridge, 1998) 171.

Western metaphysics. Objects of belief, in contrast, are not "substantial" but exist solely as relations, as pure difference without properties or attributes. Certainly the empirical object, the one covered by concepts with attributes, is present to belief, but some extra quality "X" enters into the object that is more than it, marking its participation in a fantasy. The FRE "mattress" was in a block with "Haitians," intelligible not through its attributes but through a relationship. Moreover, this "meaning" is not intended or communicated, but emerges in the field of relationships specific to a given person (the emerAgent). A fantasy object may not even be perceived apart from the disturbance of desire associated with it. This experience is related to "fetish," of which the commodity is one, according to Marx, so in principle the operations of desire and drive are familiar enough in everyday life. A theory important in our methodological hybrid—critical divination—was (poststructural) psychoanalysis, if not for its clinical claims, then for its status as a logic that is at once the end of literacy and the beginning of electracy.

The Mattress shows how an image becomes "categorical." At the micro level of form and medium of photographic recording, a third meaning is to digital recording what the pattern of words relating to a concept was to alphabetic recording (such as the variations on "dike"—justice—noticed by the Classical Greeks who abstracted the first concept out of the oral epics). That a "bed" may demonstrate a metaphysics we know from Plato's discussion at the heart of his great dialogue on justice, the *Republic*. There are three beds in his "Realism": the real bed is the Form created by god; the actual bed is the copy made from this Form (idea) by a craftsman; an image of the actual bed appearing in a work of art (mimesis) is furthest removed from the real bed. Greek metaphysics does not account for the fantasy bed triggered by the photographed mattress in "Crossroads."

[*"Objectity."*] This mattress with the X in it more than it is a different sort of object, one that Lacan called the *"objet (a)"* (small a, *"autre"*). As Jacques-Alain Miller explained, the object (a) falls outside the range of ontology, which "tells a priori what can be said about objects," based on the categories, a sorting into kinds based on what features or properties objects may share.

> But when we speak of object "a," we speak of another objectivity—let's say of another "objectity," an objectity that is not summoned opposite the subject of representation … However, this new objectity is such that one cannot avoid experiencing it. It is an object articulated not to the subject but to its division, to a subject that does not represent to itself the objects of the world but that is itself represented. For this reason, we cannot say that the structure of this object is identical to that of the "énoncé" [statement]. There is no specificity of the object in the Other, where nonetheless, the object "a" does not dissolve. It escapes categories because it does not have the same structure as the statement. By using the medieval reference re-actualised by Yankelevich, we can say that here it is a matter of a "quod," in the sense of difference between "quodity" and "quidity." We could also say that it is a question of the difference between existence and essence, or something that there is, but the essence of which one cannot define in the Other. One can say that it is—that is, "quodity"— but one cannot say what it is. There we have a kind of paradox of the "quod": something exists but without "quid."[26]

[*Hole-ism (holEism).*] The Mattress looked back at us; delivered its belated blow, the punctum, producing an effect best described as "uncanny" (something unfamiliar in that we have never seen it before, is nonetheless recognised as familiar). As Freud said, in the uncanny something that should have remained secret has come to light. Breton spoke of the uncanny

---

26 Jacques-Alain Miller, "Extimité," *Lacanian Theory of Discourse: Subject, Structure and Society*, eds. Mark Bracher, Marshall Alcorn, Ronald Corthell and Francoise Massardier-Kennedy (New York: New York University Press, 1994) 82-83.

as something "troubling." *Trou*ble. The real, in Lacan's pun ("trou" = "hole") is "traumatic."[27] In the Creole dimension of the method such effects are explained in terms of magic. This effect happens in the real. The satori Barthes spoke of, however, will not occur without further collaborative work. For now we have the fact that the theoria recognised the Mattress.

[*The Thing.*] This "thing" is "das Ding" in theory—the object of desire (the object-cause-of-desire): Mattress. "The pleasure principle is the law which maintains the subject at a certain distance from the Thing, making the subject circle round it without ever attaining it."[28] The Lacanian graph showing the triangular path of the drive around the "hole" or void of jouissance could be imposed on the river as a map for a psychogeography. The Thing or object (a) in terms of categorisation has the effect of a "strange attractor," being some part of the scene that becomes, temporarily, a point of order and coherence of the whole (hole).

Such traumatic kernels/voids are that around which the Symbolic order circulates. The holes found in the Tequesta Indian site excavated by the developers at the mouth of the Miami River uncannily refer to the importance of the hole (which is holism with a difference—addressing the silent "we" of "whole": w/hol/e). "Crossroads" grasps the river zone not as a whole, but as a hole: hence the neologism "holEism" to name the peculiar way of gathering. "One learns about the whole from the hole." And we should add, "one learns about the block from the block. Psychoanalysis uses topology to show the hole of the subject."

[*The Shipwreck Thing.*] Žižek identified the sinking of the Titanic as exemplary of the traumatic Thing, which accounts for the fascination of the wreck/wreckage. "The symptom is conceived

27 Hal Foster, *The Return of the Real: The Avant-Garde at the End of the Century* (Cambridge, Mass.: MIT Press, 1996) 136.
28 Evans, *An Introductory Dictionary of Lacanian Psychoanalysis*, 205.

as a real kernel of enjoyment, which persists as a surplus and returns through all attempts to domesticate it, to gentrify it (if we may be permitted to use this term adapted to designate strategies to domesticate the slums as 'symptoms' of our cities), to dissolve it by means of explication, of putting-into-words its meaning."[29] The zone as place and as category resisted the gentrification or reduction of the extra X that disturbed the policy makers and seemed to be the matter of what was the matter. The Thing for us shifted a series of Haitian boats, from nightscreams and the Rose-Marie Express that initiated our sense of obligation, to the trader God-Is-Able that produced the feeling of recognition; from the smuggling of aliens to the market in used goods. Used. Goods. (One has to listen with the third ear). Žižek's analogy suggests that no amount of empirical solutions can "fix" the zone, since the zone is in us, is extimate. The "cause" of zone problems, that is, is "non-local." The switch point, the swivel, the twist in the möbius band, the "lip" of the Klein Bottle, is the Mattress (in this reading, attuning this situation). Here was the zone's preliminary response to the querent. The zone says you are already fixed: in a fix. The fix is in.

The mattress pattern focused our attention on the Haitian trading vessels affected by the Caribbean Code safety policy.

14. *Look for the sublime dimension of a public policy issue.*
The consultation looks for the sublime dimension of any public policy problem (such as the policies of the Caribbean Code or the Miami River Planning Commission). The point of entry is that order of "feeling" associated with the family of "recognition." "The logic at work in the experience of the dynamical sublime is therefore as follows: true, I may be powerless in face of the raging forces of nature, a tiny particle of dust thrown around by wind and sea, yet all this fury of nature pales in comparison with the absolute pressure exerted on me

[29] Slavoj Žižek, *The Sublime Object of Ideology* (New York: Verso, 1989) 69.

by the superego, which humiliates me and compels me to act contrary to my fundamental interests!"[30]

The scene of "Crossroads" is promoted in our report to this same status (a scene become iconic of a theory—a picture theory). One purpose of the testimonial is to give access to this experience of the sublime, to make it legible to citizens and in the public schools as a force—to map the outline of the ethical obligation felt within by means of the "disaster" investigated outside. In electrate metaphysics, the accident is essential. The Miami River in me. The measure of my attunement, how things are with me (in us) is to be inferred from the *trou*bles of the river.

[*Middle Voice (Responsibility).*] The attunement happens only through an act of recognition in which the consultant takes personal responsibility for the external scene that reveals in a flash that she has "been there before." It is the effect of the middle voice, of reflexive agency. The theoria report takes the form of a metaphor, or metonym (is figural). The poetic method of research—the tuning—depends upon such recognitions. The rewriting of the sublime formula has to be modified to accommodate the traumatic nature of the mediated disaster. The River does not "express" something I already felt, but reveals a correspondence between subject and object. "True, I may be powerless to do anything about the condition of these Haitians, yet their difficulties figure and reveal to me the pressure of the obligation that otherwise I am unable to feel."
15. Make a metaphor joining the personal domain of the burning question with the policy problem of the zone.
The Mattress opened the field of Haitian shipping and led us to focus on the story of the impounded traders, caught in the "safety net" of the Caribbean Code. The connection came through Barbara's tuning. Prompted by the Mattress, she recognised (in an illumination) the relevance of Ron's (her

---

[30] Slavoj Žižek, "A Hair of the Dog that Bit You," *Lacanian Theory of Discourse*, 51.

partner's) biography to the inquiry—that at one time he served in the Coast Guard. This coincidence constituted a "lucky find" whose relevance in retrospect seemed obvious. Revelle recognised in the full sense of the "sublime object" that her story with Ron, or the feeling that she got from being an actor in this story, found its voice, its mood, in the situation of the Haitians. A mapping between the levels (Literal-Moral) turned up a block (in Lyotard's sense) of correspondences, including her identification as a fifty-something woman with the old ships no longer considered to be economically viable. In answer to her burning question ("should I leave this love relationship?") the zone showed her an impounded boat. The mystory functions as a map to link this scene with other images, to dialectise or put the subject in motion through the popcycle. As in any divination, the action that follows from the answer is open to interpretation by the querent. The key point for category formation is that the classifying feature is not "in" the image. Rather, as in the mnemonic practice of meditation, the image is a cue, a reminder whose "auratic" power is due to the network of associations that it calls to mind.

[*The Irreparable Impoundment.*] The consultation produced an analogy: Barbara's relationship with Ron is like the relationship of the Haitians with the Coast Guard. Here is the attunement. How do things stand with me? I am (we are) impounded. At the anagogical level it was easy to see that the impounded circumstances of the Haitians connected with the psychoanalytic impasse that marks the interruption of the unconscious in the smooth running of daily business. The problem or *trou*ble isolated by the policy decision (the Safety operation) was the visible dimension of trauma that extends into several other dimensions that resist both representation and repair. Specifically, Lacan's maxim that "there is no sexual relation" suggests that the impasse is "irreparable." As Agamben said about the irreparable condition of life, the world (the catastrophe) is the same whether one's state of mind is sad or happy. Uncannily, the image emerging out of the theoria resonated with the images of spleen inherited from Paris. We had come upon a scene, a screen, of repression, characterised in the theory as an experience of hopeless deadlock. A pattern arose (the point is worth repeating) linking Miami with Baudelaire's Paris and Joyce's Dublin: paralysed cities. Are we still so modern?

John Craig Freeman, still frame from *Imaging Place*. Ground level, navigable scene from North West 17th Avenue on the Miami River, 2004.

[*The Black Hole.*] Moments of "objective chance" that give rise to the uncanny acquire their power because they expose a repressed desire. The impasse of the subject's condition is evoked in the very use of knot topologies in Lacan's theory. We are bound and tied up in knots. The "subject" is not a "thing" but a trajectory, however, a path, a propensity, movement along a chain in which one link, or one signifier, is missing (expelled to the outside). Such is the inner path we follow with our geographical movements (psychogeography). During analysis, a patient runs up against a "master signifier," which "covers the subject's lack." This signifier is a placeholder of the "letter" (the sinthome is the set of such letters). The name of Barbara's childhood game recurs in a commentator's description of the symptom/sinthome. "These metonymic ruins mark the place of an absence the way extraordinarily strong blasts of energy radiate out from the spot where a black hole is swallowing up matter and energy from the universe. In the case of symptoms, including those produced by the transference-neurosis, the black hole is that of the unique being of the subject."[31]

PART FOUR: DRAWING CONCLUSIONS

16. *Extend the metaphor by searching the disciplinary knowledge base for a match with the zone attunement.*

[*Aporia*.] The experience of recognition passed from the uncanny to eureka when we "dialectised" the impounded Haitians and the impasse of Barbara and Ron with Jacques Derrida's account of aporia (blocking the popcycle discourses of Family, History, and Career). At this point the zone not only answered Barbara's burning question, and revealed the attunement of the zone, but gave guidance at a theoretical level regarding policy formation. The Haitians impounded on the Miami River constitute a mise-en-scène of a theory. This scene shows both a specific answer to the official question of the inquiry (what is to be done about the image crisis?), and a theoretical answer to the question of method as such in electracy.

Our understanding as we approach the internet project is that the tour of a problem engages the basic metaphor of "method," referring to a way or path. The figurative passage through the steps of method and the following of hyperlinks online were to be coordinated by Revelle's literal drifting through the zone. In the Greek tradition Philosophy began with

---

[31] Gilbert Chaitlin, *Rhetoric and Culture in Lacan* (Cambridge: Cambridge University Press, 1994) 199.

a sense of wonder growing from an initial difficulty (aporia) resulting from conflicting arguments. The initial state of ignorance with respect to this difficulty was compared by Aristotle to a man in chains (translations of aporia include "difficulty, question, problem, with no way out").[32] The response to the aporia was the application of "method"—an exploration of various "routes," "diaporia," a canvassing of previous opinions, leading to a proof, or solution, "euphoria, lysis, a loosening of the chains," which is the heart of the philosophical procedure. "Method" as a concept and practice (invented by Plato in *Phaedrus*) is abstracted from a mise en scene of following a path.

In deconstructive consulting the problem-solution approach to method is not replaced but is put in tension with its unthought other —the pair "aporia-impossibility." The theoria tours the zone with this sense of both "way" and "no-way" (opposition not as a static dualism but as a dynamising generator).

> What was going to be at stake in this word [aporia] was the "not knowing where to go." It had to be a matter of the nonpassage, or rather from the experience of the nonpassage, the experience of what happens and is fascinating in this nonpassage, paralysing us in this separation in a way that is not necessarily negative: before a door, a threshold, a border, a line, or simply the edge or the approach of the other as such. It should be a matter of what, in sum, appears to block our way or to separate us in the very place where it would no longer be possible to constitute a problem, a project, or a projection, that is, at the point where the very project or the problematic task becomes impossible and where we are exposed, absolutely without protection, without problem, and without prosthesis, without possible substitution, singularly exposed in our absolute and absolutely naked uniqueness, that is to say, disarmed, delivered to the other, incapable even of sheltering

[32] Horst Peters, *Platons Dialog* Lysis. *Ein unlösbares Rätsel?* (Frankfurt a.M.: Prismata, 2001) 22.

ourselves behind what could still protect the interiority of a secret.[33]

The mapping between "Crossroads" (the photograph and its title) and aporia constituted a new understanding of how to go on, in that it showed the impasse as threshold. The first lesson was that the explanatory effect of this figure moved first from the image to the theory: the deconstructive aporia became intelligible in the context of a social, lived embodiment of an aporetic condition of the river. The crossroads X or chiasm served Derrida from the beginning as a figure of a doubling and crossing at work in language and history. The X does not symbolise the unknown, he said, but is "a kind of fork (the series 'crossroads, quadrifurcum, grid, trellis, key, etc.') that is moreover, unequal, one of the points extending its range further than the other: this is the figure of the double gesture, the intersection."[34]

Aporia is for the inventional consultant what problem is for the conventional one. These two "ways" are not oppositional but complementary. A tension between problem and aporia is produced by refusing the calculative, analytical loosening of the bonds of contradiction, and instead intensifying and multiplying them. "Method" as metaphor is the passage, way, or path (odos, methodos, Weg) from problem to solution. The deconstruction of consulting works precisely on this metaphorical dimension. The point of departure of articulating this difference with method is to experience the difficulty itself as such, to witness it and meditate with it. The function of the choral image ("Crossroads" in this case) is to evoke this feeling.

> The question of knowing what it means "to experience the aporia," indeed to put into operation the aporia, remains. It is not necessarily a failure or a simple paralysis, but sterile

---

[33] Jacques Derrida, *Aporias*, trans. Thomas Dutoit (Stanford : Stanford University Press, 1993) 12.

[34] Derrida cited in Rodolphe Gasché, *The Tain of the Mirror: Derrida and the Philosophy of Reflection* (Cambridge, Mass.: Harvard University Press, 1986) 172.

negativity of the impasse. It is neither stopping at it nor overcoming it. (When someone suggests to you a solution for escaping an impasse, you can be almost sure that he is ceasing to understand, assuming that he had understood anything up to that point). Does one then pass through this aporia? Or is one immobilised before the threshold, to the point of having to turn around and seek out another way, the way without method or outlet of a Holzweg or a turning that could turn the aporia—all such possibilities of wandering?[35]

"Crossroads" gives not a solution to but an image of aporia, and in so doing "figures" the experience, thus composing a map. It is just such a map that is needed in order to tour a problem.

17. *Draw policy conclusions from the picture theory.*
The no-way of aporia is not an end or stopping point of thought but the opening of another way that may be for electracy what method was for literacy.

[*Learning From New Orleans.*] The scene of impasse does not call for answers, but for testimony at this preliminary stage. Our policy issue concerned "Haitian traders." In the frame of the emerAgency (*Problems B Us*), what do we make of this "answer" to our question (how do things stand with us)? At the limits or borders of the solutions supplied "up until now" by the Western tradition with respect to democracy and every other question, our consultation with the River revealed that we have been overlooking a resource. What is this Haitian-in-me? We are in any case no longer "merely" jewgreek, but are jewgreekcreole. What does this Creole dimension give us to work with? The continuing syncretism of civilisations is well underway and has already accomplished much. The Miami River is haunted by a New Orleans precedent that shows a

---

[35] Derrida, *Aporias*, 33.

possibility. The Haitian guests arriving in Florida, dead or alive, are harbingers of what we already will have become.

[*Syllojazz.*] "The questions of how Haitian Voodoo came to the continental United States, and the question of why jazz originated in New Orleans, are in fact parts of the same question. Jazz and rock 'n roll would evolve from Voodoo, carrying within them the metaphysical antidote that would aid many a twentieth-century Westerner from both the ravages of the mind-body split codified by Christianism, and the onslaught of technology. The twentieth century would dance as no other had, and, through that dance, secrets would be passed."[36] Jazz is exemplary for us of "possibility," the modality of "perhaps" organising the temporality of the event. What happened in music may continue in consulting and in every other discourse and institution, as "we" become jewgreekcreole. Syllogism may become syllojazz.

[*Impoundment Blues.*] The image tuning the zone is that of an impounded Haitian boat, piled high with its cargo of used mattresses. The image works categorically by means of emotion in the profound sense of atmosphere or mood. A function of this image as part of the deconstruction of method is to interrupt and supplement the instrumental mood of "anomaly" and "solution." Conventional consulting works in a kind of booster mood of progress. Inventional consultants, rather, frame problems in the mood of "the blues." The individual tuning of a problem zone specifies the image within this frame. To open "problem" with its empirical state of mind to the realm of Arts and Letters in this syncretic frame is to integrate the practical politics of public policy formation with the emotional wisdom of the Afro-Caribbean musical and dance traditions (related with the syncretic religious traditions of the Black Atlantic) whose different names in different regions and

[36] Michael Ventura, "Hear That Long Snake Moan," *Shadow Dancing in the USA* (Los Angeles: Tarcher, 1985) 120.

nations reflect the different nuances of creolisation that have occurred historically.

In the United States, the creolisation of the Judeo-Christian-Greco-Roman West with the Black Atlantic has developed in the mood of blues (the related mood in Brazil, for example, is the Samba feeling of "saudade"). The emerAgency goal is to fashion a consulting practice from the lessons of "blutopia," combining the two major impulses of African-American music: "a utopian impulse, evident in the creation of imagined places (Promised Lands), and the impulse to remember, to bear witness, which James Baldwin relates to the particular history of slavery" (Lock, 1999: 3). "Blues" is not feeling "bad," but what you do about bad feelings.

I have built a cultural narrative about the transformation of Western consciousness through African-American music by focusing on colour and alchemy. In *Shadow Dancing in the USA* (1985), Michael Ventura arrived at many of the same conclusions by constructing a historical narrative about jazz and rock 'n 'roll that focused on a return to the body through the "loa" or spirit possession of the musician and listener/dancer. The bluesmen are the secular carriers of the Hoodoo or Voodoo religion which is a hybrid of traditional West African religions and Christianity. As such, bluesmen and women tend to spirit and psyche in a manner handed down from Africa to Hoodoo; spirit possession. Where the Northern soul, from shaman to Christian priest, operates dissociatively, leaving the body to travel the spirit world, the African priest, the Hoodoo conjurer, and the bluesmen ask the "loa" to enter bodies and possess them. It is through this possession that the "loa" is known and expressed ... Blues lyrics have tremendous breadth, within which are two core streams, depression and libido. The depressive quality of the blues is the most recognisable to the majority of people, an example of which is the lament for being "done wrong" by a lover. But the blues is also highly sexual and at times exuberant. There are many "happy" blues about good time fun, including the joys of food and dance. The blues is about the passions of the flesh. Where the pathological Western mind tended to create dirty movies out of this blue, blacks turned these libidinous hurricanes into the huge body of art called the blues … It is fascinating to note that in addition to the lyric content of the blues, its music and performance practices also worked to transform the dissociative consciousness. Harmonically, the blues is based on the tritone interval which is considered the most dissonant of all intervals and thus full of tension. In Renaissance times this interval was known as the "Diabolus en musica" and for a time its use in performance was actually illegal. In the blues almost every chord contains the tritone, even the tonic. The problem of union of the opposites is managed in the blues by permeating the music with the tension of the tritone. The Christian Devil is everywhere, the dream of salvation nowhere.[37]

[*I'm Not Stuck; I'm Dancing.*] The tension between problem and aporia suggests the need to identify a "movement" that is for event what method (the road or path, whether clear or blocked) is for concept. The metaphor for aporia as "way" comes from the Afro-Caribbean scene for which the Haitian harbingers are a metonym. Referring to the "places of aporia in which I have found myself regularly tied up, indeed, paralysed," Derrida explained that he "was then trying to move not against or out of the impasse but, in another way, according to another thinking of the aporia, one perhaps more enduring."[38] The idiom of this alternative way is the phrase "il y va d'un certain pas [it involves a certain step/not; he goes along at a certain pace]."[39] This deconstructive "step" remains open to creolisation. Our consultation returns to the metaphorical root of "method" to imagine this jewgreekcreole state of mind as a "certain way of walking." Our method will emerge from the blocking of these two steps (French theory and Creole practice).

[37] Stephen Diggs, "Alchemy of the Blues," *Spring: A Journal of Archetypes and Culture*, 61 (1997).
[38] Derrida, *Aporias*, 13.
[39] Derrida, *Aporias*, 6.

Barbara Jo Revelle, from *Miami River Chora*

18. *Make an impossible recommendation.*

To shift the Miami River from the category of problem to that of
aporia, to look not for its solution but for that in it which is
impossible for us, is the advice—the direction for further work
on the new consultancy—that came out of our eureka. The
impossible reveals the metaphysical border, the negative
dimension of our identity. The zombie is the upholstery tack in
the mattress of the procrustean bed that ideology made for me,
and that I am lying in. What does this fact about my situation
make impossible? One consequence of staying on the side of
aporia was to realise that the Haitians represented not a
problem that could be solved, but a state of mind for rethinking
all problems, and "problem" as such. The generalisability of
this discovery remains to be tested: The problem is the solution
(the outside is inside).

The Miami River is a port, a crossroads, an interface joining
North and South America, as much a part of the Caribbean
basin as it is of the United States (a lounge in the Orlando
airport is named "the Floribbean"). The Haitians waiting on

their impounded, burned, substandard, sinking, mortgaged, repossessed boats, with their used cargoes collected in warehouses that have been looted, vandalised, rain-damaged, scattered, auctioned off, given away, these temporary denizens of the river, these guests, show and reveal, give the location of the port as door, passageway, and opportunity. The goal of the theoria is to find this door in a zone. It will always be blocked, and that is how one finds it (but this claim is what remains to be replicated or falsified by other theorias).

> "Opportunity" comes from the Latin "*porta*," which is an "entrance" or "passage through." The word is associated with doors and entranceways (portal, porch, portico), and an "*opportunus*," then, is what offers an opening, or what stands before an opening, ready to go through. For the Romans, a "*porta fenestella*" was a special opening that allowed Fortune to enter. The Greek root is "*poros*," which is a passageway for ships but also any passageway, including one through the skin, that is, a pore. "*Poroi*" are all the passages that allow fluids to flow in and out of the body. A pore, a portal, a doorway, a nick in time, a gap in the screen, a looseness in the weave — these are all opportunities in the ancient sense. Each being in the world must find the set of opportunities fitted to its nature.[40]

As Lewis Hyde elaborates, tricksters hang around "poroi" and are involved in both closing and opening the way. "Kairos" is the name for that hypericon of opportunity, the timing of shooting the shuttle through the rising and falling warp threads. Hyde links "poros" and "kairos" to the "lucky find." "The fabric of social and spiritual life contains, shapes , and binds our lives; a lucky find tears a hole in the cloth so that we can slip free … Against all this — against the nets of reciprocity, the grid of ethics, the weave of fate — we have the find which is a lucky break, a hole in the surrounding cloth. The lucky find is an opportunity, a pore or penetrable opening in an otherwise

---

40 Hyde, *Trickster Makes this World*, 46.

closed design."[41] Hyde's interest in the trickster stories found throughout the world is the common theme they express regarding the importance of maintaining a balance between the essential and the accidental.

[*The General Accidental.*] Hyde calls attention to the inadequacy of Aristotle's codification of categories (a major step in the invention of the "concept," and of metaphysics itself). "In the *Categories*, Aristotle argued that we ought to be able to look at any group of things, say 'apples' or 'human beings' or 'jazz recordings,' and determine what is essential to membership in the category and what isn't … Accidentals are present by chance, essentials by design. Accidentals are changeable and shifting; essentials are stable. The real significance of a thing lies with its essences, not with its accidents."[42] The trickster tradition counters this preference given to essences. The ability to work with contingency constitutes the special craft of the trickster and points to a paradox of image categories.

[*Sublime Hospitality.*] That tourism is so intimately involved with the hospitality industry makes it a good site for testing the capacity of Entertainment as the institution supporting the emergence of electracy. Derrida's introduction of the language of hospitality into the history of democracy demonstrates the practicality of thinking tourism and theory together (theoria). The history of Western thought from Aristotle to the present has theorised political gathering into communities by means of the logic of exemplarity, and the exemplum for political relationship is friendship. The model includes an oppositional interdependency between the concepts of friend and enemy (hence politics has been condemned to melodrama). The friends have always been conceived of as men, specifically as brothers, with the relationship generalised and made universal

---

41 Hyde, *Trickster Makes this World*, 133.
42 Hyde, *Trickster Makes this World*, 97.

historically in the "fraternity" of the French Revolution (the Rights of Man).

Barbara Jo Revelle, from *Miami River Chora*

[*Welcome.*] A part of the effect of "trouvaille" in bringing Derrida into the block was his opening up certain pivot words (choral words), showing an affiliation between "river" and "arrivant"—a term that could be used to describe the Haitian boat people.

> What takes place with the aporia? What we are apprehending here concerning what takes place also touches upon the event as that which arrives at the river's shore ["*arrive à la rive*"], approaches the shore, or passes the edge—another way of happening and coming to pass by surpassing. All of these are possibilities of the "coming to pass" when it meets a limit … What is the event that most arrives? What is the arrivant that makes the event arrive? The new arrivant, this word can, indeed, mean the neutrality of that which arrives, but also the singularity of who arrives, he or she who comes, coming to be where s/he was not expected … and such is hospitality itself, hospitality toward the event. One does not expect the event of

254

whatever, of whoever comes, arrives , and crosses the
threshold—the immigrant, the emigrant, the guest, or the
stranger ... Such an arrivant affects the very experience of the
threshold, whose possibility he thus brings to light before one
even knows whether there has been an invitation, a call, a
nomination, or a promise.[43]

At the historical level it seemed that Derrida was describing the
Miami River itself as an embodiment of the problematic of
borders, classification, categories: the question of what is inside
and what is outside that is central to the experience of
epiphany, attunement, extimacy, goes to the heart of Western
metaphysics. The denizens of the river are figures of the other,
are the arrivants (those who come), caught within this
problematic space or place of a frontier, limit, edge. Our own
destiny may be read (is revealed) in their "situation," and
epiphany is precisely the art of articulating situations, which
suggests that the anagogical dimension may be rendered
popularly through the allegory of the river. A tour of the
problem/aporia writes the hole of our situation (how things are
with us). It is not that the fate of God-Is-Able replaces Derrida,
but that the juxtaposition (the combination of tourism and
theory) is mutually illuminating. The juxtaposition of the river
image and aporia constitutes a picture theory. What is revealed
is that "division," the way things are sorted into kinds at every
level and scale, is mutating now.

In the politics of hospitality the "enemy" is replaced by the
stranger, foreigner, immigrant, as figures of the other (but for a
generalised other who need not be literally foreign). The
exemplary relationship for thinking this post-conventional
democracy is the host/guest relationship. As one of the
commentators stated in the Ken Burns documentary on Jazz,
civilisation may be summed up in one word: "welcome." To
state his question Derrida formalised the aporetic sentence,
which in turn draws upon the rhetoric of negative theology, to

---

[43] Derrida, *Aporias*, 33.

evoke a thought of that which is still to come, absolutely, and therefore lacks concept, shape, or eidos. The question is formulated using the structure "X without X."

> The central question of this essay would be that of a friendship without hearth. Ultimately, a friendship without presence, without resemblance, without affinity, without analogy. Is an aneconomic friendship possible? Can there be any other friendship? Must there be another? Can one answer this question otherwise than with a "perhaps"—that is, by suspending in advance the very form of a "question," and the alliance of the "yes"—in order to think and to dream before them? And must not this reflection account for a certain end of Lysis, in its final leavetaking?[44]

The tourist situation, like every other intersubjective experience, must take into account as least three positions: host, guest, "parasite" (to exploit the French pun on "noise," the channel of communication between, unpacked by Michel Serres). The Haitian begins as noise. We know from block composition that each party circulates through all positions (actants), with each function equally important to the "economy." A quick adaptation of Derrida's X to our consultation (Florida tourism) might read: a hospitality industry without consumers. Applied to the policy question of the Caribbean Code, this formula proposes the suspension of the interdiction and boarding of Haitian vessels by the Coast Guard, to be replaced with the "boarding" of Haitians at city expense: "learn about boarding from boarding." Here we have one formulation of the impossible: a key to the city for everyone on the Rose-Marie Express. This proposal must be clarified, since it resonates with the one that Socrates made at his trial (*The Apology*), when given an opportunity to name an alternative to the death penalty, after being found guilty of impiety: "free maintenance at the state's expense" was what he

---

[44] Jacques Derrida, *Politics of Friendship*, trans. George Collins (London: Verso, 1997) 155.

deserved, he said. Nothing radical here, an alien might reply who has been housed in one of the detention centres for those arriving in Florida without proper documentation.

[*Guests' Dilemma.*] The various conventional problems addressed by Miami River policy (such as immigration) cumulatively evoke the problematic of democracy and its future in the apparatus of electracy. Derrida noted that the limits of the friend-enemy model of politics have been exposed by the decline of the Cold War. This context also answers those who doubt the potential of aporia as a guide for policy, since policy during the Cold War was guided by the paradox known as Prisoner's Dilemma. This dilemma (or aporia) which originated as a parlour game was at the heart of the invention of game theory by John von Neumann, and directed thinking about nuclear deterrence (Poudstone). Prisoner's Dilemma works best when the interests of the two parties are absolutely opposed, with each party pursuing its own interest at the expense of the other (not unlike the rules of dialectical argument formulated in Aristotle's *Topics*). In fact, the policy conclusion of this dilemma was "impossible" and never enacted (the odds favoured a nuclear first strike). The politics of the stranger, in contrast, puts the interests of the other first, without expectation of reciprocity. It remains to be seen what sort of policy might be entailed by the aporia of hospitality, but its impossibility in principle is nearly the inverse of Prisoner's Dilemma. "For unconditional hospitality to take place you have to accept the risk of the other coming and destroying the place, initiating a revolution, stealing everything, or killing everyone. That is the risk of pure hospitality and pure gift."[45] Pure gift, in other words, constitutes the impossible necessity of ethics. "Learn about the present from a present."

---

[45] Jacques Derrida, *Of Hospitality*, trans. Rachel Bowlby (Stanford: Stanford University Press, 2000) 71.

Barbara Jo Revelle, from *Miami River Chora*

[*My Friend, My Other (Miautre).*] The shift from a politics of friendship to one of hospitality suggests a name for the chora to be created in moving the zone to the internet, a name that will distinguish it from Miami and Myami alike. At the level of the signifier, a series unfolds (creolising French, Spanish, English) as follows: Miami, Mon Ami, Mi Amigo, My Friend, My Other, Mi Otro, Miautre. Deconstruction supplements the dialectical logic of problem solving with a poetic stylistics of echo, rhyme, rhythm, pun, paradox (the verbal art that supports the sinthome). Against the rule of "belonging" that enforces language as a shibboleth, deconstruction opens language to the Creole remainder, to heterogeneity, dreamwork, the obliqueness of literature. The original shibboleth was the name of a river. Judging by the way Americans pronounce "Notre Dame" (noter daym), "Miautre" will be pronounced "my-odour." In other words, Miautre is "funky." Or as the poets say, the ideogram does not follow a path but creates one as it unfolds in language ("inveniere"). A macaronic pun motivates the link between Miami and this deconstruction of a politics of friendship. If we accept the luck of this series joining the words to the themes of friendship (Mi Amigo, Mon Ami) we produce a name for the Miami River as chora: *Miauture* (my other)—a place to invent (virtually first of all) the politics of hospitality. At least we have a name for this virtual civic place, designed to avert the general accident of the internet (miautre.com). The work of testimonial, however, is not that of solutions but of witness. With Miautre, the virtual community has a chance to take place.

Andrew J. Mitchell

Torture & Photography: Abu Ghraib

Torture & Photography

In April of 2004 the CBS news show *60 Minutes II* broadcast images from the Abu Ghraib detention facility outside Baghdad. The images appeared in print a week later in an article by Seymour Hersh in *The New Yorker*. The prison which introduced the word "rape room" to the public imagination was operational again, though this time on the side of the Global War on Terror (GWOT). The photographs showed guards mishandling the detainees, physically, emotionally, and, given certain prescripts of Islam, spiritually. They are photographs of torture, the logical result of unrestricted political power over life and our entrance into the Information Age of digital technology.

President Bush's memorandum on the humane treatment of al Qaeda and Taliban detainees reveals the sovereign logic at work. After first accepting the legal conclusions of his administration that the Geneva Conventions do not apply to the conflict with al Qaeda and the Taliban, he nonetheless asserts that "As a matter of policy, the United States Armed Forces shall continue to treat detainees humanely and, to the extent appropriate and consistent with military necessity, in a manner consistent with the principles of Geneva."[1] As a result, the locus of the protections has shifted. The Geneva Conventions do not apply to the human *qua* human, but only according to the arbitrary and good will of the sovereign.

Technology, too, surrounds the events of Abu Ghraib, from the digital photographs themselves, transmitted half-way across the globe, to General Miller's goal of "a worldwide-integrated detainee database."[2] The Abu Ghraib photographs are, in a sense, the shadow of this goal. Technology has led us into the Information Age and it is hungry for the information that interrogation and torture deliver; it will not take "no" for an answer.

What follows is an attempt to make sense of the heaps of memos, facts, and photos surrounding Abu Ghraib. It is an inquiry into photography, torture, and the relations between them, a hope that somewhere we might be touched by humanity. These words are dedicated to the faces of the enemy and the ways in which those faces show themselves to the digital camera.

---

[1] Memorandum from George W. Bush, re: "Humane Treatment of al Qaeda and Taliban Detainees" (February 7, 2002), *The Torture Papers: The Road to Abu Ghraib*, eds. Karen J. Greenberg and Joshua L. Dratel (Cambridge: Cambridge University Press, 2005) 135.

[2] Report of MG Geoffrey D. Miller (September 13, 2003), Annex B: Information Technology Solutions, *Torture Papers*, 459.

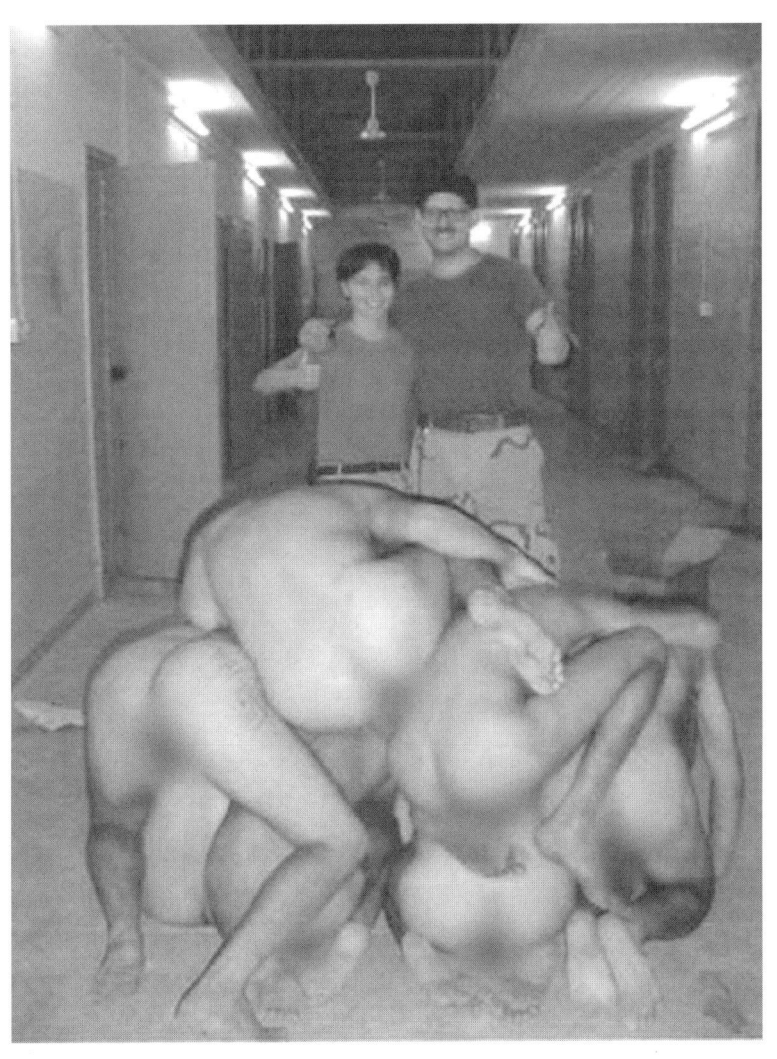

263

Prophylactics

The gloves call attention to the filth that they themselves created. The logic of this scenario can equally be applied to photography. Film separates the doer from the deed, *there is a doer* of the deed. But the gloves provide a film that allows us to touch the world without being touched. This is not a symmetrical relationship. We can touch the world in gloves, but we cannot be touched by it. One can always ask, did I do this? Was I the one who punched them down and shoved them into piles? I may have done it, but it did nothing to me, for it never touched me. This is a showing of thumbs and holes, where the doers do, but are not touched, and where what is done should not be seen.

Does the camera's film allow us to touch the world without being touched? It certainly allows us to accumulate and pile up our (lived) experiences of the world. Lived-experience (*Erlebnis*) is always denigrated in favour of the transformative experience of *Erfahrung*. But the same life who lives its experiences makes the journey of *Erfahrung*. Does the camera record *Erfahrungen* or only the *Erlebnis*? Does life itself bear an inherent political determination, which is what we understand by "rights," or is humanity something only arrived at along the path of righteousness? How are we touched by film?

The questions which the photographs from Abu Ghraib raise are not simply questions about the representation of torture, nor even simply about the use of photography and representation from within torture as such. What is troubling in these digital photographs from Abu Ghraib are the questions they raise concerning a world already transformed into so many piled bodies, a world that can only reveal itself as tortured, and this by the very technology that has travelled out from Iraq and into the wired homes of America to bring us these insistent images of cruelty and abuse. The camera calls attention to the filth that it itself creates. The insistence with which it does so is troubling. It is not that we are troubled by the demand to respond which emanates from these images, but that the demand to respond is precisely the order of the interrogator to the victim he tortures. The camera wears its gloves, too. As we see in this image, the arseholes are all blurred.

266

Spectator Moralist

Photography is inherently a conservative enterprise. The photographer, according to Susan Sontag's *On Photography*, is interested in maintaining the status quo, "it is a way of at least tacitly, often explicitly, encouraging whatever is going on to keep on happening."[3] The photographer immortalises the passing moment and aesthetically delivers it to eternity, a static realm where all is reconciled and nothing is to be done. "To take a picture is to have an interest in things as they are," Sontag writes, "including, when that is the interest, another person's pain or misfortune."[4]

In fact, due to its place within our consumer culture where a free market has been declared upon our attention, photography leads to an atrophy of our moral sense. "Things as they are" must always get worse. The images that battle for our attention strike us with ever increasing force, ever more pain-fully, regardless of our response. Our attenuated attention span demands it, they say. Sontag finds a "leading tendency of high art in capitalist countries" to be "to suppress, or at least reduce, moral and sensory queasiness."[5] Photography cannot help but do this when left unsupervised in such a system.

While we might object that photographs do distress us, do touch us, the photograph itself will cancel this distress en route to eternity. Photographs "can and do distress. But the aestheticising tendency of photography is such that the medium which conveys distress ends by neutralising it."[6] It neutralises our distress by bringing it to a standstill, by making the world stand over against us. This distance brings an indifference. We are passive before images that imprison reality. In her last book, *Regarding the Pain of Others*, Sontag expresses this in terms of a supposed link between ourselves and those who suffer in the photograph, "So far as we feel

3 Susan Sontag, *On Photography* (New York: Farrar, Strauss and Giroux, 1973) 12.
4 Sontag, *On Photography*, 12.
5 Sontag, *On Photography*, 40.
6 Sontag, *On Photography*, 109.

sympathy," she writes, "we feel we are not accomplices to what caused the suffering. Our sympathy proclaims our innocence as well as our impotence."[7]

The photograph demands our sympathy at the very moment that it betrays our trust. Nothing will ever satisfy its relentless demands and enjoinders. We are pummelled by images.

---

[7] Susan Sontag, *Regarding the Pain of Others* (New York: Farrar, Strauss and Giroux, 2003) 102.

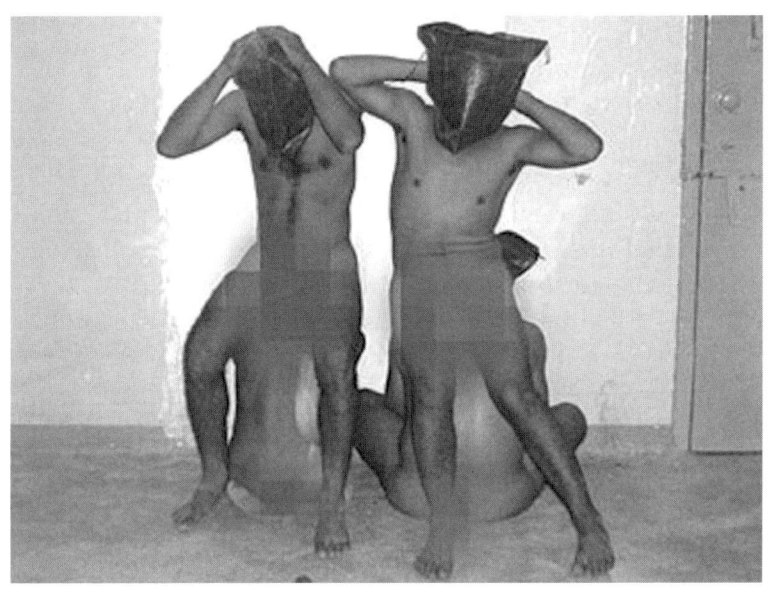

Torture Poses

"When they torture him they took gloves and they beat his dick and testicles with the gloves. soldier came and put electrical wires on my fingers and toes and on my penis and I had a bag over my head. And he took the hood off and he was describing some poses he wanted me to do. they pushed the first one on top of the others to look like they are gay and when they refused, Grainer beat them up until they put them on top of each other and they took pictures of them. They started to take photographs as if it was a porn movie.

And they treated us like animals not humans. They forced me to eat pork and put liquor in my mouth. They ordered me to curse Islam and because they started to hit my broken leg, I cursed my religion. They ordered me to thank Jesus that I'm alive. And I did what they ordered me. This is against my belief.

They started torturing them and taking pictures and they were enjoying that. Grainer was putting the phosphoric light up his ass. Then when I heard the screaming I climbed the door because on top it wasn't covered and I saw [name blacked out], who was wearing the military uniform putting his dick in the little kid's ass. And the female soldier was taking pictures. They tied him to the bed and they were inserted the phosphoric light in his ass and he was yelling for God's help.

I was trying to kill myself but I didn't have any way of doing it. They were taking pictures and writing on our asses. I couldn't read his name because he put tape over his name. No one showed us mercy. They forced me to slap him on the face, but I refused cause he is my friend. And they were taking pictures of me during all these instances. And everyone was taking pictures of this whole thing with cameras. this night which we felt like 1000 nights."[8]

---

[8] Amalgam of detainee deposition statements as obtained by *The Washington Post* and reprinted in Mark Danner, *Torture and Truth: America, Abu Ghraib, and the War on Terror* (New York: New York Review Books, 2004) 225-248.

The camera is not an accidental partner to this torture. Photography stages the world and contorts it into poses. It makes the world homo-sexual, making of everything it captures the same representational image at the disposal of a sadistic delight in objectification. Photography is unrelenting and merciless, taking pictures of the most inhumane moments, shining its light where no one wishes to be seen or to see.

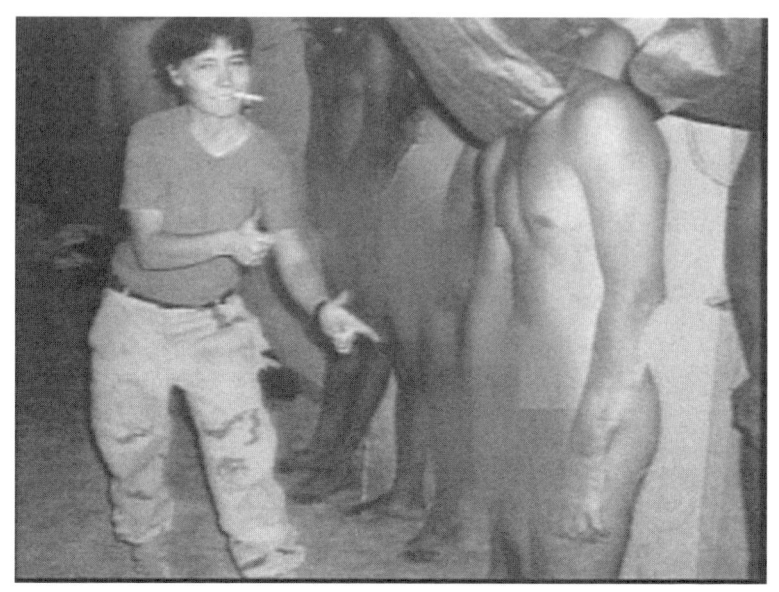

272

Speaking the Truth and Showing the Truth

What distinguishes the image of torture from the language of it? Which is better able to indicate the thing itself, to point into the obscurities of pain, while maintaining the cool of the Brechtian observer, cigar—or cigarette—firmly in cheek? Does either possess a relation to pain other than the smugly deictic? In her book, *The Body in Pain*, Elaine Scarry considers the relationship between pain and language as encountered in torture. From the very outset, however, Scarry opposes the physical reality of the body to the cultural world of the mind. But in this antagonism, the photograph is able to interpose itself.

To the physical body that feels pain is opposed the world of language, culture, meaning; to the body Scarry opposes the world itself. Consequently, the body becomes a headless body and the head's connection to that body is hidden from it. The opposite of the world's expansion, the body is the most extreme point of contraction and deflation of the world. The body is what dangles outside the world. To address pain, therefore, Scarry has to set it at odds with language. Her whole book rests on this, "Physical pain does not simply resist language but actively destroys it, bringing about an immediate reversion to a state anterior to language, to the sounds and cries a human being makes before language is learned."[9] Pain is always at the other side of language.

The photograph is preternaturally silent. Scarry notes that the silence one finds in images of screams, "coincides with the way in which pain engulfs the one in pain but remains unsensed by anyone else."[10] This silence is likewise something that the image shares with the body, "only in silence do the edges of the self become coterminous with the edges of the body it will die with."[11] While language objectifies pain and

[9] Elaine Scarry, *The Body in Pain: The Making and Unmaking of the World* (New York: Oxford University Press, 1985) 4.

[10] Scarry, *The Body in Pain*, 52.

[11] Scarry, *The Body in Pain*, 33.

bestows meaning, something pain inherently lacks according to Scarry's dualism, the photograph is able to present the body without foisting a linguistic meaning upon it. The photograph speaks to the body in the "language" of the body. But what the photograph ultimately gives us to understand is that the body is meaningful apart from all language, even the language of gestures. It points to the difference between speaking the truth and showing the truth, and to the world of sense between them.

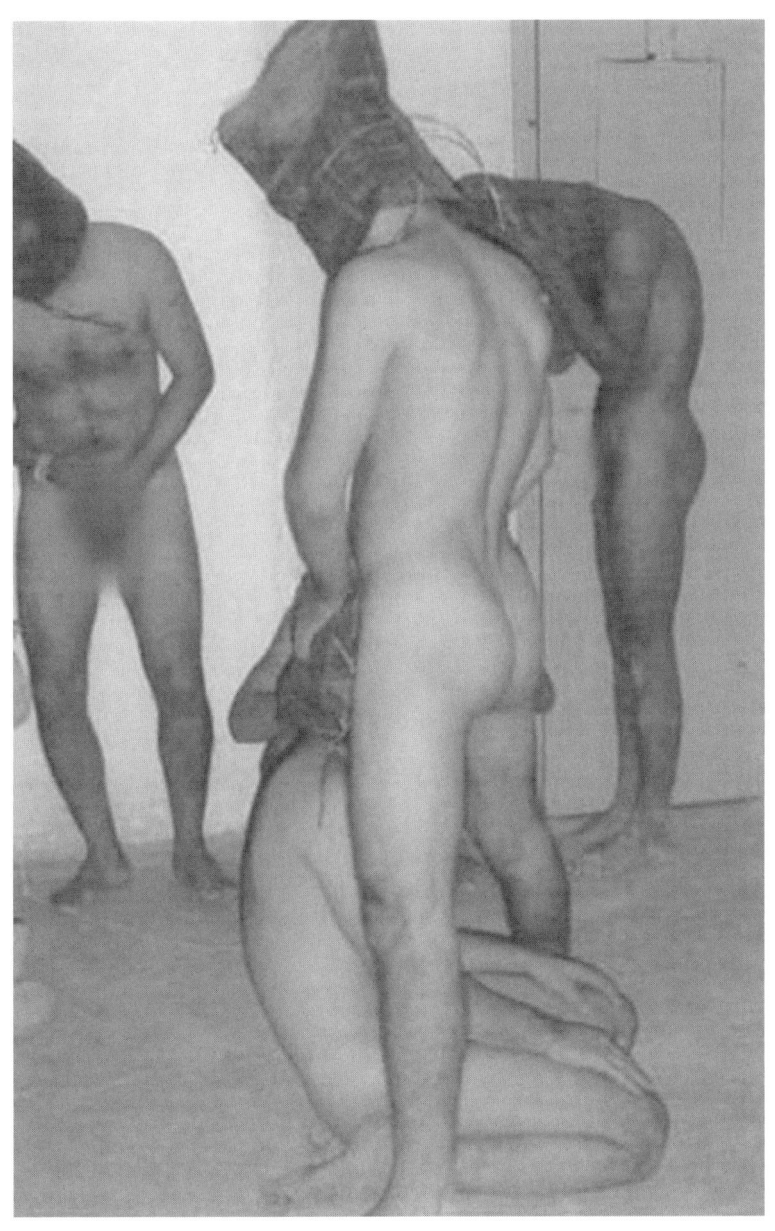

The Touch
They stand like Medieval penitents in the background, not even watching what is going on, unable to watch. One feigns exhaustedly at masturbation, as instructed, the other simply holds his fallen head in his hands. Before them a scene of simulated fellatio, a standing hooded man holding the head of a kneeling hooded man to his groin. And yet I am touched by this photograph, not solely by the arrangement of bodies, nor even mostly, but by the touch that takes place in the midst of them.

This touch communicates to me, even through the film of the hood, I know that this contact was the most tender yet experienced. Even through the film, I can be touched by that touch. It is both the ethical stance of the detainee, "they wanted me to hit him, but I wouldn't because he is my friend," and the faith of the counsel in rejecting blanket approval of category three interrogation techniques, the strongest available, "Our Armed Forces are trained to a standard of interrogation that reflects a tradition of restraint."[12] I discern these effects through the film.

But while I can be touched, I cannot touch. The relation again is asymmetric. In viewing the photograph, I suffer the prophylaxia of film. I am struck by the force of it and made filthy by it, implicated by it—I am touched by it. But where can I touch? It is so suffocatingly close that I can find no point of contact. I am touched without touching and thus indebted. I cannot reciprocate its touch in kind. I cannot be a friend, I cannot show my restraint. I am implicated and indebted by this film and try as I might I cannot cancel this debt. I will always be the one who was touched by this photograph.

But is it possible to speak about a touch across film? Is it legitimate to speak of gloved hands touching someone? of bare hands on a hooded head? of myself before this photograph? I must assume that it is, otherwise torture would be impossible

---

[12] Danner, *Torture and Truth*, 237; Memorandum from William J. Haynes II, re: Counter-Resistance Techniques (November 27, 2002), in Greenberg and Dratel, *Torture Papers*, 237.

and I have a photograph of torture before me. More, this touch across film is what renders us susceptible to torture in the first place. We can still suffer, even through the film. There can be no end to humiliation, no end to abuse, but this also means that we can always be touched.

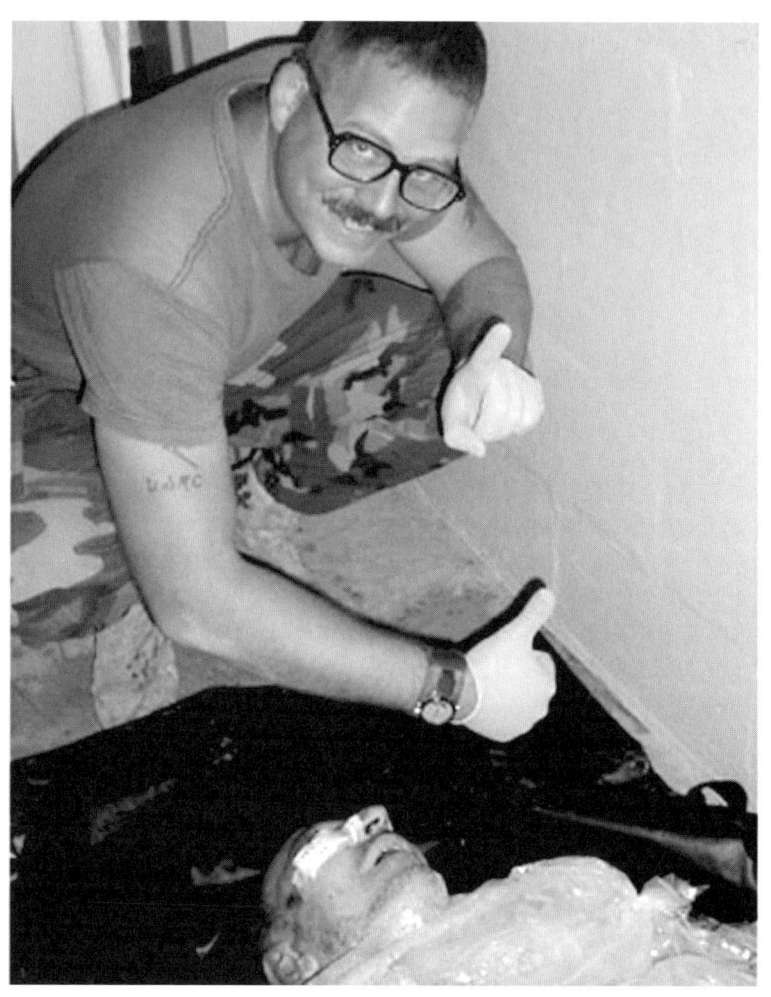

The Digital Spectacle of Torture

When interrogation becomes execution, when the detained, as the man pictured here, are tortured to death, then it is impossible to keep the camera at bay. The world has become a tortured world, stripped of its conceptual wrapping in the language of rights. Nothing remains private (the Red Cross report exposes the conditions under which the detainees were summarily rounded up, with guns drawn, and no information to the families). When we strip the world and force it to stand publicly in place, when we distance ourselves from our own acts, the world is photographed already. US Defence Secretary Rumsfeld sees, but does not comprehend, "we are constantly finding that we have procedures and habits that have evolved over the years from the last century that don't really fit the 21st century. They don't fit the Information Age, they don't fit a time when people are running around with digital cameras."[13] But they do fit this age of increased intrusions and media saturation, where the digital standard renders obsolete all material data formats before it and promises a consummate unity of information. As Rumsfeld notes, "with 24-hour news and digital cameras, something like this can have an impact that is just enormous."[14]

The world becomes a torture image. For Foucault, the connection between torture and publicity is nothing new. In the Ancien Régime, justice had to show itself infinitely superior to any individual who would dare to contravene it. Public torture, Foucault states, "justified justice, in that it published the truth of the crime in the very body of the man to be executed."[15] We find in this publication the mechanism of a power "that was

---

[13] Donald Rumsfeld, Testimony before the House Armed Services Committee (No. 108-28), Operations and Reconstruction Efforts in Iraq (7 May, 2004), http://commdocs.house.gov/committees/security/has128000.000/has128000_0f.htm.

[14] Rumsfeld, Testimony before the House Armed Services Committee.

[15] Michel Foucault, *Discipline & Punish: The Birth of the Prison*, trans. Alan Sheridan (New York: Vintage Books, 1979), 44.

recharged in the ritual display of its reality as 'super-power.'"[16] Foucault draws conclusions from this public display of torture on the part of a "super-power" which should give us pause for thought: "The ceremony of punishment, then, is an exercise of 'terror.'"[17] Perhaps not only in the Ancien Régime are all super-powers terrorists.

The torturing power requires publicity along with public spectators and the digital image brings an ever greater number to participate in the torture and guarantee its power. Far from not fitting the Information Age, our methods of torture eerily accord with it, as made visible upon the dead man here.

---

[16] Foucault, *Discipline & Punish*, 57.
[17] Foucault, *Discipline & Punish*, 49.

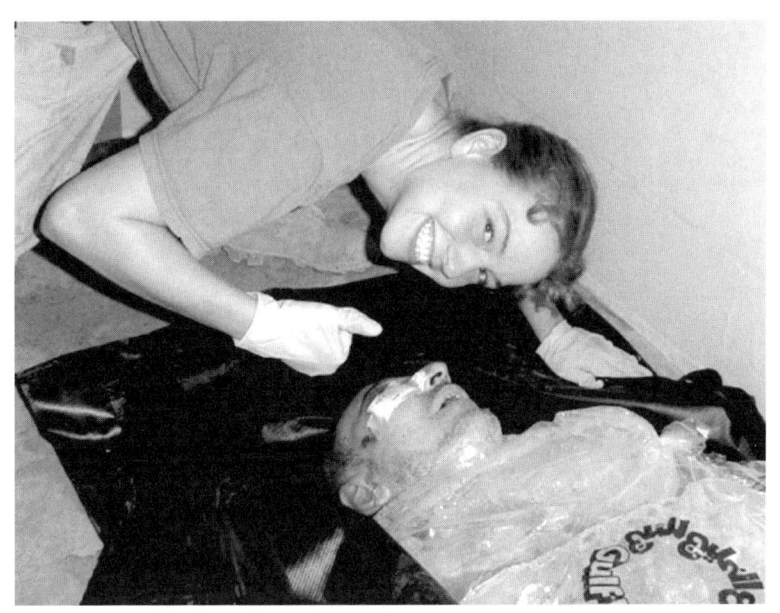

On the Geneva Conventions

Reading the official memoranda surrounding the detention of prisoners in the GWOT, with the US government actively arguing for the inapplicability of the Geneva Conventions to detainees and, upon securing this, immediately compiling defences to projected allegations of torture, is disheartening.

The contracting parties of the 1949 Geneva Conventions agree to respect them "in all circumstances,"[18] providing that POWs "must at all times be humanely treated," with "respect for their persons and their honour" and protected against "public curiosity."[19] But as Alberto Gonzales correctly surmised, our situation today "renders quaint" some of these provisions (the profit-reinvesting camp canteen).[20] Yet the US goes against the spirit, if not letter, of the laws in deciding, via technicalities, that since the Conventions apply to states, they do not apply to al Qaeda and the Taliban. With complete latitude in the handling of detainees, the discussion turns ineluctably to torture.

The new war requires information and Rumsfeld's repeated references in his press conferences to the "Information Age" should be heard with the interrogation techniques of counter-resistance in mind. As Jay Bybee writes the President, "certain acts may be cruel, inhuman, or degrading, but still not produce pain and suffering of the requisite intensity to fall within Section 2340A's proscription against torture."[21] For the required intensity, pain "must rise to the level of death, organ failure, or the permanent impairment of a significant body function."[22] Rumsfeld cannot say that we torture, "I'm not a lawyer. My impression is that what has been charged thus far is abuse,

---

[18] Geneva Convention III, Relative to the Treatment of Prisoners of War, 12 August 1949, article 1.

[19] Geneva Convention III, articles 13-14.

[20] Memorandum from Alberto R. Gonzales, re: "Decision re Application for the Geneva Convention on Prisoners of War to the Conflict with al Qaeda and the Taliban" (25 January, 2002), *Torture Papers*, 119.

[21] Memorandum from Jay S. Bybee, re: "Standards of Conduct for Interrogation under 18 USC §§ 2340-2340A" (1 August, 2002), *Torture Papers*, 172.

[22] Greenberg and Dratel, *Torture Papers*, 176.

which I believe technically is different from torture."[23] The bar for torture is set so high that nothing short of death achieves it. We are abandoned to unending abuse.

What is disheartening in these memos is not that the US sought to elude a commitment to human rights in order to torture. What is disheartening is how so many other parties have done the same, how the Geneva Conventions themselves only apply to those outside them when "the latter accepts and applies the provisions thereof."[24] Nowhere is there any concern for humanity, *not even in the Conventions themselves.*

---

[23] Donald Rumsfeld, Defense Department Operational Update Briefing (4 May, 2004), http://www.dod.mil/transcripts/2004/ tr20040504-secdef1423.html. The terrorists themselves would seem to understand this distinction, as Rumsfeld points out at this same briefing, "I'm not in the position to say whether—there are other allegations of abuse. That is a pattern and a practice of terrorists, to allege abuse. We've seen that in their training, that they do that."

[24] Geneva Convention III, article 2.

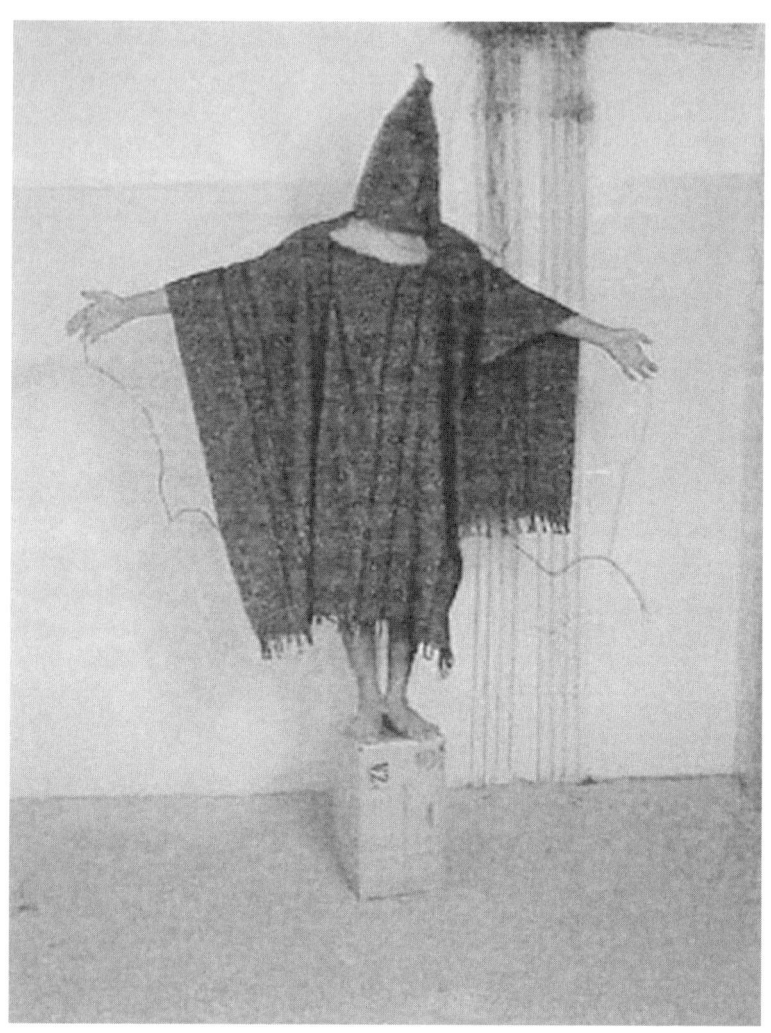

The Face of Torture

When Bataille's history of erotism in the plastic arts, *The Tears of Eros*, draws to its close, the topic turns to torture photography. Here Bataille considers "the most anguishing of worlds accessible to us through images captured on film," a 1905 photo in his possession of a Chinese man suffering the torture *hundred pieces*.[25] In this, the victim dies by dismemberment and the pincering away of the flesh from the trunk that remains. Bataille's photo shows the man still alive, legless, armless, and with the flesh torn from his chest exposing the rib cage. It is a gruesome photo, to be sure, and upon first seeing it, Bataille writes, "I was so stunned that I reached the point of ecstasy."[26] Bataille's statement attests to the ability of the photograph to silently communicate sovereign violence to the ecstatic viewer.

The silence of the photograph shares in the "profound silence peculiar to violence, for violence never declares either its own existence or its right to exist; it simply exists."[27] This fact is documented in the photograph in a manner impossible for language to convey, even the language of Sade. Sade's verbose attitude is "diametrically opposed to that of the torturer."[28] The torturer is silent, Bataille specifies, and "If he bothers with his fellow men at all, he talks the language of the State to them," i.e. an anonymous, non-revealing language.[29] Such silence of the torturer is not incompatible with the camera.

For Bataille it is only the face that communicates this ecstasy. The image of torture extends beyond the frame and communicates with the viewer due to the ecstatic moment captured there, exhibiting both "divine ecstasy and its opposite, extreme horror," as well as "an infinite capacity for reversal"

[25] Georges Bataille, *The Tears of Eros*, trans. Peter Connor (San Francisco: City Lights Books, 1989) 205.

[26] Bataille, *The Tears of Eros*, 206.

[27] Georges Bataille, *Erotism: Death & Sensuality*, trans. Mary Dalwood (San Francisco: City Lights Books, 1986) 188.

[28] Bataille, *Erotism*, 188.

[29] Bataille, *Erotism*, 188.

between them.[30] In the face, the ambivalence of the sacred comes to expression and opens the photograph beyond itself. But in attending solely to the face, Bataille looks away from the wounds, which remain dumb facts and inexpressive blossoms. The pain that concerns Bataille is consequently a bodiless pain. Bataille cannot attend to this body, cannot see torture where the face is covered, and cannot recognise that the silence of violence can also be faceless yet communicative nonetheless.

[30] Bataille, *The Tears of Eros*, 207, 206.

On Standing

Standing in place is a "stress position," approved as a category two interrogation technique for up to four hours at a time. At Abu Ghraib, standing became the order of the day. "Every time one of them fell on the ground they drag them up to stand on his feet."[31] Prisoners were cuffed to the bars of their cell and left to stand until they could stand no longer; after that they just hung by the wrists. "Then he hung me to the door for more than eight hours. I was screaming from pain the whole night."[32] Hooded prisoners with electrical wires attached to their fingers, toes, and genitals were threatened with electrocution should they fall.

Maintaining an upright posture has long served as a mark of human distinction. Herder notes that it allows the human to look about him and above him, Hölderlin that this "looking up" (*Aufschauen*) exposes us to the beyond, Freud that the achievement of the upright posture is a first step toward culture. The phenomenologist Erwin Straus states, "Because upright posture is the leitmotiv in the formation of the human organism, an individual who has lost or is deprived of the capacity to get up and keep himself upright depends, for his survival, completely on the aid of others. Without their help, he is doomed to die."[33] Humans cannot stand for long. We cannot support our own weight. We must rely upon the world and others for support, physically and emotionally. Our human stance is simultaneously a human dependence.

But is the world any different? Does it, too, not need its rest? our support? And what then of photographs? Do they not bring the world to a standstill? Or are they just for our delight in a world made perpetually to stand, a tortured world? The photograph is the perfect art-form for a world where not only human rights are suspended, but human bodies, too.

[31] Danner, *Torture and Truth*, 234.
[32] Danner, *Torture and Truth*, 228.
[33] Erwin Straus, "The Upright Posture," *Phenomenological Psychology* (New York: Basic Books, 1966) 139.

Photographs reveal an exhausted world; the world collapses into photographs. Straus rightly notes, "gravity is never fully overcome."[34] Humanity is literally a delicate balance. The stance which establishes us cannot do so forever. And yet Rumsfeld writes upon a memo regarding approved interrogation techniques, "However, I stand for 8-10 hours a day. Why is standing limited to 4 hours? D.R."[35]

---

[34] Straus, "The Upright Posture," 141.
[35] Memorandum from William J. Haynes II re: "Counter-Resistance Techniques" (27 November, 2002), *Torture Papers*, 237.

Commenting upon President Bush's military order providing for the indefinite detention of non-US citizens Giorgio Agamben charges that, "What is new about Bush's order is that it radically erases any legal status of the individual, thus producing a legally unnameable and unclassifiable being ... Neither prisoners nor persons accused, but simply 'detainees,' they are the object of a pure de facto rule."[36] Bush's decision, arising out of his determination that "an extraordinary emergency exists for national defence purposes," is a sovereign decision for a state of exception to juridical law.[37] Its living corollary is the "bare life" of the detainee, which Agamben traces back to an ancient Roman legal determination of sacred life, "that is, life that may be killed but not sacrificed."[38] What sort of life is this?

It would be wrong to think of it as a reduction of the human to an animal existence, despite the guards taunts of "dog," their insistence that the detainees bark on command, or their riding around upon the backs of them. The animal at least belongs to humanity, if only as the blackness against which it first sees itself. The human is the *animal rationale*, after all, and this determination installs an unspoken bond between man and animal. In this photo we see all the players in this drama of bare life. There is the human, the guard, man the tool user, the domesticator, intent, aggressive, and the master of life. There is the animal, obedient, equally aggressive, disciplined and trained, ready to act at the master's command. Finally, there is the detainee, bare life, threatened, cornered, kneeling and with hands tied behind its back. He does not return the gaze of man or of animal. He is entitled no protection. He is the outside

[36] Giorgio Agamben, *State of Exception*, trans. Kevin Attell (Chicago: The University of Chicago Press, 2005).

[37] George W. Bush, Military Order of 13 November, 2001, *Torture Papers*, 26.

[38] Giorgio Agamben, *Homo Sacer: Sovereign Power and Bare Life*, trans. Daniel Heller-Roazen (Stanford: Stanford University Press, 1998).

appearing now on the inside, cowering and susceptible, but nevertheless at the centre of the axis of sovereign power.

Is it possible that in the dehumanising treatment of the detainee what is lost is his status as *animal rationale*? that a new existence could take shape here, one unrecognised by both the man and the animal and recognising itself in neither? Victim no longer, he would cast off this old, all too metaphysical life like a shadow, the only one here who does so.

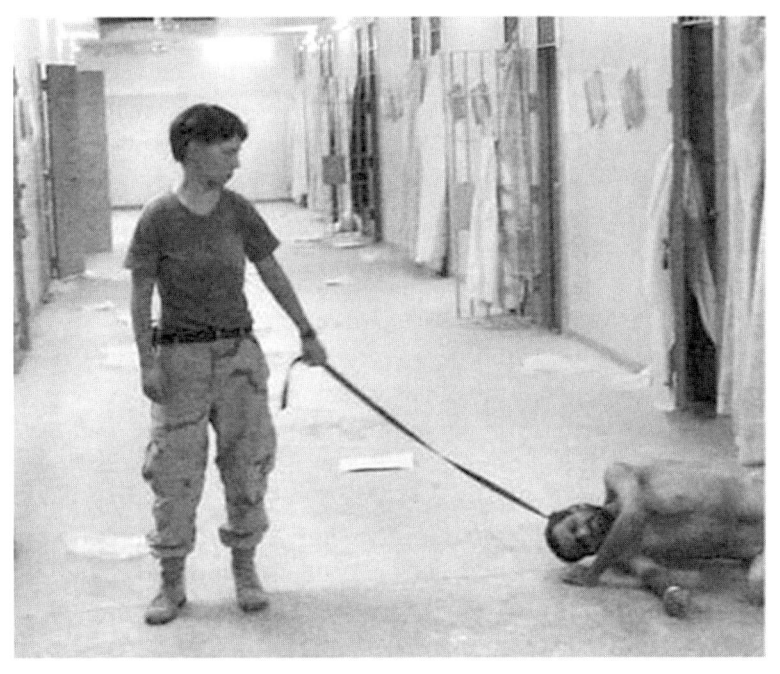

Humanity, Encore un effort!

We can talk and talk of inalienable rights and they are inalienable so long as they are in force and they must be enforced by the threat of the same violence they would protect you against. But when they are taken from you, then you never had them, since you can never lose them when they are inalienable. But even if humans are attributed inalienable rights, there is no guarantee that one is found human. Humanity is something to be achieved.

And don't we protect ourselves, perhaps too much, from what are termed "inhuman" acts? An inhuman act is a river, is the warmth exuding off puppies who suckle at the teat. Humans do not commit inhuman acts, and yet these acts occur. Our very objections remove humanity once again, sequester it away to an undisclosed location and leave the perpetrators behind dehumanised, the victims alone without recognition. Once again, humanity is to be achieved. The inhuman is human, and perhaps, too, the river.

We will not achieve humanity until we recognise that humanity is nothing to be achieved, that our dismissal of the "inhuman" deprives the perpetrators of their humanity. When humanity is something that we can lose, we have already lost it. Is not the depravity of the crime increased when we do not allow the excuse of inhumanity? Who expects humane acts from something inhuman? Only a fool. Let us maintain them in their humanity and hold them responsible all the while. Humanity is inalienable, and so too your guilt.

Here is to a humanity that connects us and tethers us the one to the other! Humanity must be absolute if it is to have any sense at all—to unconditional humanity then! This does not put an end to dehumanisation; on the contrary, it renders it unending. Things can always get worse. Your humanity can never be taken from you, but what little of it that remains can always be reduced further. Treasure it! There is always, too, the scintillating irritant of hope, that someone will take a stand, will see the photos, will leave them on another's bed, that they will be sent home, forwarded to the press, shown on prime-time television, and printed with a distribution of millions. Who would have the humanity to hope for that?

Transfiguration: to No Longer Support the Troops

There is a tacit and unquestioned agreement within society today that we will support the troops. They are automatically accorded the accolades of heroes, vehicles are festooned with ribbons, advertisers voice their support, and the President makes every effort to reaffirm this tide of emotion. Support for the troops is legion, unconditional, is it still possible to ask why?

Did the troops not have a choice? Do we not do those we wish to support a grand injustice by denying them the very privileges of autonomy? They chose to serve. Our celebrations of the troops quickly become celebrations of abdication of choice. We celebrate the relinquishment of choice. How much of the support for the troops sounds in our ears like an expression of relief.

It will certainly be objected that these are our poor, our disenfranchised, that the military is the only way for them to receive an education. The objection is its own refutation. Rather than support this deplorable state of affairs by proxy, I withdraw my support from the troops and the system that would leave a country's youth without support. Support for the troops has functioned to indefinitely postpone discussion of the justifications of war and the social system that provides it with troops. Why is the military the only means for receiving an education, why not public service in one's home community? To support the troops in these conditions is to support the system that refuses them support, is to not support the troops at all.

Others will object that it is precisely the nature of a hero to follow orders without question, whatever the cost. This, at least, was heroism in war. And yet, as the President claims, "the war against terrorism ushers in a new paradigm."[39] In this, heroism has no place. Unconditional support requires unconditional humanity, until then we live in a world bereft of heroes, until

[39] Memorandum from George W. Bush re: "Humane Treatment of al Qaeda and Taliban Detainees" (February 7, 2002), *Torture Papers*, 134.

then we can only no longer support the troops, which is not to not support them at all (for we have lost this not at all), but perhaps to not yet support the troops. Until then there is the nightmare of torture and photography, which the photographs from Abu Ghraib so eloquently demonstrate. We can not yet support unending abuse. I no longer support the troops.

Arthur & Marilouise Kroker

Cloner

for Kathy Acker

It's a sweet moving, easy livin' summer evening, the twilight in the city air lingering on an endless repeat cycle, and I'm stompin' St. Catherine's Street on my Harley-Davidson Screaming Eagle.

Born in '63, the year Kennedy was assassinated, I've always been hooked on those too late at night b&w rebel with or without a cause biker movies, 'specially Marlon Brando in his beautiful bod, Greek god-look, eyes to dream about days. Friends tell me that a woman, 62 inches vertical, has no business straddling a max cc, turbo-charged, neon red, chrome-plated, road hugging Daddy like a Screaming Eagle, but I just put on that moody Brando pout with my DOT helmet and black leather jacket and laced up the side pants and silver-tipped blast throttle boots, set the jet carb on full gas intake and ignite. Sort of a retro 50s take on the e-wire 00's, or maybe a girl flesh fresh from life in the wires out for a spin with all the boys.

But before I get ahead of myself, let me tell you how I got the name Cloner. It was about five years ago and I was on another bike, a K-line BMW, cruisin' a desert highway mid-winter. Never even saw that transport creaming my way. All I remember is the silver grill, high-top sun-tinted windows,

* Previously published as "Screaming Eagle," *Life in the Wires: The CTheory Reader*, eds. Kroker & Kroker (Victoria: NWP, 2004).

snarling cougar roof design, gonna kill you, gonna maul you good, eat you right up, you're in my lane, and my lane is the whole fuckin' road kind of speed noise. I can still smell to this day burning tires, melted chrome, and the fear of me splashed on the highway.

Woke up in Phoenix with half my face ripped off, and all I could think of was "Shit I don't have any insurance."

No big deal, I'm told.

The surgeon tells me it's my lucky day. Turns out I'm one of those bike wrecks I've always read about. Something about donor tissue.

I think to myself organ donors? Aren't I still alive?

Then I hear the word, SynSkin, the new artificial flesh grown in bio-gen labs from the foreskin of baby boys. And you know what the surgeon tells me: "A single male baby foreskin produces enough SynSkin to cover four football fields."

That's a lot of skin, and not much foreskin.

I'm lying there broken-bodied, torn face, feeling real bad, no Marlon Brando pout, but still something clicks in my DOT crushed head, and I can't help but admire the ingenuity and audacity of Big Science marching ahead, or in this case marching right over my face. Because as it turns out, the surgeon's got an Alien 5 suggestion. "How would you like to grow a new face, or at least half-a-face? No charge."

"Sure, I think to myself, 'cause it's probably experimental."

And it was. And it was great. Took about four weeks for the foreskin, or I should say SynSkin, to clone the remains of my face.

That's about the time I started calling myself Cloner.

My Face

Artificial face for a time in which machines have migrated into the flesh.

Before the accident, I was thinking hard about consciousness, about the bicephalic brain split into right- and left hemispheres, about McLuhan's theory that ever since the Gutenberg Galaxy we've lived in a right-hemisphere world where all the values associated with uniform visual culture—specialisation, privatisation, the individuated ego, the eye not the ear—have been stamped on our memories, speech patterns, gestures, bodies, and, most of all, on our faces. Eye faces without ears or tears or memory smears.

Maybe that was why in the hospital in Phoenix, drugged down tight and mind drifting free, I had this strange recurring dream. I was always double-headed, double-faced—a high-distortion camera red eye and a blue-screen liquid ear—zooming outwards from an earth-bound tissue patch, coiling together, leering, touching, embracing, and then always splitting apart. And the difference that split wide open the face ear and the face eye was a real screaming eagle with its no-blink stare and its shriek-shriek hunting scream and its razor-tooth talons doing max damage to the twirling double-headed flesh spiral.

Didn't much like that swirly dream, but I trapped its message good in my dream-catcher, and so when the surgeon asked me if I had any "special preferences" for my SynSkin face, I just told him that I wanted an ear for an eye and an eye for an ear and a Screaming Eagle for a mouth in between. Maybe not really, but it sure would be nice.

Probably having read his McLuhan and knowing that revolting against the press-ganged, screwed down and screwed up, uniform visual culture Gutenberg face has to begin somewhere, sometime, he just said that he'd "see what he could do." Maybe he even understood that what I really wanted was a wetware face as a kind of flesh bridge between software flesh and the hardware road.

A Post-Biologics Face
Which is exactly what I got. My left profile was the same as always, sort of a memory box stuffed with flesh reminders of

who I used to be, an eye and an ear and a tongue and some bad-assed scrapes and too-bruised bluish skin. Sort of a camera eye in permanent position fixed-focused on facial features that moved to the more ancient rhythms of time's decay. The right-side face, my SynSkin face, was magnificent. It was as if the surgeon had Francis Bacon'd my skin, laying over the stripped down bones a liquid skin hologram, like a mutating slide dipping and weaving and flesh-blending. Put my face in front of the liquid array of a computer screen or under the black light of a dance club, and what you get is me hologrammed into the image of an eye for an ear, an ear for an eye, with this trip hop angry Screaming Eagle taking up the remainder.

I looked in the mirror, and thought to myself. Great!

Because who wants a perfect face anyway? The face has outlived its usefulness. We've been morphed and graphed and pixellated and mutated and serialised and downloaded and zip-drived and pinholed and infrareded and surveillanced and ABM recorded. What's left is just some empty orifices, a hole for air, a canal for sound, sockets for light, a tongue for taste, and a mouth to spit away the difference.

Zoe Beloff

Natalija A. & Eva C.

Mental Images or Psychic projection

I work with many forms of moving images: stereoscopic16mm film, projection performance, installation and interactive works. Each time I begin a project, I find myself attempting to reinvent cinema. I ask myself how can I bring a story to life on the level of both narrative and apparatus. My fascination with case histories of mediums and the insane lies in their ability to graphically conjure up unconscious imagery in ways that inspire me to rethink cinema.

Case histories purport to be scientific documents that describe symptoms and offer explanation from a rational perspective. I'm not interested in simply illustrating them. Instead I find myself drawn to the other side, the perspective of their objects of study. In my installations I wanted to see the world through the eyes of Eva C. a materialising medium and Natalija A. a schizophrenic, to conjure up phantom figures or disturbing hallucinations with an impossible intimacy. I wished to show how these women produced a kind of creative

* Notes and reflections on two moving image installations: *The Influencing Machine of Miss Natalija A.* (2001) and *The Ideoplastic Materialisations of Eva C.* (2004).

resistance, a provocation, a going beyond what could be managed by doctors who studied them.

It is their excess that opens up new perspectives on moving images. They show us how projection is more than simply the technology of a machine throwing light on a screen. It is also intimately bound up with mental projection and unconscious desire. At the same time I wish to show how these cases can be regarded as a distorting mirrors that reflect back symptomatically yet with uncanny clarity the crossroads of media technology and psychology of their time.

Time and Space

In classical cinema, moving images open up a window into another world beyond the screen. To enter this alternate universe, viewers must imaginatively leave their bodies behind. Disembodied, they find themselves taken on a journey, caught up in the multiple perspectives of numerous characters. Just as suddenly as it began, the illusion vanishes and the audience awakes as it were from a dream, thrust back into their skin, subject once again to the mundane laws of time and space. However this is simply one economy of the moving image, which has existed for only the last hundred years.

An installation projected in a gallery, opens up opportunities to conceptualise moving images very differently both in terms of the relation of the images to the space around them and the perception of their duration.

A film appears to exist only while we watch it. In contrast an installation is there when the viewer arrives and are still there when they leave. I think about creating projects that makes sense of this kind of duration. When the viewer enters the séance room of Eva C. the characters are always there, the way they are in a diorama. They are neither living nor dead, but rather in a state one might call "reanimated." Time is circular rather than linear.

It is important to me that a moving image installation exists in relation to the space that contains it. Otherwise it would be nothing more than a film projected on a gallery wall. I am inspired by ideas about moving images prior to the invention of classical cinema. My work attempts to realise forms that could only be imagined in the past. In so doing I aim to create bridge between past and future. The ancestors of my installations are phantasmagorias, dioramas and the waxwork displays. My installations exist spatially in direct relation to the spectator. For example it is very important that the figures in Eva C. are projected both 3D and life size. They appear to exist in the space of the gallery in the same way that the spirits conjured up in a séance appeared to move freely among the sitters.

I aim to create both an emotional identification with Eva C. and Natalija A. and at the same time play within suspension of disbelief. I'm drawn to working with stereoscopic imagery precisely because on the one hand it is an optical trick, one sees something that is quite simply not there. On the other hand the illusion is far from seamless. It is of course obvious to the viewer that they are not seeing reality but artifice, "life reconstituted."

Eva C. — A Photographic Body
The Ideoplastic Materialisations of Eva C. is a re-enactment of ten séances held between 1906 and 1913 with the French medium Eva C. Her career under the name of Marthe Beraud began in Algeria where the phantoms she produced were very much an embodiment of European fantasies of the Orient. Clearly she captivated Charles Richet, the Noble Prize winning French physiologist and psychic researcher who travelled to Algeria specifically to investigate her. Here he apparently witnessed a phantom known to the circle as Bien Boa, floating above the floor wrapped in a sheet, crowned with a helmet and sporting what Richet described as "a thick black artificial beard covering his mouth and chin" as well as "The Egyptian Queen," a young

Eva and the Coachman—still from *The Ideoplastic Materialisations of Eva C.*

and beautiful woman who apparently laughed heartily and seemed greatly amused by the French professor. Scandal ensued when the coachman was accused of playing the ghost. However Richet stuck to his story that the manifestations where quite genuine, insisting that he couldn't find a trap door anywhere in the séance room.[1]

Several years later the medium reappeared in Paris holding séances for a select audience of savants at the home of Juliette Bisson, a wealthy sculptress and psychic researcher. Her chief exponent was Baron Albert von Schrenck Notzing who gave her the name Eva C. His book *The Phenomena of Materialisation:*

[1] Charles Richet, *Thirty Years of Psychical Research*, a translation of *Traité de métapyschique by Stanley De Brath* (New York: Macmillan, 1923) 504-510.

The Phantom Bien Boa—still from *The Ideoplastic Materialisations of Eva C.*

A Contribution to the Investigation of Mediumistic Teleplastics contains detailed accounts of her séances as well reproductions of hundreds of photographs of her in the process of materialisation.

As well as being an ardent psychic researcher, Schrenck Notzing was a medical doctor specialising in sexual pathology. During the séances the scientific method became lured into a strange dance with sexuality. Photography as simultaneously document and metaphor bound them together. Under the assumption that the camera could not lie, anything became possible. Eva herself was conceptualised by the Baron as a kind of living camera who brought forth images from behind the black curtains of the cabinet in the corner of the séance room, a space that did indeed bear a resemblance to the dark chamber of the camera obscura. Under the red safe lights, whitish malleable ectoplasm took the form of face and hands in states of metamorphosis and like unfixed photographs faded away as mysteriously they had appeared.

> Illumination with red light, aggregating about one hundred candle power. Eva had hardly been hypnotised on her chair by Mme. Bisson when she breathed loudly and stertorously, with every sign of a deep trance. The teleplastic creative process began at once. At the place in the curtain which had been made familiar by practice, a white luminosity became visible. Eva then tried gradually to expose the image to the light by rolling up the left curtain flap with her left hand, and thus gradually allowing the red light to fall upon the object, obviously fixed inside. To my greatest astonishment I seemed to recognise in the masculine face, shown with the well-known drapery of veiling, but sketched as with black chalk on a flat surface, the features of Alexander Bisson, the husband of my collaborator who had died in 1912.[2]

Perhaps the most extravagant photograph in the book is the Baron's prized picture of the naked medium with a phantom that might be most accurately described as a cardboard cut out in a bathrobe. If this did not tax our credulity, before publication Schrenck Notzing had it meticulously retouched to remove all trace of Eva's breasts. Thus, in an extraordinary twist of logic, he asks us to accept the photographic proof of phantoms in bathrobes but not of the bodies of young ladies. A perverse struggle between the flaunting and the hiding of the symbols of sexuality is literally played out on the body of the photograph itself.

---

[2] Baron von Schrenck Notzing, *Phenomena of Materialisation: A Contribution to the Investigation of Mediumistic Teleplastics*, trans. E.E. Fournier d'Albe (London: Kegan Paul, Trench, Turbner and Co., 1920) 164.

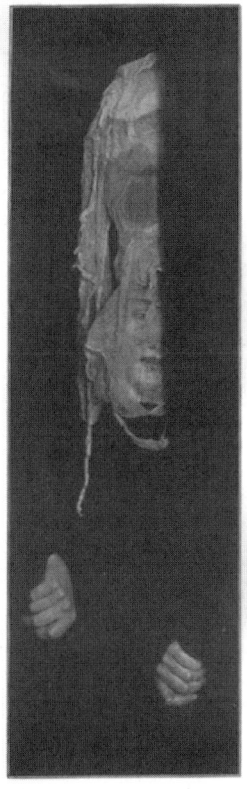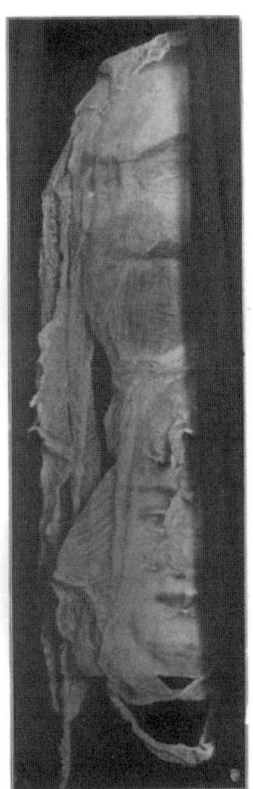

Schrenck Notzing's photograph of 1 June 1912 – materialisation of M Bisson
from *The Phenomena of Materialisation*.

Indeed the Baron's fascination with Eva's body as a kind of photographic sexual organ went deeper still. It appeared when she and Mme Bisson held private séances together ectoplasm oozed from her nipples and once she even produced a head from between her legs. Schrenck Notzing feared phantoms lurking in an even darker chamber of Eva's person, phantoms that could make a fool of him. Thus before each séance he searched her with "gynaecological thoroughness" to make sure that she had not hidden any fake ectoplasms in her vagina.

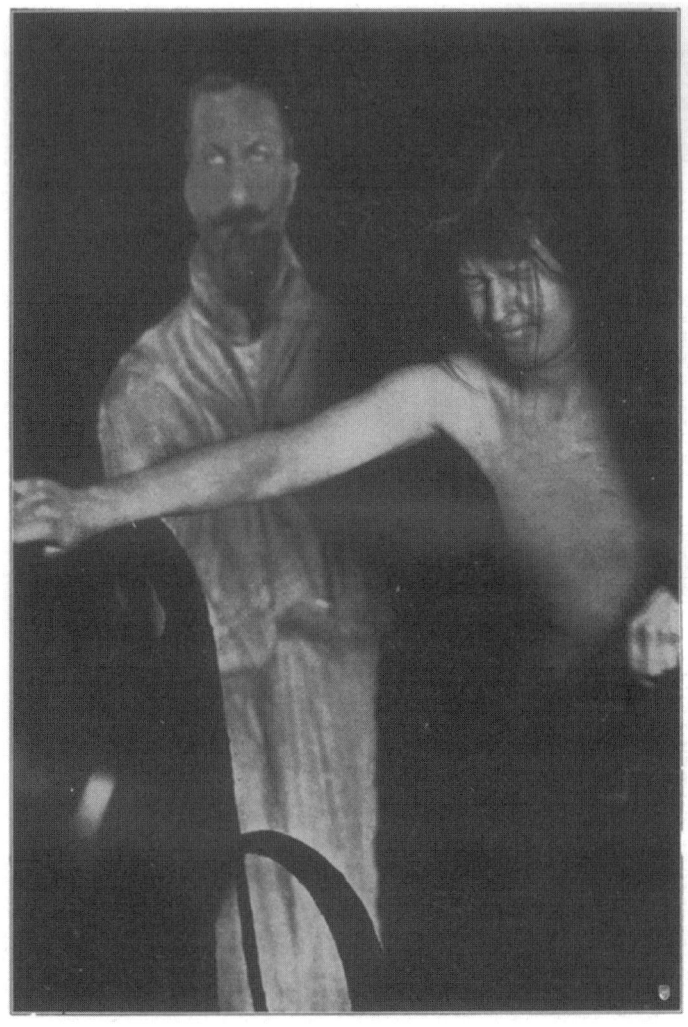

Mme Bisson's photograph of 23 February 1913 – phantom with nude medium (retouched). From *The Phenomena of Materialisation*.

The wealthy researchers treated Eva with the utmost condescension. "She thinks of herself as a machine" the Baron declared.[3] Though he might have said more accurately, "I think

---

[3] Schrenck Notzing, *Phenomena of Materialisation*, 99.

Eva materialises a head — still from *The Ideoplastic Materialisations of Eva C*

of her as a machine." By removing all trace of agency from Eva, by treating her as a machine for the production of phantoms he justified the authenticity of her manifestations in the same way as the photographs that documented her performance.

In my installation I wished to show how Eva, freed from agency, was able to operate outside the social rules. I suggest her lovers included Arabs and women, her séances were extravagant artistic and erotic performances. These played out in the home, a space where women could take centre stage. What is remarkable is that this extraordinary sexual energy was never remarked upon. I believe because it could not be spoken about, it could be acted out. Ultimately beyond formal considerations what fascinates me about materialising mediums was the way in which they opened up a space where the unconscious could be graphically manifest.

An Artificial Resurrection

The form of my installation suggests how photographic illusionism can appear to conjure up the impossible. For a long time I have been fascinated by the way in which nineteenth century media was conceptualised as a way to prolong life after death. In 1877 the editors of *Scientific American* extolled the phonograph's ability preserve the voice long after the demise of the speaker. The article also suggests that if stereoscopic images were projected simultaneously with sound, the illusion of life would be complete. "It is already possible by ingenious optical contrivances to throw stereoscopic photographs of people on screens in full view of an audience. Add the talking phonograph to counterfeit their voices, and it would be difficult to carry the illusion of real presence much further."[4] In this sense media was seen as a mechanical medium that would conjure up virtual presence with more reliability than the spirit medium.

Storyboard drawing for scene five of *The Ideoplastic Materialisations*

Technically my project is a four channel stereoscopic surround sound installation. 3D projections create the illusion of life size black and white figures that appear to inhabit a continuation of the real space of the gallery. The performance was staged and shot proscenium style; that is there are no cuts in the scenes, the actors are shown full body.

---

[4] The 22 December 1877 issue of *Scientific American* cited in Francis Jehl, *Menlo Park Reminiscences: Volume I* (New York: Dover Publications, 1990) 168.

One could describe the scene as a virtual diorama. It's illusionism is very much related to the kind of diorama one might see in a wax work display or history museum. In fact the early twentieth century saw the creation of the great illusionistic dioramas at places like the American Museum of Natural History that seemed unnervingly lifelike to contemporaries. One can think of the natural history diorama is an artificial world where science meets sideshow, since this is very much what happened in the séances of Eva C. the diorama seemed an important reference. At the same time my installation suggests a little vaudeville stage or a living room theatre.

To the side and in front of the stereoscopic projection, close ups of figures and the ectoplasmic manifestations appear and disappear with lightening rapidity on two invisible black scrims. They reference both how Eva C's materialisations were perceived by the sitters and also Balzac's idea that objects radiated pictures of themselves. In his novel "Cousin Pons" he wrote that Daguerre's invention proved "that a man or a building is incessantly and continuously represented by a picture in the atmosphere, that all existing objects project into it a kind of spectre which can be captured and perceived."[5]

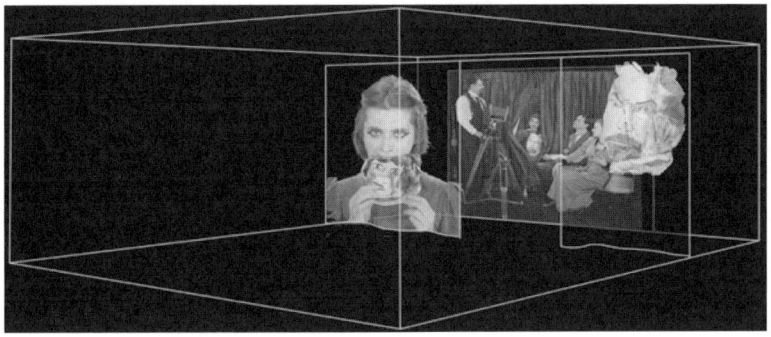

Diagram of *The Ideoplastic Materialisations of Eva C.*

[5] Balzac cited in Tom Gunning, "Phantom Images and Modern Manifestations: Spirit Photography, Magic Theatre, Trick Films and Photography's Uncanny,"

In the gallery, the viewer opens a curtain and enters a darkened room. One might say that like the sitters in a real séance, they are caught up in suspension of disbelief. They know that what they are witnessing is nothing more than an illusion yet none the less they see three dimensional figures that appear to exist however ethereally in their world, an artificial resurrection of people and events of a hundred years ago.

Mysterious Rays

Just as photography was in its early days considered uncanny so too the concept of television had occult overtones. As far back at the 1870's Sir William Crookes posited the fourth state of matter 'the radiant state' to explain fluorescence. The direction of his experiments in this field would lead ultimately to the development of cathode ray tubes.

The whole idea of waves or rays transmitted information was a new and mysterious concept that was seized upon by scientists, psychic researchers and schizophrenics alike. All kinds of rays were posited, Tesla and Marconi's radio waves transmitted audio information, Röntgen rays that penetrated the flesh, Schrenck Notzing discusses the work of a Dr. Kotik of Moscow who believed that thinking is accompanied by the emission of brain-rays having a great penetrative power, apparently the small particles of these psycho-physical emanations were denoted by Dr. Kotik as "psycho-physical atoms" or in accordance with the newest views as "psycho-physical electrons."[6] Baron von Reichenbach posited Od rays which bore some relation to Mesmer's magnetic fluid to explain the paranormal.

In his essay *Psychic Television* Stefan Andropoulos points out that the German word for television *Fensehen* also refers to "remote viewing" in the paranormal sense of clairvoyance and

Fugitive Images: From Photography to Video, ed. Patrice Petro (Bloomington and Indianapolis: Indiana University Press, 1995) 43.
6 Schrenck Notzing, *Phenomena of Materialisation*, 32-33.

notes that the concept of "ether waves" was used to explain both psychic and technical television.[7]

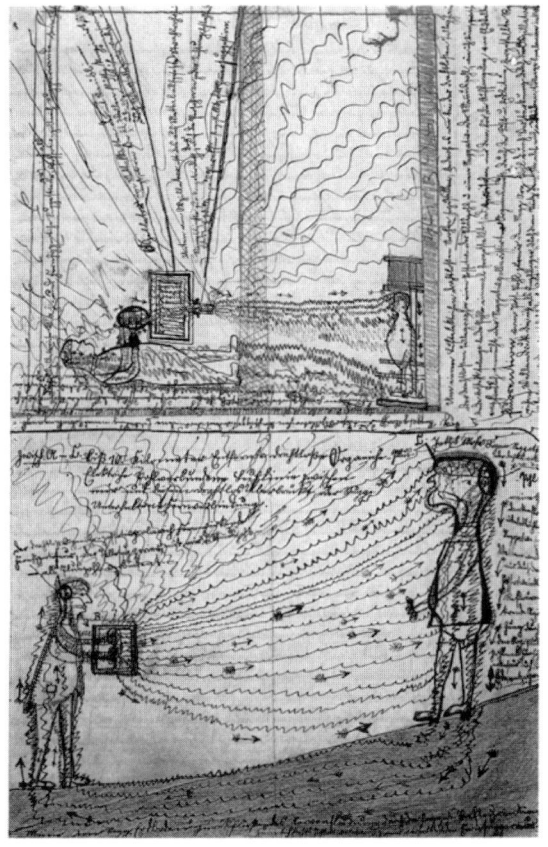

Proofs by Jakob Mohr (diagnosis: dementia praecox paranoides) 1910.
From the Prinzhorn Collection.

Natalija A. — A Televisual Body
If we can think of Eva as a kind of camera extruding images from her orifices, the subject of my earlier installation, Natalija A. might be conceptualised as a "televisual body" being both transmitter and receiver.

[7] Stefan Andriopolos, "Psychic Television," *Critical Inquiry* 31.3 (Spring 2005).

In 1919 this former student of philosophy visited Victor Tausk, a Viennese psychoanalyst and early follower of Freud, complaining that a bizarre electrical apparatus operated secretly by physicians in Berlin, was manipulating her thoughts through the use of waves rays or mysterious forces. It was a torture machine, plaguing her with disgusting smells, dreams, thoughts and feelings. When someone struck the machine she felt a corresponding blow to her body.

In his essay *The Influencing Machine,* Tausk gave a new interpretation of this common schizophrenic delusion of being persecuted by a machine. He believed that it represented the patient's own body that had become alien and strange to her. Treatment did not last long. After three sessions Natalija believed that the Tausk too had fallen under the influence of the "diabolical apparatus" and never returned.

I was initially inspired by two quotes. The first by Victor Tausk, "Machines produced by man's ingenuity and created in the image of man are unconscious projections of man's bodily structures."[8] The second by the Nazi in charge of the nascent television industry in Germany Eugen Hadamovsky who declared in 1935, "Now in this hour broadcasting is called upon to fulfil its biggest and most sacred mission, to plant an image of the Fuhrer indelibly in all German hearts.[9] I imagine Natalija taking this statement completely literally.

In my project I wished to make connections between the experience of hallucination, transference in psychoanalysis and the development of real influencing machines in the form of radio and television in 1930's Germany – extending the definition of psychosis from the individual to society. At the same time I wanted to find a way for the viewer to viscerally experience her perverse technological transformation in all its

---

[8] Victor Tausk, *The Influencing Machine* in *Incorporations*, eds. Jonathan Crary and Sanford Kwinter (New York: Zone, 1992 [1919]) 569.

[9] Eugen Hadamovsky cited in William Uricchio, "Rituals of Reception: Patterns of Neglect. Nazi Television and its Postwar Representation," *Wide Angle* 10.4 (1988): 51.

horror, to conjure up her lonely and terrifying hallucinations. She described the diabolical apparatus as machine that was also a body, its limbs drawn on a coffin shaped trunk, whose inner parts consisted of electric batteries.

My installation consists of a large stereoscopic diagram based on Natalija's description of her influencing machine as well as early television apparatuses. Inside the diagram is a small panel onto which video is projected. When the viewer wearing red/green glasses, looks down at the diagram, they see an actual three-dimensional structure. They touch a designated point on this virtual machine with a wand and all at once moving images appear on the screen, sound blares from the apparatus. They remove the wand and the projections vanish. Different points on the diagram trigger different video fragments.

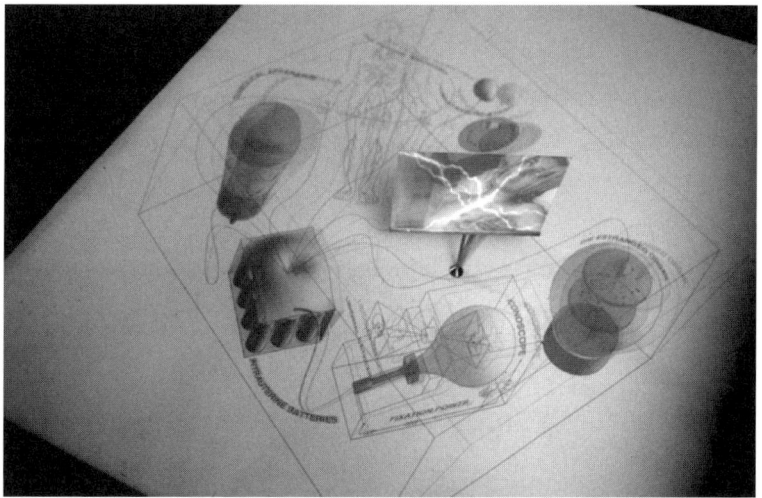

The Influencing Machine—3D diagram and video projection screen.

From the moment the viewer puts on the glasses they see things that others in the room cannot see, almost as though he or she were actually hallucinating. Through interacting with the apparatus, poking and prodding its "virtual organs" they find

317

themselves viscerally implicated, placed in the position of the sinister physicians/technicians (always male) whom Natalija thought were probing her mind.

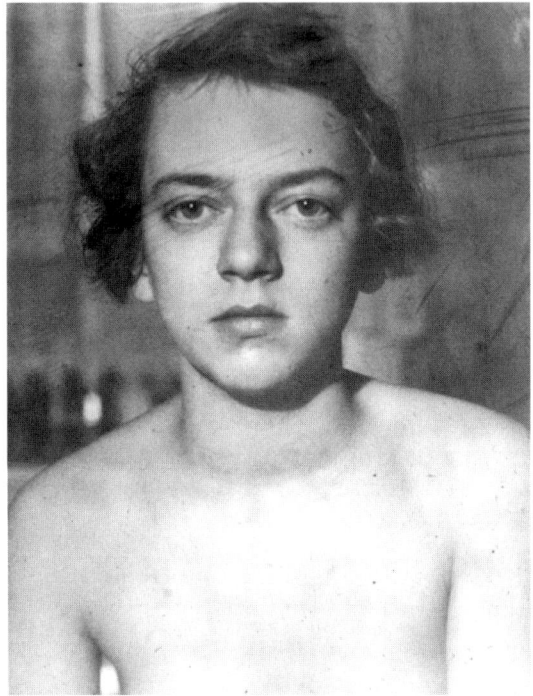

A medical photograph of an anonymous girl.

One or Many Natalija's?
Unlike the character of Eva C. who is played by an actress, there is no one Natalija with whom the viewer can identify. Instead in the video fragments we see many women, from German home movies from the 1920's as well as technological, pornographic and medical films of the era. They all could be Natalija whom I wish to portray not as a person but perhaps more accurately as a condition of modernity. Waves and rays radiating through the atmosphere penetrating everyone and anyone, all potential Natalija's, all potential victims of media manipulation. She was perhaps nothing more than a very

sensitive antenna. The most emblematic image for me was that of an anonymous young girl taken from a stack of medical photographic negatives that I found at the flea market.

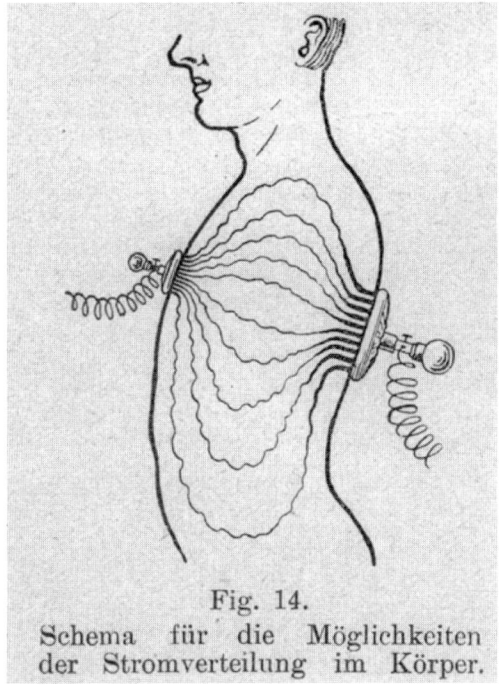

Fig. 14.
Schema für die Möglichkeiten der Stromverteilung im Körper.

From J. von Mering's *Lehrbuch der Inderen Medizin*.

A Dialog with Media History

Attempting to conjure up the past I aim to create a dialog with how people pictured themselves and their world. In *The Ideoplastic Materialisations of Eva C.* I did not attempt convey some kind of "unmediated reality" rather I wished to show how séances might have been "performed" as drama in the nineteen teens. I asked the actors to listen to early spoken word recordings. Though historically the Baron and his circle would have conversed in French and German, I was interested less in the language than in grain of the voice. The upper classes had a very different rhythm of speech and intonation than contemporary speakers. It is this that I wanted the actors to convey, for I believe the voice is just as evocative as any costume in conjuring up an era. In terms of movement and performance, the actors studied the serial films of Louis Feuillarde. I was interested in the fact that each of actors used a series of poses and gestures that they would repeat in the appropriate circumstances.

In *The Influencing Machine of Miss Natalija A.* I worked with media from the nineteen twenties and thirties subtly altering it, imagining how it might be perceived by the mind of a schizophrenic. The 3D diagram is based on pictures of early television apparatuses from Audel's *Radioman's Guide* and medical illustrations from J. von Mering's *Lehrbuch der Inderen Medizin*, a German Medical Textbook distorted by Natalija's description of her influencing machine.[10] Here diodes take on organ like properties, an exposed nervous system is tethered by

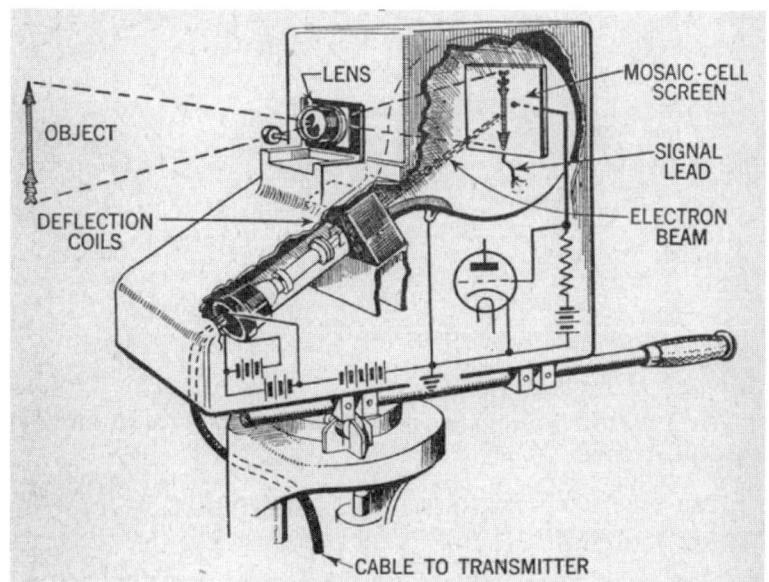

From Audel's *Radioman's Guide*.

---

[10] Edwin P. Anderson, *Audel's Radioman's Guide: covering theory construction and servicing including television electronics* (New York: Theo Audel &Co., 1944); J. von Mering *Lehrbuch der Inneren Medizin* (Jena: Gustav Fischer, 1921).

electrical cables, psychoanalytic and electronics terminology fuse.

When I work with found or archival footage, I don't wish to destroy or claim authorship for another filmmaker's work. Rather all I aim to do is open up long forgotten documents to slight psychological distortion revealing a perhaps previously hidden meaning. Creating Natalija's video hallucination's I cut into fragments of German home movies with excerpts of medical and technical films, like *Extirpation of a mediastinal teratoma: a training film shot on the Surgical Division of the Wilhelminen Spital, Vienna* 1927; *Transmitting Pictures by Wire* 1928; and *High Speed Photography of the Larynx* 1928. I imagined Natalija as a kind of very sensitive psychic antenna picking up picking up signals from extreme ends of the radio spectrum. For the soundtrack I collaged sounds from short-wave "Numbers Stations" believed to be coded Intelligence messages, recordings of long wave atmospheric and geomagnetic radio interference as well as the kind of popular German songs from the period, that might most tryingly get stuck in your mind.[11]

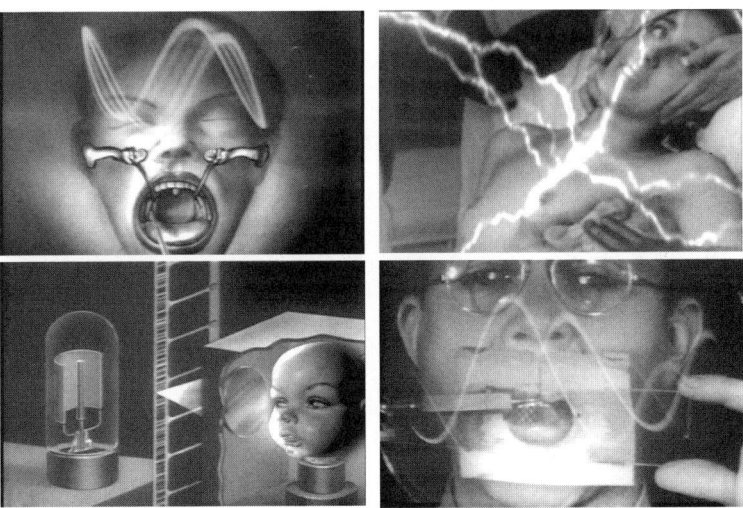

[11] For further information on Number Stations see
http://www.irdial.com/conet.htm.

The Gallery as Museum

As I have mentioned, museums of natural history in which science and entertainment go hand in glove are a key source of inspiration. I present my projects a series of carefully "scientific" exhibits, to foreground the spirit in which the séances were conducted. Before entering the séance room of *The Ideoplastic Materialisations of Eva C.*, viewers are presented with a brief introduction citing the sources of information on Eva C. and a series of eight framed doubled pages, reproduced from *The Phenomena of Materialisation*. Thus it is clear that what I am creating is a recreation, and the bizarre materialisations are contextualised historically.

On display is a 35mm hand-cranked projector from 1912. In the projector is a loop of film — a recreation of a series of frames shot by Schrenk Notzing with a Pathé Cinematograph showing Eva C. extruding some ectoplasm from her mouth. The viewer is invited to crank the projector and bring the tiny image to life. I wanted to make a connection between this early incarnation of cinema where the viewer created their own illusion by interacting with the machine and its most modern manifestation multiple synchronised DVD projections used to create the séance scenes and in so doing perhaps reanimate our contemporary apparatuses with the sense of the uncanny.

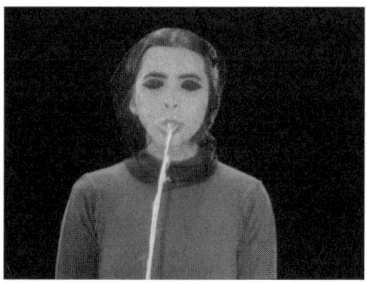

35mm hand-cranked projector and frame of 35mm film.
From *The Ideoplastic Materialisations of Eva C.*

The Influencing Machine of Miss Natalija A also contains a brief wall text explaining the sources of the project and how to interact with my virtual machine. As well as the stereoscopic diagram there is also a vitrine where various artefacts characterised as Natalija's "estranged organs" are displayed. These include vacuum tubes, a model kidney and a crumbling plaster baby face, all of which appear in the video "hallucinations." The vitrine was inspired by a display one might see in a medical museum. Natalija's "diabolical apparatus" was both real and metaphoric. It was in part her own flesh and blood self, in part psychosis and perhaps also an awareness of the encroachment of actual electronic influencing machines. Similarly, in their own way, my installations are constructed of technologies, phantom figures and mental images.

Jane Lewty

Syntonic Desire: Unheard Tales of Transmission in Radio's Wake

In 1912, the philosopher William Ernest Hocking summarised that any attempts in communication are "launches in solitude in the direction of an assumed reality; which reality, if it exists, is no less solitary."[1] It follows that Guglielmo Marconi's initial desire for his invention, wireless, was that it be used by "men on lonely lightships [...] to render less painful their isolation."[2] He hoped that the invention "which knew no frontiers" might "fulfil what has always been an essentially human need" — for reciprocal exchange. The first trans-Channel wireless exchange on 27 March 1899 had proved to Marconi how various agents could distort the message: "Gniteerg morf Ecnarf ot Dnalgna hgowht eht rehte."

The Dover operator is said to have written down exactly what he heard. Following this attempt, Marconi filed for a patent in 1900 which sought to achieve "syntony" by aligning both transmitter and receiver; thus giving a measure of order to wireless advances. "Syntony" is another term for selective

---

[1] William Ernest Hocking, *The Meaning of God in Human Experience* (New Haven: Yale University Press, 1912) 245.

[2] From a speech at City Hall, New York, 1927. Cited in Orrin J. Dunlap, *Marconi, The Man and his Wireless* (New York: Macmillan and Co., 1937) 289,

tuning; that which makes it possible to locate a spot on a particular wavelength in the radiofrequency spectrum and at none other. Thereafter known as 7777, the patent gave license to attempt the ultimate aspiration of the individual mind, that is, to commune with another, irrespective of boundaries.

Speaking of his aim for 7777 — "to cause intelligible communications with one or more stations out of a group of several receiving stations"[3] — Marconi commended the findings of Alexander Graham Bell, who had based his own device on the membrane of an eardrum. Conspicuously, Marconi's first transoceanic messages were "read" through a telephone receiver, a corporeal appendage which somewhat neutralised the horror of the new medium. Telephony already implied the walled-in self, expectantly signing to an absent other with no guarantee of *consensus in idem*. Wireless opened up a vacuum filled with innumerable signals, of which the one tracked may or may not be the one summoned.

The pivotal work by Sir William Crookes, "Some Possibilities of Electricity" (1892) had foregrounded the lack of secrecy innate to what he called "telegraphy without wires," assuming rightly that, at some point in the future, advanced methods of tuning would facilitate "mutual receptivity."[4] Aware that a wireless transmitter would send out waves in all directions, Crookes was ever anxious to prevent "surreptitious straying" — a vitally revealing phrase which recurs with every media projection, and

---

[3] Dunlap, *Marconi*, 93.

[4] William Crookes, "Some Possibilities of Electricity," *Fortnightly Review* 51 (1 January-1 June, 1892): 173-181. Crookes (1832-1919), a distinguished physicist and chemist, had discovered the element thallium and designed the radiometer (a device for measuring radiant energy) in addition to pioneering the cathode ray tube, a crucial component in the invention of television. Concurrently a believer in Spiritualism, he served as President of the Society for Psychical Research, 1896-1899, a sideline shared by the elite of British physicists who collectively approved of a transcendent principle of order — the ether. There is hardly any figure in the history of early radio who does not refer to the article of 1892 as having been greatly influential.

specifically in radio. Already, the idea of dissemination—or broadcasting—via "telegraphy without wires" is deemed to be unsatisfactory. This is apparent in Crookes's insistence on a junction with "other sentient beings." The experiment recorded in the 1892 article occurs within the confines of a house; it resembles a séance, with the messages clandestine and controlled. It is noteworthy that Crookes, the figure who introduced the promise of a wire-less state where mass communication was inevitable, does not envisage the use of radio frequencies for anything other than one-to-one dialogue. Future commentary was influenced by this opinion, as shown in pieces such as "Wireless Telegraphy and Brain Waves" by James T. Knowles which appeared in *Living Age* (July, 1899); a popular concept furthered in Upton Sinclair's lengthy investigation *Mental Radio* (1930) which hoped to find "reality" behind spiritualist practices by linking them to the human brain, "a storage battery, capable of sending impulses over the nerves by means of some other medium, known or unknown?"[5] In 1907, professional psychic Frederick Fletcher estimated that "if a machine produces etheric waves capable of cognition and communication, then the same possibility should exist within ourselves."[6] The overriding theme of such writings is joy at the ability of modern science to locate infinitesimal human traces, and its journeying into a dimension extended by any two separated points of contact.

An important figure within this climate is Camille Flammarion (1862-1927), originally an astronomer, who founded the Paris Society of Psychological Research in 1891, and became a president of the British Society for Psychical Research (SPR) between 1923-1924. In his novel *Lumen* (1897), Flammarion extrapolates a metaphysical system to contain and dramatise his scientific data, offering ideas on thought transference, on the

[5] Upton Sinclair, *Mental Radio* (London: T. Werner Laurie, 1930) 9-10.
[6] Frederick Fletcher, *The Sixth Sense: Psychic Origin, Rationale and Development* (London: Fowler Ltd., 1907) 8.

continuation of the disembodied soul and its serial reincarnation as alien life forms. Lumen—a spirit—is deeply preoccupied with movements of the ether, believing that "a soul vibrating under their influence perceives them as well." Consequently, he is able to measure attractions of the mind through "a process [belonging] to the psychic order" which renders "transmission instantaneous."[7]

Constantly mobile and fluctuating, Lumen holds great knowledge of communication amid the spheres. He argues that humanity need not be so remote in its "dark cavern" if it would only "advance into the air with a velocity superior to that of sound," or rather, by arresting the travel of sound waves before it left the lips of a speaker. Only then could the essence of human thoughts be relayed in a similar fashion to spectrum rays "across million and million of miles" to its intended destination: the mind of another, whether they be dead or alive.[8]

William Crookes had confidently extended the definition of ether as proposed by James Clark Maxwell, by locating electricity as the primary mode, perhaps a manifestation of the void itself.[9] Crookes's 1892 article mentions invisible wave-forms within the ether "or in some still more subtle substance" which—to his contemporaries—elicited an understanding into telepathy and clairvoyance. Some years later, in 1924, *Scientific American* magazine staged an experiment titled "Thought Transference from the Broadcasting Studio," where members of the public were invited to reproduce words, pictures and ideas emanating from the "senders" who were positioned next to the

---

[7] Camille Flammarion, *Lumen* (London: Heinemann, 1897) 100.

[8] Flammarion, *Lumen*, 222-223.

[9] "Nature's abhorrence of a vacuum was a sufficient reason for imagining an all-surrounding aether … To Descartes, the bare existence of bodies apparently at a distance was a proof of the existence of a continuous medium between them … Aethers were invented for the planets to swim in, to constitute electric atmospheres and magnetic effluvia." James Clerk Maxwell, "The Ether," *Collected Papers*, ed. W.D. Niven (Cambridge: Cambridge University Press, 1890) 763.

microphone. The task was a failure, owing to the promiscuous nature of the radio medium which was said to "swallow up" any merging of minds. "One cannot get undisputed possession of the air at any rational hour of the day or night," the author complained.[10] So, at this stage, the wireless signal was a symptom of the desire to relay messages, as James T. Knowles wrote, "through space, for great distances from brain to brain."[11]

Significantly, this remark was not in relation to telepathic endeavours, but the work of Marconi, a visionary who nevertheless hesitated to recognise the public nature of the private voice. His defects were characteristic of innovators who, in the words of Oliver Lodge, were, instead, "deafened by the chords [they could] summon at will."[12] Slow in adjusting to the practical, business capacities of the broadcast voice, Marconi initially baulked at abandoning the dream of direct wireless for a world-wide relay system, as favoured by cable companies and sponsors. His rapid improvements to early devices—the four sevens—were fuelled by, firstly, what the Futurists called "the ancient nostalgic torment of long distances" and a comparable concern that anyone with a radio receiver could eavesdrop upon, or "crash" a message of importance. Even worse, two senders could blot each other out. As aforementioned, Marconi's intent was to fix waves in the radiofrequency

[10] J. Malcolm Bird, "Telepathy and Radio: Results of the Scientific American Test of Thought Transference from the Broadcasting Studio," *Scientific American* (June 1924): 382, 443.

[11] James T. Knowles, "Wireless Telegraphy and Brain Waves," *Living Age* 222 (8 July 1899): 100-106.

[12] Oliver Lodge, *Modern Views* (London: Cassell, 1923) 359. Lodge (1851-1940) was also a pioneer of early radio technology. His work at University College Liverpool included the development of a radio detector using tuned circuits; and in 1897 attempted to detect radio waves from the sun. He improved upon Edward Branly's connection of glass tubing, batteries and a voltmeter; this became known in radio parlance as the "coherer." During a Royal Institute lecture in 1894, Lodge demonstrated radio telegraphy a year before Marconi's trials.

spectrum; to assert *the place* on the dial from *where* an absent voice may be emanating.

Despite such efforts, it was admitted that cross-interference would remain a feature of this innately chaotic system whose sound waves wreaked disturbance upon each other regardless of portals and other directives. They obscured the specific location, which would veer tantalisingly within reach, and then sink beneath the surging frequencies. Styled as the "main prospector of the ether,"[13] Marconi may have granted ingress to another level of existence, but he could never slice through it with certainty. His future modifications to wireless revolved around the issue of accuracy; destined, as he was, to sending "a lot of messages that never got anywhere."[14] Evidently, point-to-point wireless verified survival; the flicker of consciousness which manifested itself in a click or a vibration. The uncomfortable burden of solitariness was intensified by the failure to detect faint stirrings of a sympathetic caller. In 1908, another radio technician, Ernst Ruhmer, surmised that after pioneering efforts were all forgotten, "when copper wires, gutta-percha covers and iron bands are only to be found in museums," a wireless operator of the future might "call with an electric voice [heard] only by him who has a similarly tuned electric ear." On finding no reply, "he will know that his friend is dead."[15]

Sir Oliver Lodge, another president of the SPR (1901-1902), could not maintain the degree of pragmatism which characterised Crookes's enquiry into hidden forces; instead, he retained a staunch belief of survival after bodily death. Janet Oppenheim remarks that Lodge became outmoded, in that he

[13] Dunlap, *Marconi*, 75.
[14] Marconi, address to directors of Radio City Rockefeller Centre, June 1927.
[15] Ernst Ruhmer, *Wireless Telephony in Theory and Practice* (London: Crosby, Cockwood and Son, 1908) 301.

"clung" to the ether while physics progressed.[16] In his opinion, the living and the dead would surely exist as independent, isolated fragments were it not for the cohesive agent which summoned impulses through a copper wire. Recalling his development of the coherer at University College, Liverpool, in 1883, Lodge described "picking up lots of communications from ordinary telephone lines, and [hearing] people ordering potatoes for dinner and other such absurdities."[17]

This talent for eavesdropping would prove beneficial. A black-bordered telegram dated 14 September 1915 announcing the death of his eldest son in battle, confirmed a message received during a séance of 8 August through a medium, Alta Leonora Piper. This tragedy, and its aftermath, resulted in Lodge's book *Raymond or Life After Death* (1916), an elegy unswerving in its belief, which provided solace to those painfully aware of separation reinforced by telegrams and half-heard news. The First World War had turned Europe into a vast communications network where the movements of bombardments and offensives reported by wireless focused the attention of the home front, creating a near-synchronised drama. Radio technology was not only heralded as the fastest method of news-gathering but also as a potential site of verification and retrieval when the message was ominous.

Shortly before his death in 1931, Thomas Alva Edison, father of the phonograph, had promised to return via his own improved device, as reported in a *New York Times* article, "Mr Edison's Life Units Hundred Trillion in Human Body May Scatter After Death-Machine to Register Them." The newspaper asked the inventor to ascertain the fate of dead soldiers whose relatives still grieved: "People everywhere are anxiously awaiting word from you."[18] An authorless volume published in

---

[16] Janet Oppenheim, *The Other World: Spiritualism and Psychical Research in England, 1850-1914* (Cambridge: Cambridge University Press, 1985) 381.

[17] Letter to J. Arthur Hill (5 July 1915) in *Letters of Sir Oliver Lodge* (London: Cassell, 1932) 83-84.

[18] *New York Times* (23 January 1931).

1918 had outlined the same theme. In *Thy Son Liveth: Messages From a Soldier To His Mother*, a young American is killed in France, but speaks to his family through the wireless set, with whose mechanics—during his previous existence—he was greatly obsessed. Therefore, a spiritualist tract from a reputed wireless pioneer such as Oliver Lodge extended the interplay of electricity and psychic ritual which already imbued the cultural consciousness. Radio orchestrated, registered, and kept vigil over the scene of mass warfare in a practical sense, but it also suggested that the souls of the dead could be arrested and channelled from the trenches.

Motifs of Oliver Lodge's doctrine persist throughout *Raymond*, chiefly, his description of "waves of vibration" during a séance and the portrayal of "Ether or a still more myriad existence: a region in which communication is more akin to telepathy."[19] Despite this, occlusions and blockades in the spirit-medium discourse often prevented messages from being understood. During a séance, there is generally a guiding spirit, known as the "control," who uses the medium as a vessel. He or she admits other spirits into the periphery, many of whom also possess the medium for a time. The effect is akin to an oscillating radio waveband, whose frequencies often collide and are subject to interference. Lodge explains that his son, Raymond, must channel through "Feda" the control, and suffer the vagaries of Alta Leonora Piper and her colleagues. "[Raymond] wants to know," writes Lodge of a direct-voice sitting (which elicited a gentle "Ray-mnd" from the medium in trance), "did the voice sound like mine?"[20] Later sessions raise further objection from Raymond himself:

> I didn't like it much. I didn't use his tongue. I used his larynx without his tongue and without his lips [...] and that's why

19 Oliver Lodge, *Raymond or Life After Death* (London: Methuen, 1916) 208.
20 Lodge, *Raymond or Life After Death*, 173.

tones of the medium's voice come in and why it's so often coloured by the medium."21

This amounts to a grotesque semi-possession, where the spirit of Raymond inhabits selected part of a corpus. He projects inaccurate, perhaps guttural sounds, implying that errors in communication are multiple even in the afterlife. Speaking and hearing through layers of distortion results in polluted exchange as Raymond finds that "the different sound of voices confuses me and I mix [the message] up with questions from another's thoughts."22 It is unclear whether he refers to agitation in the spirit world or a busy séance where all sitters wished to interact. Trying new ways of "getting through," his words are "twisted" by "Feda"; he loses the "Power" and is broadcast incorrectly.23 A fate certainly shared by every beneficiary of Oliver Lodge's work on telecommunications. Lodge may have wished his son to resemble an electric signal, composed of an immaterial substance which has no property of "age, or wear and tear," as he depicts the ether in *My Philosophy*.24 This applies to excerpts in *Raymond*, where shattered limbs are said to be reconstituted in certain spheres. On one occasion, Raymond's visit to a higher plane is related, where he contracts into a tiny shape (an atom?) flowing down a "river of electricity or force, going all ways at once."25 Death, here, is perceived not as a cessation, but as a liberation of energy. Dialogue in Raymond's "world" occurs at a refined level, unhampered by the devious ministry of flesh, such as gesture and facial expression which were, of course, obsolete. Here, infers Lodge, is the opportunity to achieve soul-to-soul transfer, but only if the conditions are favourable and the elements co-operative.

21 Lodge, *Raymond or Life After Death*, 177.
22 Lodge, *Raymond or Life After Death*, 108.
23 Lodge, *Raymond or Life After Death*,154.
24 Oliver Lodge, *My Philosophy. Representing My Views on the Many Functions of the Ether of Space* (London: Ernest Benn, 1933) 220.
25 Lodge, *Raymond or Life After Death*, 184.

The most outlandish, yet undisputed, example of wireless as a pervasive feature or idea within the séance, appears in a small edition for the Psychic Book Club in 1927. *The Blue Room: Being the Absorbing Story of Voice-to-Voice Communication in BROAD LIGHT with Souls who have passed into the GREAT BEYOND* is a series of case notes by a Clive Chapman and a journalist friend "G.A.W." It recounts frequent conversations with a band of spirits characterised by their voice modulations and ability to sing hymns alongside musical instruments. Chapman concluded hazily that spirits used "their own power in combination with the power around the medium, together with the utilisation of sound waves."[26] A set tone, or vibration, was set up during the playing of a piano which effected the transmission. If the music were to cease in mid-flow, then "Dorothy," the control, was displeased, as the sudden shift nullified efforts from the spirit world to tune-in.

Like Marconi's maxim regarding patent 7777, successful contact in *The Blue Room* is only possible when certain chords are struck and minds duly sensitised, which results in "perfect harmony all round."[27] During a voice-to-voice interview with one of the spirits, the journalist G.A.W supposes that human transactions are vastly inferior, as "thoughts carry millions of miles [...] like a telephone" in the other dimension, only impeded by clumsy signalling from our earthbound circle.[28] This premise of telepathy in the spirit world was offered by Flammarion's *Lumen*; whereas Oliver Lodge proposed a form of ideal broadcasting among the spheres, used when "He" [Christ] wished to speak, "not in words but [...] mind to mind." Raymond apparently asks, "if it were words, why should a thousand of us all get a message at once?"[29]

26 Clive Chapman and "G.A.W," *The Blue Room* (London: Special Edition for the Psychic Book Club Ltd., 1927) 48.
27 Chapman and "G.A.W," *The Blue Room*, 100.
28 Chapman and "G.A.W," *The Blue Room*, 103.
29 Chapman and "G.A.W," *The Blue Room*, 182.

In *The Blue Room*, extracts from Chapman's diary reveal the subliminal influence behind his faintly ridiculous testimony. On 27 September 1925, he ponders a dream of a previous night, wherein a ship complete with wireless aerial battled through stormy seas towards a corresponding radio station on an island. Upon hearing a random voice proclaiming true enlightenment, Chapman concludes that science is in fact an auxiliary to the supernatural:

> Perhaps it may mean that those on the other side have been able to link up with our wireless stations and that before long, the world will get some startling messages through [...] The wireless station on the island represents those souls tuned-in to the faith, receiving and sending out messages of hope, and the words I heard must mean that communication has been established by the faith of those who believe, and that direct communication will be opened up, most likely through our wireless machines.[30]

Disappointingly, reports of any enlightening trials are confined to a single entry, 5 October 1926, where the radio is present during a session "giving lots of volume, while in between these wireless items I played the piano." From the space opened by the dial, when the room was silent of terrestrial nose and ecstatic hymns, Chapman claims, "we all heard a voice speaking in a whisper ... very, very close."[31] This is surely an example of collective persuasion. The only uncanny visitant of Chapman's blue room was likely to be generic radio interference—static—and not an auditory hallucination.

These amateur séances surely imitate the awed hush and sinister energies of Rudyard Kipling's story "Wireless" (1902) which underscores the parallel between technology and paranormal practices. One of the first imaginary works to

---

[30] Chapman and "G.A.W," *The Blue Room*, 146.
[31] Chapman and "G.A.W," *The Blue Room*, 151.

explore radio's phantasmal presence, it centres around an apothecary where a long-range wireless installation is attempted after dark. Marconi's trials have recently taken place at Poole, further up the Dorset coast, in the Haven Hotel which boasts a mast of 110 feet. At the outset of "Wireless," it is pointed out that "they" are once more conducting a legitimate operation with stronger batteries than ever. The experiment in the apothecary seems arcane; carried out by a Mr Cashell, who may conceivably be one of Marconi's assistants at the Haven Hotel. He invests his home battery, the coherer, with mystical capabilities, unaware that it was always the weakest link in the circuit that produced Hertzian waves, often reacting wildly to incoming vibrations, regardless of source. The narrative, however, revolves around Mr Shaynor, the pharmacist, who is dying of consumption. Swallowing pastilles which emit a noxious blue fume, "very like incense," he begins drafting a letter to his unrequited love, while Cashell strives to make wireless contact.[32] "There are a good many kinds of induction," Cashell announces meaningfully as electricity crackles through the instrument. In the adjoining room, Shaynor lapses into a stupor, scribbling lines from Keats's "Eve of St Agnes," not in the way that "a vile chromo recalls some incomparable canvas," but producing an ideal reprint, or echo. He receives impulses from the dead poet's mind on the moment of composition, garnering poetry from a specific wavelength which will inevitably veer out of range:

> "Not yet—not yet," he muttered, "wait a minute. Please wait a minute. I shall get it," then—
> Our magic windows fronting on the sea,
> The dangerous foam of desolate seas...
> For aye—

---

[32] Rudyard Kipling, "Wireless," *Traffic and Discoveries* (London: Macmillan, 1904) 213-239.

The current falters, Shaynor is cut adrift and sputters out with a screech, jerking his body like a stray wire ripped from its port. Meanwhile, Cashell's endeavours are ultimately futile; he captures "just enough to tantalise" from two ships moored in the Channel who obstruct his own frequency directed inland.

> The Morse instrument was ticking furiously. Mr Cashell interpreted ... "Can make nothing of your signals." A pause. "M.M.V.M.M.V. Signals unintelligible ... Do you know what that means? It's a couple of men o'war working Marconi signals ... They are trying to talk to each other. Neither can read the other's messages, but all their messages are being taken in by our receiver here ..."

The boundless ether allows words to stray. Cashell's target is never reached; instead he is compelled to eavesdrop on one-way traffic flowing into his coherer from ships who have failed to syntonically adjust transmitter and receiver. Cashell's device becomes the invisible third valve, yet, along the coast in Poole, someone is waiting for *his* call of "T.R. T.R." in vain. "Wireless" is a primary text of ruptured communication, implying that all attempts are abortive; Shaynor will never even send his love letter. The subtle claim is that poetic "induction" (transference from one circuit or body to another) is statistically more successful than radiotelegraphy. The capacities of wireless are utilised to reactivate the mind of a sentient being—if not the one desired—which flashes through live wires and a concordant medium.

Characterised by confused discourse, marginal writings such as *The Blue Room*, "Wireless" and Lodge's *Raymond* pre-empt areas of concern within later modernist works of literature. Their treatment of the unknown, which incorporates the mystery of electricity and radio technology, qualifies the need for "syntony" in the early twentieth century, for identical minds in concert which would theoretically replace the evasive, perhaps battle-torn body. Since knowledge is available in separate minds, and, in the opinion of spiritualists, readily transferred by telepathy in other worlds, then the body was, in effect, an occluding agency. Only angels communicate without the bridge of physical contact or twists of spoken language; they exchange their interiority in a silent stream of intelligence, unaffected by discrepancies in time or distance—a fitting logo for Deutsche Grammophon in 1898. However, in the paradox of modernity, a body is often sought after regardless of its "occluding" capacities; as noted, Edison's death-rattle was preserved phonographically and the first wireless transmission received through a pseudo-eardrum.

Within the social fabric and creation of modernist literature, the fear of communication breakdown was usually figured as loss of the other. If meaning is in the *mind* of the beholder, a mismatching of intention occurs during verbal intercourse, summarised in 1923 by C.K. Ogden and I.A. Richards who blamed a "veritable orgy of verbomania" for the "impasse of solipsism" in modernity.[33] Hugh Kenner rightly attributes this to the "new century's pervasive experiences, that of being talked to by people we cannot see."[34] *The Waste Land* (1922) is widely considered to be a vast telephone poem or mangled séance; its disembodied voices emerging from the text as pure utterance and returning misunderstood. Oddly, it is the "cocktail party problem" which became a fundamental problem of early radio drama; in the attempt to glean words from spatially disparate sources in order to reproduce a non-exclusive aural environment, one would be unable to select a *single* sound to which to attend. Wireless had restored the dream of telepathy but also highlighted the inexactitude of words, and, furthermore, the failure to reach their intended destination. After all, the dyadic nature of all communication ensures that when a gap is surmounted, the distances become

[33] C.K. Ogden and I.A. Richards, The Meaning of Meaning: *A Study of the Influences of Language upon Thought and the Science of Symbolism* (New York: Harcourt and Brace, 1923) 20.

[34] Hugh Kenner, *The Mechanic Muse* (Oxford: Oxford University Press, 1987) 34.

more prominent. Synapses are faulty in much modernist discourse; interpersonal connections are incomplete, often silent, but ceaseless amid the ether:

> Giles said—without words, "I'm damnably unhappy."
> "So am I," Dodge echoed.
> "And I too," Isa thought.

An exchange from Virginia Woolf's *Between The Acts*, where each spectator of the pageant is trapped in the circumference of self, with no opportunity to cohere their perceptions of the day, their lives, the pageant itself.[35] They are silent broadcasters, emitting rays to no-one. Woolf recognises that if shared consciousness—a soul-to-soul transfer—is the criterion of success, then communication is impossible, and we therefore stick in the impasse of solipsism. It is arguable that the condition of modernist writing—that which fuses, diminishes, amplifies—was deeply wrought by the symbiosis of science and the paranormal. Thought transference between kindred spirits—whether alive or dead—is the *primus inter pares* of communication, qualified by the ambiguity of radio: its potential and promise; its intimacy juxtaposed with a long-range remoteness. Writers became secondary mimics, for, with the advent of sound storage, the dead found an oracle greater than the printed page, while overhead signals clashed through Marconimasts—the true carriers of information. Furthermore, wireless raised the phantom of Socrates who had warned of misfires in the earliest communication technology: the written word itself. Challenged by new media which restaged human interaction, writers implicitly and explicitly sourced radio, for its transmissions, interchanges, and failed dispatches. In this respect, etherised patients became a condition of modern subjectivity: wired up, yet solitary and ever inclined to eavesdrop.

---

[35] Virginia Woolf, *Between The Acts* (London: Penguin, 1992) 205.

Notes on Contributors

Louis Armand is Director of Intercultural Studies in the Philosophy Faculty of Charles University, Prague. His is the author of *Technē: James Joyce, Hypertext & Technology* (2003); *Incendiary Devices: Discourses of the Other*; and *Solicitations: Essays on Criticism and Culture* (2005). www.louis-armand.com

Zoe Beloff is an artist working in film, stereoscopic projection performance, and interactive media. She has collaborated with composer John Cale, sound artist Ken Montgomery and the Wooster Group theatre company (who she worked with to create *Where There There There Where*). In 2002 she presented *Shadow Land or Light from the Other Side*, a stereoscopic film based on the life of the 19th century medium Elizabeth D'Espérance at the 2002 Whitney Museum Biennial. She teaches film and digital media at Queens College in New York. www.zoebeloff.com

Arthur Bradley is a lecturer in the Department of English at Lancaster University. He has published widely on continental philosophy and is the author of *Negative Theology and Modern French Philosophy* (2004).

Simon Critchley is Professor of Philosophy in the Graduate Faculty of the New School University, New York, and at the University of Essex, and Directeur de Programme at the Collège International de Philosophie, Paris. He is the author of *Ethics-Politics-Subjectivity: Essays on Derrida, Levinas, and Contemporary French Thought* (1999); *Very Little, Almost Nothing: Death, Philosophy, Literature* (1997); *The Ethics of Deconstruction: Derrida and Levinas* (1992) and *Things Merely Are* (2005).

Ben Goertzel is currently a Research Professor at Virginia Polytechnic University, and also CEO of two software firms, Biomind LLC (a maker of AI-based bioinformatics software) and Novamente LLC (which does AI software consulting and also hosts the Novamente AI project, an ambitious attempt to create an AI system with general intelligence at the human level and beyond).

Ivan M. Havel is Director of the Centre for Theoretical Studies, Prague. His fields of interest include theoretical computer science, artificial intelligence, cognitive sciences and related philosophical issues. Before the communist regime in Czechoslovakia collapsed in late 1989 he hosted discussion groups in his apartment in Prague, and from November 1989 till June 1990 he was engaged in political work as a member of the Council of the Civic Forum. Since 1990 he has been the editor-in-chief of the scientific journal *Vesmír* and a member of Academia Europea.

Arthur and Marilouise Kroker are the editors of the online journal *Ctheory*. Their books include *Panic Encyclopedia: The Definitive Guide to the Postmodern Scene* (with David Cook, 1989) and *Digital Delirium* (eds., 1997). ctheory.concordia.ca

Jane Lewty is currently Assistant Professor in 20th century non-US literature at the University of Northern Iowa. She recently completed a postdoctoral fellowship at University College London and is working on a monograph on radio in modernist literature.

Christina Ljungberg has worked in Cultural Programming with Swedish and Canadian Television and now teaches English literature at the University of Zürich, Switzerland, with research interests in visual and cognitive semiotics. Her publications include *To Join, to Fit and to Make* (1999) and *The Crisis of Representation* (with Winfried Nöth, 2003).

Tom McCarthy is a writer, artist and General Secretary of the International Necronautical Society, a semi-fictitious organisation played out across the worlds of art, literature and media, whose activities have included the construction of a radio broadcasting unit in London's Institute of Contemporary Art. His publications include *Navigation was always a Difficult Art* (2002). www.necronauts.org

Andrew Mitchell is a postdoctoral teaching fellow in the humanities at Stanford University. He is the translator, with François Raffoul, of Martin Heidegger's *Four Seminars* (Indiana University Press, 2003). His recent publications include "Heidegger and Terrorism" (*Research in Phenomenology* 35) and "Fassbinder: The Subject of Film" (*Cinematic Thinking: Philosophical Approaches to the New Cinema*).

Donald F. Theall is University Professor Emeritus at Trent University, Canada. He is the author of *The Medium is the Rear View Mirror:*

Understanding McLuhan (1971); *Beyond the Word: Reconstructing Sense in the Joyce Era of Technology, Culture and Communication* (1995); *James Joyce's Techno-Poetics* (1997); and *The Virtual Marshall McLuhan* (2001).

Darren Tofts is Associate Professor of Media & Communications at Swinburne University of Technology, Melbourne. He is the author (with artist Murray McKeich) of *Memory Trade: A Prehistory of Cyberculture* (1998); *Parallax: Essays on Art, Culture and Technology* (1999); and editor (with Annemarie Jonson and Alessio Cavallaro) of *Prefiguring Cyberculture: An Intellectual History* (2003). His most recent book is *Interzone: Media Arts in Australia* (2005).

Gregory L. Ulmer is Professor of English and Media Studies at the University of Florida. His books include *Heuretics: The Logic of Invention*; *Teletheory: Grammatology in the Age of Video*; and *Applied Grammatology: Post(e)-Pedagogy from Jacques Derrida to Joseph Beuys*. Along with photographers Barbara Jo Revelle and John Craig Freeman, he is a member of the FRE: www.floridaresearchensemble.net

McKenzie Wark is a lecturer in Media and Cultural Theory at New School University in New York City. He is the author of *Virtual Geography: Living with Global Media Events* (1994) and *Dispositions* (2002). *A Hacker Manifesto* was published by Harvard University Press, 2004.

Slavoj Žižek is Senior Researcher at the Institute for Social Sciences at the University of Ljubljana, Slovenia, and is the leading figure of the "Ljubljana School" of Psychoanalysis. He is the editor of *Cogito and the Unconscious* (1998) and the author of *Tarrying with the Negative*; *Enjoy Your Symptom!* and *The Sublime Object of Ideology*. www.lacan.com